MW00364827

The UFO Guidebook

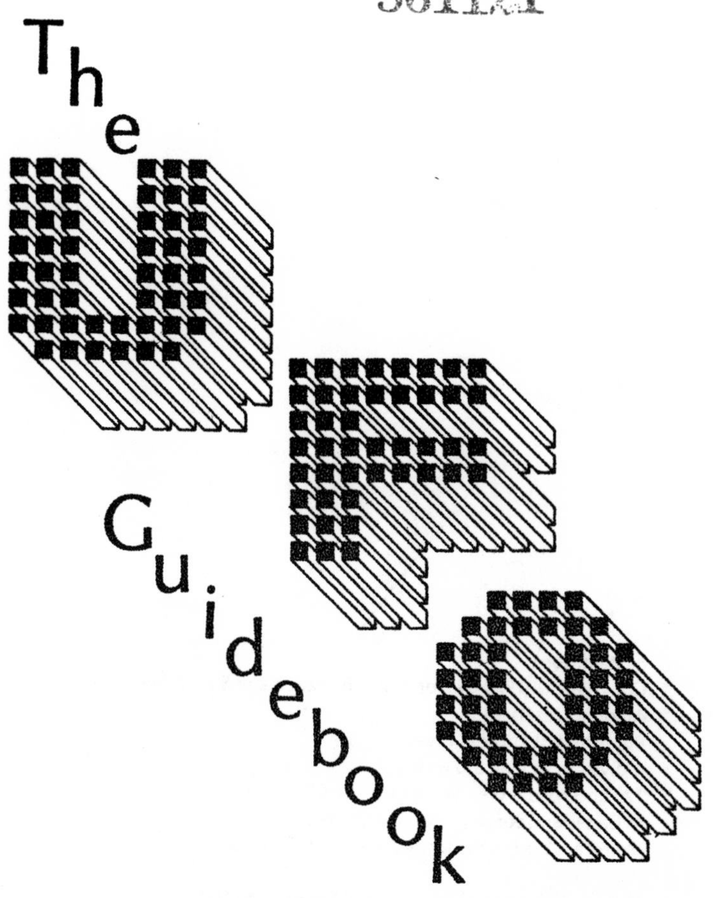

Norman J. Briazack

and Simon Mennick

The Citadel Press

Secaucus, N. J.

First edition

Published by Citadel Press
A division of Lyle Stuart Inc.
120 Enterprise Ave., Secaucus, N.J. 07094
In Canada: George J. McLeod Limited, Toronto
Manufactured in the United States of America

Library of Congress Cataloging in Publication Data

Briazack, Norman J
The UFO guidebook

Bibliography: p. 245
1. Flying saucers—Dictionaries. I. Mennick, Simon, joint author. II. Title.
TL789.B717 001.9'42'03 78-17825
ISBN 0-8065-0636-9

INTRODUCTION

Ufologists are not certain when UFOs first made their appearance. The more audacious ones argue that there is evidence to indicate that UFOs were around as far back as ancient times. The pillar of cloud and fire, for example, which is mentioned in the Bible in the Book of Exodus, is considered by Barry H. Downing to have been a UFO. But there is an inherent difficulty in attempting to prove the presence of UFOs in the past by relying on ancient and medieval records. There is always present the danger that ufologists may read unwarranted meanings into the records. Despite the high level of culture of many ancient and medieval peoples, their science and learning were for the most part limited to their surroundings and constricted by their limited cultural needs. They did not know as much as modern man does; and, therefore, it would have been easier for them to misidentify or to inadequately describe natural phenomena, including the aerial type.

It was only during the 1600s that man began to enter the modern age. He started on this path by discovering the works of the ancients. Spurred by a rekindled interest in the natural world, man initiated the most significant revolution in history—the scientific revolution. It would sweep away old superstitions and usher in a modern technological world. Due to the ever-increasing scientific sophistication, reports of strange aerial phenomena from this period acquire greater significance. But even these reports—as, for example, the report of a strange fiery object over Robozero, Russia, in 1663—should be taken cautiously. Man had only embarked on the road of science, and the old bonds of ignorance were still strong.

It was not until the twentieth century that man progressed sufficiently to break the bonds of superstition and ignorance, and to look seriously at the Universe not only in awe, but also in a spirit of adventure and exploration. Man now had the basic and necessary instruments of an advanced civilization. He had the radio, the telephone, the airplane, radar and sonar. In the second half of the twentieth century, he mastered and controlled nuclear energy, developed the laser, and constructed rockets and space vehicles.

In short, by the mid-twentieth century, man had both the experience and the scientific sophistication to recognize truly mysterious aerial phenomena. Though records of sightings of mysterious aerial phenomena before this time can be considered and used cautiously to support the case for UFOs, most ufologists would agree that it was not until World War II that the first indisputable UFO sightings occurred. During bombing missions over German-occupied Europe and Japanese-controlled Asia and Oceania, Allied pilots reported being followed by strange mysterious blobs of light, which they called foo fighters. At times, there would be a formation of these foo fighters, at other times, only one. Intelligence considered them to be secret German and Japanese weapons of an unknown purpose.

It was only after the war had finished and the victorious Allies had examined captured Axis records that it was learned that the Germans and Japanese were both equally puzzled by the foo fighters, considering them to be secret Allied weapons. Each side had thus believed that the foo fighters were secret aircraft of the other side. Since Allied Intelligence knew that the aircraft were neither British nor American, the mystery deepened and a new explanation had to be offered for the sightings. Intelligence subsequently revised its conclusions. The sightings of the foo fighters were now labelled as illusory, the result of combat fatigue.

Man was then only beginning to take his first tentative steps into space. The idea that foo fighters might have been interplanetary spacecraft did not seriously occur to anyone. The alternative explanation that they were paraphysic in nature or that they originated from a parallel dimension was similarly not given serious consideration. Science had relegated superstition and demons to the garbage heap of history, and to look to these explanations seemed patently ridiculous and unthinkable.

The explanation that the foo fighters were illusory in nature sufficed for a while because it seemed the most reasonable and, indeed, the only acceptable explanation available. But strange things continued to happen. The disappearance on December 5, 1945, of five Navy TBM-3 Avenger torpedo bombers on a training mission out of Fort Lauderdale, Florida, and the subsequent mysterious disappearance of the rescue plane, a PBM Martin Mariner, focused public attention on a part of the ocean which has since become infamous as the Devil's Triangle.

These disappearances were followed by other equally mysterious ones. The government seemed helpless to solve the mysteries and to prevent further disappearances. Scientists could only speculate on what had happened to the vanished craft and men. The public was slowly being forced to the conclusion that science did not have an explanation for everything and that the government was not all-powerful. The sightings of strange aerial objects continued, but the idea that they were under intelligent control or of extraterrestrial origin still was not seriously considered.

An important change was also taking place in the attitude of the American public toward space. During the war, the major belligerents had all been intensely interested in rockets, and the Germans had been advanced in this respect. Their rockets had caused devastating damage to Britain. Towards the end of the war, both the USSR and the U.S.A. attempted to capture as many German rocket scientists as possible, realizing that rockets might hold the balance of military power in the future. The scientists were brought to the respective countries to continue the experiments. The motivation was purely military, but it payed extra dividends. Experiments were progressively developing even bigger and better rockets.

As early as the 1930s, the more imaginative motion pictures had depicted space travel, but the idea was dismissed and regarded as merely fantasy and science fiction. But the success with rockets was beginning to make space flight a reality. Individuals with vivid imaginations realized that there was no reason why rockets could not be constructed to carry men on space voyages to other planets. The idea of space travel and trips to other planets no longer sounded totally ludicrous. Books, films, and articles began to deal more frequently with the subject.

Simultaneously, there was a growing awareness of the fact that astronomy had long stated that there were millions of stars in the Universe, many of them invisible to the naked eye. The possibility that there were other intelligent beings in the Universe was an old idea, but now it assumed a greater importance. People began to reason that if man was thinking of traveling to other planets, perhaps advanced beings on other planets were also thinking of visiting Earth and that perhaps they had already done so. Slowly, attention was being focused on the mysterious aerial objects.

The change in attitude was swift and dramatic. During World War II, the idea that foo fighters could have been of extraterrestrial origin had not even been considered. Yet several years later, the public was prepared to accept the possibility that life existed on other planets and that alien beings might be visiting Earth.

June 24, 1947, marks a revolution in the thinking of man on the subject of nonhuman intelligent beings. On that day, Kenneth Arnold, flying his private plane past Mount Rainier, sighted a formation of luminous, flying, disc-shaped objects. He related his experience to a waiting newsman who dubbed the objects "flying saucers." The name stuck and the phenomenon achieved worldwide significance. From that day, ufology was officially born in America.

Three concepts were now linked—that of space travel, that of beings on other planets, and that of the mysterious objects which Arnold had sighted. Flying saucers were quickly labeled as being extraterrestrial in origin. This seemed like the only reasonable explanation, for the government seemed helpless to explain the phenomenon. It seemed certain that these mysterious objects, which were apparently under intelligent control, were not manmade, and that they could have come only from outer space.

In those early years, the most obvious point of origin was considered to be a planet in our solar system, Mars and Venus being the two most likely candidates. These two planets had still not been explored, and the possibility seemed reasonable. However, space probes sent to these two planets in the 1970s by the U.S.A. and the USSR established that no intelligent life existed on them. Those who still ascribe to the theory that UFOs are from our solar system believe that Europa, a moon of Jupiter which has certain Earth-like characteristics, is a likely possibility. Most other ufologists, however, now prefer to believe that UFOs originate from other planetary systems.

Because of the large number of sightings, the widespread speculation about their origins, and the potential danger which they posed to national security, the U.S. government took an active interest in these mysterious flying objects. The Air Force was directed to investigate UFOs. From the start the Air Force consistently denied that UFOs were spacecraft from another planet. They maintained that UFOs were usually misidentifications of known natural phenomena. Other cases were explained as the result of hoaxes, hallucinations, or the unreliability of the witnesses.

The government involvement in the investigations helped to spur an unprecedented amount of interest in the subject, the result being the release of a large number of books, articles, and movies on the subject. A new field of interest and study had come into being—ufology. And a new expert was spawned—the ufologist. Talks and lectures were soon being given on the subject. Newspapers and magazines began to deal with the subject, often in an intelligent manner. The field of ufology, once looked down upon as the domain of crackpots, was slowly gaining respectability.

The initial theory shared by most ufologists was that UFOs were from another planet. The mid-fifties saw the rise of a new major theory on UFOs. This was the paraphysic or parapsychological explanation. Adherents of this theory rejected the claim that UFOs were from another planet. In its place, they advanced the theory that UFOs were from a parallel dimension. Alongside these two main theories there arose several other ones. These theories, however, have found few adherents.

The Hollow Earth theory claims that inside the center of Earth there exists an advanced civilization, and that UFOs are spacecraft from this civilization. Another theory has advanced a biological explanation, arguing that UFOs may be a form of life. Ivan T. Sanderson championed this theory and made a good case for it. Still another theory holds that UFOs are the handiwork of the survivors of Atlantis, who, it is maintained, have an undersea base from which UFOs are dispatched.

Increased sightings of UFOs in the 1960s, the ever-increasing public interest in the subject, and the pressure from eminent scientists and other public figures, forced the government to initiate a study of the UFO phenomenon under the guidance of a private organization.

The project was given to Colorado University and placed under the direction of Dr. Edward Condon. This was the first and only officially sanctioned nongovernmental study of UFOs. The report was released in January 1969. It was condemned by some scientists, writers, and ufologists, and praised by other equally eminent persons. Basically, those ufologists who believed that UFOs originated from another planet were disappointed with the report. Those ufologists who believed that UFOs were from a parallel dimension felt that the report substantiated their arguments.

Dr. Condon's two basic conclusions were that the Air Force was not covering up the UFO investigation and that there was no evidence that UFOs were from another planet. He leaned towards the parapsychological explanation, thereby placing UFOs in the same category as various other occult or paranormal phenomena. However, some of the scientists who examined the actual case studies disagreed with Dr. Condon's conclusions, arguing forcibly that the evidence indicated that the UFOs were real and of extraterrestrial origin.

The release of this report had far-reaching consequences in the field of UFO research. The Air Force, basing its actions on the report, officially closed its own UFO investigation, Project Blue Book. Unofficially, however, the Air Force continues to investigate UFO sightings. The release of the report tended to discourage further UFO research, and UFO research centers in foreign countries closed down as well. Ion Hobana reports, for example, that the liaison office of the Bucharest Observatory, the scientific UFO circle in Rumania, ceased its activities after publication of the Condon Report.

For a while, the report also dealt a serious blow to private UFO research in this country. Scientists who had become interested in the subject now shied away. However, other prominent scientists, such as Dr. J. Allen Hynek, continued to criticize what they consider to be the official conspiracy of silence designed to keep the truth about UFOs from the public. The National Investigations Committee on Aerial Phenomena (NICAP) blasted the Condon Report and the continuing failure of the government to deal objectively and seriously with the UFO phenomenon. Since 1969, ufologists have been pressuring the government for a new study on UFOs, though no progress has been made in this direction.

Sightings of UFOs have continued to proliferate. Hundreds of thousands more people now claim to have seen UFOs. Many more sightings at close range, and numerous cases of actual contact, have also been reported. There has yet to be a UFO flap as great as that of the mid-sixties. The 1970s have, however, witnessed a new, explosive surge of interest in the subject. Erich von Daniken has had much to do with rekindling public attention and interest in UFOs and intelligent beings from outer space. His books, while not dealing strictly with modern UFO sightings, deal with the theory that astronauts from distant planets visited Earth in its remote past. A TV special, "In Search of Ancient Astronauts," based on von Daniken's book, *Chariots of the Gods?*, did much to popularize and to boost interest in this field.

Since the theory of "ancient astronauts" is intimately connected with the UFO problem, public interest simultaneously focused on UFOs. Von Daniken has been responsible for a renewed interest in all aspects of the UFO subject. Books published earlier on UFOs and related phenomena began to be reprinted. New UFO books appeared. Established national publications carried articles on the subject. Perhaps most significantly, several specialized UFO magazines made their appearance. Ufologists have been invited as guest speakers on TV and radio shows. Though the UFO mystery still remains, ufology has in the past several years attained a high level of respectability and public acceptance the likes of which it has never before enjoyed.

Men have landed on the moon and space probes have been sent to distant planets. The idea of men traveling to other planets no longer sounds ludicrous. Scientists are openly talking about the possibility that there are other inhabited planets. By 1966, scientists were certain that Barnard's Star, six light-years away, possessed a planetary system, when they confirmed the discovery of three dark companions. All these developments have directly affected ufology. Many people who earlier scoffed at the idea of UFOs are now at least willing to admit the possibility that the objects are of extraterrestrial origin, and that they may be piloted by intelligent beings.

As in the 1950s, today two schools of thought continue to dominate the field of ufology. One school maintains that UFOs are from another planetary system, the second school of thought argues that all the evidence points to the fact that UFOs are from a parallel space-time continuum. The extraterrestrial origin theory has been somewhat modified, however. The theory that UFOs originate from within our solar system has been replaced by the theory that UFOs are from another planetary system.

Thirty years have passed since the UFO phenomenon first achieved national prominence, but the mystery of the phenomenon still persists. No ufologist knows for certain what UFOs are or from where they originate. Existing scientific concepts have been found inadequate to explain them. Ufologists are in agreement that UFOs represent either a new phenomenon for man or an old phenomenon of which man has only recently become aware. Whichever may be the case, UFOs do present a new challenge to man, and it is clear that new concepts and theories will be necessary to explain them.

Though the mystery of the UFOs still persists, much progress has been made in the past thirty years towards solving the mystery. Much data is now available and the field of the possible origin of UFOs has been narrowed to: a) another planetary system, b) a parallel dimension, c) an indigenous civilization, and d) a form of life.

Perhaps the most important fact is that ufology has become an institutionalized and organized field of study, though still in an embryonic form. There now exist national organizations devoted to the study of the UFO phenomenon.

Progress has also been made in gaining some facts about UFOs. When the public first became aware of UFOs in the late 1940s, they represented a total enigma. The accumulation of data, the cumulative results of meticulous and painstaking research, the interviews with witnesses and contactees, the analyses of UFO reports, and the collation of facts from physics, chemistry, biology, etc., revealed some patterns to the UFO phenomenon.

As a result, ufologists presently know that: a) there is a relation between color changes exhibited by UFOs and changes in their velocity, b) electromagnetism is involved in some way in the propulsive system of the UFOs, c) UFOs are under intelligent control and are operated either directly by beings or by remote control, d) no communications between UFOs have ever been reported—or if they have, then such has never been officially acknowledged—though UFOs are evidently aware of commands given to pilots, for they have been known to respond to them as, for example, in those cases where UFOs have sped away after intercept commands were given to fighter pilots, e) some UFOs emit radioactivity and possibly also inaudible infrasonic and ultrasonic waves, f) UFOs clearly want to make their presence known to man, but for reasons not entirely understood they wish to avoid official contact, g) contact is usually via telepathy rather than through verbal communication, and h) hypnosis is often used during a contact, and posthypnotic suggestions are often given the contactees.

These are but some of the findings that ufologists have uncovered during the past thirty years. The steady accumulation of additional facts will, it is hoped, one day lead to a solution of this baffling mystery.

It is hoped that this book will be another positive step in the continuing effort to solve the UFO mystery. It is not intended to be simply another case study of UFOs, a field which has already inspired numerous works. Rather, the book is intended to be a reference book, a guidebook on the UFO subject. In the past thirty years, ufology has adopted from other scientific disciplines or has itself produced many new theories, concepts, ideas, and terms. The goal of this guidebook is to collate the language and the terminology dealing with UFOs. More than 400 terms have been included in this encyclopedia, which will present a brief discussion of each term, cross reference terms to other related terms, show how the term is related to UFOs, and where applicable show the consequences of this relationship to other fields of study and to human affairs.

Perhaps the most fascinating feature of ufology is that it is an umbrella discipline which encompasses and involves many other fields of study. Religion, physics, theology, biology, psychology, sociology, anthropology, and archaeology are all involved in the study of UFOs. No other field of study can lay claim to such a wide involvement of other disciplines.

From the start, ufology was handicapped because it lacked a standard reference book that would compile and discuss the relevance and interconnection of the basic ufological terms and concepts. It should be stressed, however, that ufology does not have a separate vocabulary distinct from all other disciplines. Due to the fact that it involves so many other disciplines, concepts and terms from other fields of study are also of interest to ufologists. Angel, demon, pulsar, laser, hypnosis, telepathy, electromagnetism, etc., are all concepts intimately associated with any serious study of the UFO phenomenon. These terms are all discussed and analyzed in this handbook. However, this UFO handbook does not as such concern itself with these related terms, which also belong to other disciplines. It deals with these terms only to the extent that they touch upon the UFO mystery, showing their connection with ufology.

In addition to using terms which are common to other fields of study, ufology has also developed its own distinct terminology. UFO, ufonaut, saucerian, flying saucer, oint, flap, and window area are all terms native to ufology. Most of these terms and concepts have been widely used in the field of ufology for over two decades.

However, even with the terms adopted from other disciplines and with the terms created by ufology, there still has been a dearth of sufficient terminology to effectively deal with the UFO subject. Language is an indispensable tool in the advancement of knowledge. The lack of an adequate comprehensive language has hampered the field of ufology. Ergo, it has been necessary in this handbook to create several neologisms. These neologisms have not been arbitrarily concocted. Rather, they were created to fill a vacuum. In ufology there have existed several concepts for which there were no adequate and appropriate neutral words by which these concepts could be defined. The concepts themselves were not created, only the words to identify them. These neologisms include: aconin, befap, blisk, dimensionalism, manadim, naphology, naturalia, nebecism, starism, and zeroid. In each case there existed a need for such a term.

Nebecism refers to the theory that Earth was and/or still is being visited by technologically advanced beings from another planet. Dimensionalism refers to the theory that Earth has been and still is being visited by beings from another parallel space-time continuum. To correspond to these two schools of ufology, two other neologisms were created. Befap refers to a being from another planet, whereas manadim refers to an alien being from another dimension.

One additional term was coined, this to refer to intelligent sapient beings other than man. There existed no adequate word to describe such intelligent beings. A number of terms in use, such as alien, extraterrestrial, ETI, galaxian, celestial, saucerian, and ufonaut, were found to be inadequate as generic appellations. Ergo, the term aconin, short for "another conscious intelligence," was created to fill this vacuum. In this handbook, aconin is used as a generic term. In meaning, it encompasses any intelligent being besides man. It encompasses both befaps and manadims, but is not specifically identified with either designation. In other words, both befaps and manadims are aconins, but aconin does not specifically refer to either a befap or to a manadim.

Zeroid was created as a designation for a space animal. Starism refers to that nascent philosophy which believes it is man's destiny to reach and to colonize the stars. Blisk was coined as a unit of light velocity.

Disciplines such as chemistry, history, physics, sociology, anthropology, and psychology are recognized and respected as practical and useful studies. In large part, their respectability stems from the fact that they present verifiable theories. But this has not always been the case. In medieval times, many of the sciences were looked upon as works of the devil. Scientists were punished by the authorities and were often made to repudiate their findings. Presently, however, the mere application of the term "science" or "scientific" suffices to endow a field of study with respectability.

Along with these accepted disciplines there exists a vast amorphous area of interest and study, such as astrology, spiritism, ufology, reincarnation and numerology. These fields are not considered sciences, and they lack respectability in the academic community. Scholars and scientists tend to look askance on persons interested in these areas. Though these fields of study deal with phenomena which are either real or purportedly real, one major handicap from which they suffer is that their respective areas of interest are not given to experimental verification. This lack of experimental verification has lessened their status. The lack of an umbrella term to cover all these fields of interest has also contributed towards lessening their status. This encyclopedia cannot show how to achieve the necessary experimental verification, but it has attempted to solve the related problem of terminology. In this connection, the neologism "naturalia" was coined. Naturalia is used as a class designation to encompass all manner of mysterious and unexplainable phenomena.

Perhaps the single most important neologism introduced here is "naphology." Naphology is intended to be a field of study or a branch of science which studies and deal with all manner of naturalia, i.e., mysterious and unexplained phenomena. It is intended to be a serious, scholarly, and scientific study of all reported phenomena which are not subject to experimental verification and for which there are no accepted explanations. In short, it is a scientific inquiry into the unknown.

The desire of naphology is to find answers, not to perpetuate myths. Its goal is to accumulate data and to determine if it is possible, and if so, then how, to experimentally verify unexplained phenomena.

Some of the areas of interest to naphologists are already being probed by the various established branches of science. A new branch of psychology, parapsychology, is probing the effects of psychic phenomena and psychokinetic energy. These fields touch on spiritism and ufology. Advances in this field, therefore, have a direct relation to ufology, a branch of naphology. Conversely, it is hoped that some of the data and theories of ufology will be of interest to parapsychologists.

Language is an indispensable tool of man. It is used by man to express ideas, thoughts, feelings, and concepts. Often a solution to a problem may be delayed because there is lacking an adequate language to deal with it. Each scientific and scholarly discipline has found it necessary to create its own language to deal with some of the concepts and ideas with which it is concerned. The same is true of ufology.

By codifying the language of ufology and by creating neologisms necessary to express a given concept, it is hoped that the next progressive step will have been taken towards putting ufology, as a branch of naphology, on a more scientific and scholarly level. It is hoped that by so doing, this handbook can aid in resolving the UFO phenomenon. It is hoped that naphology can serve as a bridge between the accepted sciences and that world of phenomena which science has hitherto ignored.

Ufology has produced its serious scholars as well as its share of nonsensical and ridiculous ones, persons lacking basic analytic skill and tools. Some UFO books are replete with wildly exaggerated theories and unsubstantiated beliefs, as, for example, the theory that neo-Nazis, bent on conquering the world, have a base on the bottom of the Atlantic Ocean, and that it is they who are responsible for the UFOs.

This UFO handbook has not attempted to champion any one ufological theory. It has taken the concepts and terms in use by ufologists, along with concepts and terms from other disciplines which relate to ufology, and has presented a concise explanation of each. It has presented in a succinct manner the basic theories as well as the objections and alternatives to these theories. Wherever possible, this encyclopedia has attempted an exegesis, i.e., a critical analysis of a term, thereby showing the strong points or weak points of each theory and concept. It has further collated the various concepts into a usable system by cross-referencing each term with other terms and concepts relating to and dealing with the same topic. It is hoped that this approach will permit it to become a valuable tool in the field of ufology, especially in furthering serious discussion and research into the subject matter.

It was an especially enjoyable experience to find, after cross-checking the various terms, that solutions already existed for some problems. Some nebecists, for example, have made a strong case that the Piri Reis Map shows alien influence in the remote past. Critics have argued forcibly and convincingly, however, that its origin is no mystery and that it is not as accurate as nebecists would have people believe. A solution to this mystery does not disprove the nebecian theory as a whole; it merely questions one of the proofs offered. In several other instances, a concept which has figured significantly in ufology has been labeled as solved. Case in point is the Great Red Spot on Jupiter. For decades it remained an enigma to scientists, and some ufologists attached great significance to it. Frank Edwards compared it to a giant eye focused on Earth. A number of ufologists maintained that it was a giant spaceship ready to evacuate Earth in time of disaster. Pioneer 10 examined the Red Spot and found it to be an 18,000-mile vortex. One mystery has thus been solved, and it can no longer be used by ufologists. Other such mysteries which have been solved are mentioned in this study.

It is hoped that the advance of science and scholarship will solve further mysteries associated with the UFO phenomenon. Each mystery solved narrows the list of possibilities. By progressively eliminating the least viable options and the solved mysteries, the main and important factors will be pushed to the forefront. This will permit naphology to better focus on the issues and to clarify the main problems.

This handbook has also kept in line with the developing changes of conception brought about by the advent of the space age and by ufological investigations. At one time, man used to say "the earth," but more and more this designation is becoming obsolete, being replaced by the designation "Earth." The difference in connotation between each term is quite significant, and in this UFO study the latter form has been used when reference is made to our planet.

As a handbook of ufology this reference book does not present its own theories. Its lifeline is the ever-developing field of ufology and the various other scientific disciplines which ufology involves. New concepts, new theories, and new discoveries in these fields will directly affect ufological research and analyses. By the same token, it is hoped that this encyclopedia will focus serious interest in the UFO phenomenon, and that some of the findings of ufology may have application to other fields of study. Indeed, most serious ufologists, such as Major Donald E. Keyhoe and Professor Clifford Wilson, present convincing arguments about the relevance of the UFO problem. Keyhoe is a nebecist and deals with the military and psychological hazards of keeping the public uninformed about UFOs. Dimensionalists, as, for example, John A. Keel and Clifford Wilson, present their UFO findings more in relation to religion and philosophy.

The UFO phenomenon is by no means near a solution. But, then, no mystery has ever been solved without serious scholarly study. When UFOs first made their appearance they presented a new challenge. Thirty years later, ufologists have done well at the task of taking the first steps towards resolving this great mystery. Ufologists, though not always agreeing with each other, have clarified the issues. We now know certain basic facts about the UFOs. There exist organizations devoted to the study of the phenomenon. Several specialized UFO publications exist, reporting new sightings and facts. Newspapers also report on the subject from time to time. It is hoped that a UFO study such as this will be an additional progressive step in helping to resolve the mystery.

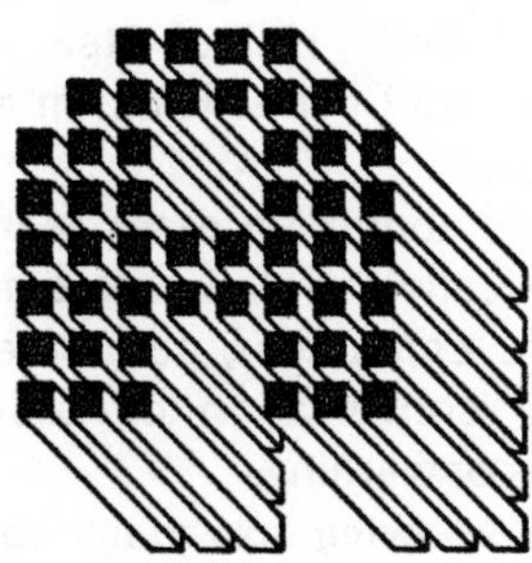

ABDUCTEE. The victim of an UFO abduction. These cases form the most interesting of the UFO encounters. In an abduction case, there is alleged to be an actual kidnapping of a human or humans by ufonauts for the purpose of examination and subsequent release or, possibly, for the purpose of permanent captivity. Human abductees who aren't released by the ufonauts may be utilized by them in one of several ways: servitude, source of food, source of amusement, and zoological or museum specimens.

Among the several kinds of UFO encounters, cases of reported abductions are extremely rare. The overwhelming majority of UFO reports are sightings of strange and moving aerial lights. Reports of landings and sightings of ufonauts are less frequent. Abduction cases belong to a special category of contact cases. Every abductee is also a contactee, but a contactee isn't necessarily an abductee.

There is one crucial difference between an abductee and a contactee. In a contact case, ufonauts reportedly contact some person and engage in friendly conversation with him or impart some message to him, invariably a warning to the human race to reform. The ufonauts may invite the contactee aboard the UFO for a trip into space, but will then return him safely back to Earth. Perhaps the most famous contactee was George Adamski.

In an abduction case, the ufonauts forcibly kidnap human victims. They are taken aboard the UFO against their will and are subjected to examination, study or experimentation, often of a sexual nature. Among the more famous abduction cases are those of Barney and Betty Hill of New Hampshire, Antonio Villas-Boas of Brazil, and Charles Hickson and Calvin Parker of Pascagoula, Mississippi.

The purpose behind abduction cases seems to be a desire by the ufonauts to physically violate in some manner the person of the abductee. Unlike contactees, abductees are not as a rule engaged in friendly conversation or issued any knowledge, predictions, greetings or warnings.

There is no way of knowing how many abduction cases occur annually. The only ones recorded are those which have been volunteered by those abductees who were released by the ufonauts. There is no manner of determining the number of abductees who are never released. Indeed, some ufologists have suggested that many of the missing persons on police files may actually be abductees. What happens to abductees who aren't released remains a mystery.

The difference between abductee and contactee cases leads to the speculation that two different phenomena may be involved. Abduction cases argue strongly for the extraterrestrial ufological theory. Ufologists who share the extraterrestrial theory tend to give more credence to the abduction cases, while downplaying the contactee cases.

On the other hand, ufologists who view the paranormal or the dimensionalistic theory as a viable explanation for UFOs see no basic difference between abduction cases and contact cases. They give credence to both types of encounters and believe that the same type of mysterious phenomena may be involved.

See: Adamski; Contactee; Dimensionalism; Hill.

ABSOLUTE EVENT HORIZON. The designation given to that area of a black hole from which light and radio waves cannot escape because the enormous gravitational pull of the collapsed star bends these waves back into the star.

See: Black Hole.

ACONIN. A neologism formed from "a(nother) con(scious) in(telligence)." This is a general term referring to and identifying all the different kinds of intelligent beings, other than human beings, which may exist in other parts of the Universe and in other parallel universes, assuming that different space-time continuums do in fact exist. A number of other terms exist to identify specific types of aconins.

See: Angel; Befap; Celestial; Elemental; Manadim; Ultraterrestrial.

ADAM. In the religious view as presented in the first book of the Bible, the Book of Genesis, Adam was the first man. He was created by God in His image.

With the rise of science, a new theory arose, that of evolution. According to this theory, a group of apes possessed the biological potential to become men. As a result of an interaction of natural selection, mutation, and environmental pressures, these apes evolved over the course of millions of years into men.

At first religion condemned evolution. Now, however, religion has been able to reconcile itself in part to the concept of evolution. But it makes one important qualification. It is willing to concede evolution, but argues that at the same point in man's evolution, God intervened and gave man a soul. It is this soul, religion tells us, which distinguishes man from animal.

The advent of the space age, coupled with the widespread sightings of UFOs, has engendered a new type of theory, that of nebecism. There are several nebecian theories on the origin of man. One nebecian school believes that man originated on another planet and was subsequently brought to Earth. A second nebecian school adheres to the evolutionary theory of the origin of man, but argues that befaps arrived on Earth and influenced the course of evolution. These visitors may have done this by destroying some biological lines of competing sapient life. For example, some nebecists argue that these befaps destroyed Neanderthal Man, thereby making it possible for the human lineage to inherit Earth.

Another possibility is that by genetic manipulation of a selected group of ape-men, these befaps speeded up the course of evolution of intelligent life on Earth. The first man or group of men to be the subjects of such an experiment were known, according to the nebecian theory, as adams, or collectively as Adam.

See: Evolution; Nebecism; Sendy.

ADAMSKI, GEORGE. One of the first modern-day UFO contactees and certainly one of the most famous. His name is now itself part of the lore of ufology. He reportedly saw his first UFO through a telescope in late 1946. These telescope sightings continued for years. Then in November 1952, he went to a desert in California in the belief that there he would find UFOs and establish contact with them. He claimed that his venture was successful and that he had established personal contact with a ufonaut, allegedly from Venus. This being expressed concern over nuclear testing on Earth.

Controversy surrounds Adamski to this day, over a decade after his death. Some consider him an outright hoax, others believe in him, revere his memory, and view him as a modern prophet of sorts.

ADVANCED BEING. Any civilization capable of interstellar space travel would necessarily be an advanced civilization. However, it must be stressed that the concept of "advanced" applies only to the technological achievements of these interstellar visitors. Ufologists, however, frequently refer to the saucerians themselves as "advanced" beings, and many ufologists suggest that man could learn much from these beings.

That these UFO beings would be advanced in the technological sense is indisputable, but it is an error to assume that they are similarly advanced in all respects. Given enough time, man will be able to equal the technology of the saucerians, as technology is basically a product of progress in knowledge, a matter of time, and a desire to learn and advance. That these saucerians possess a superior technology may be due solely to the fact that they evolved earlier than man and have had a headstart in accumulating scientific knowledge.

Man, however, may be morally, biologically and physically superior to these beings. Assuming that these UFO beings do in fact exist, the fact that they have made no attempt to conquer or to colonize Earth may indicate that they fear man for some reason.

It is also a mistake to assume that man has much to learn from them. Obviously, man could use some of their technological knowledge, assuming they would be willing to share it. But perhaps their moral and cultural values are not applicable or desirable for man. It may even be that their values are inferior to human ones. Their basic values, for example, may be totalitarian in nature, whereas those of man are freedom-oriented. As far as we know, these beings may perform ritual and institutionalized cannibalism or sacrifices. Just because an aconian civilization has attained space travel, it does not necessarily follow that this civilization is superior in all respects to human civilization. Nor does it necessarily follow that their standards are those by which human values or standards should be judged.

Ufologists have all too often approached the problem of contact from the point of view of the inferiority of man and the superiority of the aconins. They are also confident that the aconins will share their knowledge with man and help him. They share the unfounded and potentially dangerous view that the aconins are basically altruistic in nature. They look for salvation in the UFOs and see in them a panacea for all human ills.

If man progresses technologically to the point where human technology is equal to or near the technological level of the saucerians, man cannot continue then to regard the aconins as advanced beings. The UFO beings are "advanced," therefore, only in the sense that they possess superior technological knowledge; only in this sense and in no other.

AERIAL PHENOMENA RESEARCH ORGANIZATION. A UFO study and research organization founded in 1952 in Sturgeon Bay, Wisconsin by Jim and Coral Lorenzen. This was the first major UFO organization to be founded. Dissatisfied with the explanations for UFO incidents emanating from the Air Force, they decided to establish for research purposes and study an organization devoted to recording and disseminating information about UFO sightings. Since July 1952, the organization has issued its APRO Bulletin.

See: APRO Bulletin; Lorenzen.

AF. Acronym for Air Force.

See: Air Force.

AIR FORCE. The branch of the U.S. armed forces which was officially charged with investigating the UFO phenomenon. Publicly, the Air Force does not affirm the possibility that UFOs are spaceships from other planets. Its official position is that UFOs can be explained as natural phenomena or as objects misidentified by unqualified observers. Illusions, hallucinations, hoaxes, and frauds are also offered as common explanations.

Privately, however, the Air Force seems to hold a different opinion. Some individuals, as, for example, Dr. J. Allen Hynek, who was formerly associated with the Air Force program to investigate UFOs, revealed that there was tremendous pressure to cover up the truth about UFOs. If these sources are correct, then the indication is that privately the Air Force believes in the existence of UFOs.

It is believed that the Air Force does not want to admit the existence of UFOs because they are a phenomenon which it can neither explain nor control. Such an admission would be an acknowledgment of the Air Force's impotence. Another commonly given reason as to why the Air Force does not want to admit to the existence of UFOs is that it does not want to frighten the public. According to leading UFO authorities, the Air Force believes that the public will never be ready to accept the truth about UFOs.

Ufologists also argue that there are strong indications that the CIA has put pressure on the Air Force to debunk UFO reports. It is further maintained that the CIA, with its extensive network of contacts, has also contributed to the effort to keep the truth about UFOs from the public. The unofficial justification for the secrecy is that national security is involved. However, ufologists argue that such a justification is untenable. In fact, they maintain, failure to tell the public the truth may prove to be a greater danger than an open admission of the existence of UFOs.

See: CIA; Debunker.

AIRSHIP. In ufological lore this term refers to the mysterious flying craft which made their appearance over various parts of the United States beginning Thanksgiving week of 1896. These craft were usually cigar-shaped and huge, much like the "mother ships" of modern ufological lore.

The flap extended well into 1897. The sightings were widely written up in the periodicals of that time. There were no airplanes in those days, so the possibility that these airships were actually planes can be discounted. The possibility that these airships were human-built blimps or dirigibles can also be dismissed. There were only a few crude dirigibles then in existence, and the reports of the construction, maneuverability and speed of the airships precludes the possibility that they were these crude, human-built, lighter-than-air craft.

Contact was made with the occupants of these ships, who frequently carried on conversations with the humans. The occupants can be classified into three types: 1) human-appearing men and women, 2) "oriental" type of human-appearing individuals, and 3) nonhuman occupants.

Dimensionalists for the most part believe that these airships were the nineteenth-century equivalents of our modern-day UFOs, designed by the manadims to lead people astray into believing that they were actual craft, when in reality they were from another dimension. The flap was apparently another in the long line of seemingly pointless games that these beings have been playing upon a gullible mankind through the centuries.

The subject of airships is dealt with extensively by John A. Keel in *Why UFOs: Operation Trojan Horse.*

See: Dimensionalism; Mother Ship; UFO.

ALIEN. A term often used by ufologists to designate an intelligent being from another planet who visits Earth. A major shortcoming of this designation, however, is that it is also applicable to people. People born in one country who then emigrate and settle in another country are also called aliens. This double meaning of alien deprives this term of the unequivocalness and exactness required in a scientific field.

See: Aconin; Advanced Being; Befap; Manadim; Saucerian.

ALPHA CENTAURI. The sun's nearest stellar neighbor, Alpha Centauri is a triple-star system about 4.3 light-years from Earth. If UFOs are indeed from other planetary systems, Alpha Centauri would be the nearest star system from which these befaps could have come to Earth. If these beings have conquered the problems posed to space travel by aging and propulsion, it would be possible for them to travel to Earth without too much difficulty.

ANCIENT ASTRONAUT. A term used by ufologists and others to refer to those extraterrestrials who are supposed to have landed on Earth in antiquity and to have helped man along the path towards progress and civilization.

ANDROID. A type of robot which would physically resemble a human being. Ideally, it would be a perfect mimic of man in both appearance and behavior. Externally, an android should be indistinguishable from man. The fundamental difference between an android and an ordinary robot would be not in the degree of sophistication but in the structure of its outward appearance.

An android would be a robot in every respect, except for the fact that instead of a metallic outer layer, it would have a soft and pliable skinlike layer molded from a plastic-type substance.

The construction of an android is presently beyond the technological capabilities of man. But if such a machine should ever be constructed, its primary function would be to serve man.

The question of android beings also arises in connection with UFOs. Some of the UFO beings which have reportedly been sighted were described by witnesses as being metallic in appearance or as exhibiting rigid movements. If true, this would suggest that these beings were robots. Some of them may have even been androids which were mistaken for natural biological beings. Theoretically, it is possible to create an android. All that is required is a more advanced technology. It is possible that an advanced civilization may have used robots, and perhaps androids, on long interstellar journeys, such as to Earth, which required many light years to complete.

The very possibility that androids may exist raises ethical and moral questions. If an android exhibits all the behavioral characteristics of a biological being, is it then a real being or a mere machine? As a complete, self-sufficient unit capable of analysis and the storage and retrieval of information, a robot or an android might develop a distinct personality, possibly even an instinct for self-preservation.

This is a problem that man must sooner or later confront. For if he does not encounter androids in outer space, then man will in time surely fashion with his own hands androids here on Earth.

See: Bionic; Cyborg; Robot.

ANGEL. The word is derived from the Greek work "angelos," meaning messenger. In the Jewish and Christian religions an angel is one of a class of spiritual beings who are attendants of God. They frequently appeared to men either in person or in dreams, bringing him God's word.

One ufological theory argues that ancient man mistook humanoid astronauts for angels and gods. In this view, an angel was not a spiritual being but rather a physical being, i.e., an astronaut from another planetary system.

Another view is presented by ufologists who believe in the existence of either parallel space-time continuums which may be inhabited or of intelligent and conscious energy. They believe that these parallel worlds may be inhabited by intelligent beings. Therefore, dimensionalists are able to accept the idea of angels as beings with either a nonmaterial nature or with a physical nature different from that of man.

See: Dimensionalism; Heaven; Nebecism.

ANGELS' HAIR. The popular name given to one of the more baffling phenomena associated with UFOs. Angels' hair is the long weblike filament of white cottonlike or silky material which has been reported to be discharged by UFOs. What it is, what purpose it serves, or what connection it has with UFOs, remains a mystery.

Shortly after it falls on the ground or on trees, it disappears. If angels' hair is touched or handled by human hands it also quickly disappears. This propensity to disintegrate if exposed to air or handled in any way has hindered attempts to thoroughly analyze it.

There is nothing scientifically unusual about the ability of angels' hair to disappear. Strictly speaking, it does not disappear but merely changes chemical form. Angels' hair is probably a highly perfected type of biodegradable material.

Reports of fallen angels' hair go back to ancient times. Through the centuries tons of it have fallen to Earth, only to vanish. Only a few known specimens have been preserved by speedily placing them in airtight containers.

Strands of angels' hair may reach fifty feet. Preliminary analysis of several specimens indicates it contains boron, silicon, magnesium, and calcium. It is similar to borosilicate glass.

It is still a mystery, however, why angels' hair should be released by UFOs and why it would disappear quickly after being released. Some ufologists have suggested that it may be a type of exhaust or waste.

It is entirely conceivable that thorough scientific analysis of angels' hair may provide man with important information concerning the nature and functions of UFOs. The importance of angels' hair is that it provides tangible evidence of the reality of UFOs.

ANTARCTICA. The most mysterious and least explored of the seven continents, Antarctica, the fifth largest continent, is covered by ice the entire year. It is not owned by any country but has been set aside for peaceful scientific purposes. Several nations maintain research facilities there.

Of interest to ufologists is the fact that UFOs have occasionally been seen over the continent and emerging from or going into the surrounding oceans, sometimes right through the ice.

This has led to speculation by ufologists that there may be a UFO base located either somewhere on the continent itself, beneath the surface, or undersea. Another proposed theory for the not infrequent sightings is that Antarctica is a point of entry or window for UFOs flying to Earth and wishing to avoid the dangerous Van Allen radiation belts which encompass the whole planet except at the poles.

Ufologists also find strange the fact that so many different countries would spend the time, money, and manpower to study a barren and generally insignificant piece of frozen wasteland. They hint that these governments may in reality be aware of the presence of UFO bases or of the fact that Antarctica serves as a window for UFOs, and that they are there for the covert purpose of monitoring the activities of these UFOs.

Also of interest are the mysterious valleys, called polar deserts, which scientists are studying in Antarctica. These valleys are free of ice and snow the year round, even though the temperatures in these valleys occasionally drop as low as -70° F. Scientists believe that this absence of snow and ice is due to the flanking mountains which keep precipitation out, and to strong winds, occasionally of hurricane force, which scatter whatever snow does manage to gather.

Equally mysterious are the lakes which are found in these polar deserts. For some unknown reason, they are very salty, much saltier in fact than the Great Salt Lake in Utah. In addition, even though the lakes are covered with six to twelve feet of ice during the Antarctic winter, the bottoms of these lakes may register warm temperatures of 72° F.

Scientists do not at present have any adequate theory by which to explain this phenomenon. Some ufologists, however, have speculated that this unusual warmth may be generated by UFO bases located beneath the surface.

Further exploration, study, and full candor on the part of the government will be necessary before a definitive answer can be found.

ANTIKYTHERA MECHANISM. The name given to a device found in 1901 by two Greek divers off the small southern Greek island of Antikythera. The divers found the wreck of an ancient ship from which they brought up some bronze and marble statues.

From a study of the artifacts found, it has been estimated that the wreck occurred during the first century B.C. The divers also brought up some corroded bronze fragments which were thought to be meaningless until Professor Derek J. de Solla Price did an extensive study of them. He published his findings in the June 1959 issue of *Scientific American.*

The device, estimated to date back to about 80 B.C., is said to have been a computerlike mechanism with dials and gear wheels, which was capable of calculating the motion of stars and planets.

This mechanism constitutes one of the proofs cited by the nebecists in their claim that ancient astronauts visited Earth. They maintain that man was incapable of constructing such a device by himself or of knowing all the details concerning the motions of the stars and planets. They argue that such a device could have been constructed only from instructions supplied by befaps directly or from information which had been preserved for centuries by a select group, such as priests.

It should be pointed out, however, that if the mechanism was indeed constructed with the aid of knowledge supplied by befaps, then these beings were not aware of the existence of Uranus, Neptune, and Pluto, for the mechanism shows no evidence of such knowledge.

APRO. Acronym for Aerial Phenomena Research Organization.
See: Aerial Phenomena Research Organization.

APRO BULLETIN. The publication of the Aerial Phenomena Research Organization. It has been published since July 1952 and contains reports of UFO sightings, landings and contacts. The bulletin publishes both American as well as foreign UFO reports. These sightings are carefully researched by reliable and competent sources.
See: Aerial Phenomena Research Organization; Lorenzen.

AQUARIUS. Aquarius is both a constellation and a sign of the zodiac. It is currently in vogue to say that man is living in the Age of Aquarius. This simply means that the sun rises in the sign of Aquarius on the day of the vernal equinox.

The equinoctial sun will begin rising in the constellation of Aquarius about the year 2700 A.D. However, the equinoctial sun has been rising in the *sign* of Aquarius since about 1950.

Some nebecists argue that man will regain the Golden Age during the present Age of Aquarius. These individuals claim that there are ancient texts which relate the stay of befaps on Earth and their calculation, made before they departed from Earth, that in Aquarius man will equal them, i.e., become like the gods. In nebecian terminology, this is held to mean that man will have entered the space age and will be capable of space travel, including the ability to undertake interstellar journeys.

See: Golden Age; Sendy.

ARCHAEOLOGY. This is the science which systematically studies prehistoric and little-known cultures by excavating sites and then analyzing whatever artifacts may be found there. By this method, archaeologists attempt to piece together a history of the structure of the vanished culture.

Archaeology has recently come under severe criticism by some nebecists, notably by Erich von Daniken, who argue that it ignores important evidence in the form of legends, myths, pyramids, etc., in formulating theories about the life and cultural development of early man. This group of nebecists maintains that these various ignored sources of information prove that Earth was visited milleniums ago by beings from other planets.

If nebecism is one of the main opponents of archaeology, then the reverse is likewise true. Archaeology is one of the main scientific challenges to nebecism, a field of study still in its infancy. Archaeologists and anthropologists argue that prehistoric and ancient man, though not as knowledgeable as man today, was intelligent and was capable of many constructions and feats of wonder. Consequently, they maintain that all prehistoric and ancient finds and remains can be attributed to man and not to "ancient astronauts."

See: Nebecism, and Pyramid.

ARES. On August 15, 1976, the village of Ares, France inaugurated a landing field for UFOs. Located at the edge of the Bay of Arcachon, the field is marked by boundary lights. This is believed to be the first such public UFO spaceport on Earth. Its purpose is to provide a hospitable field for UFOs to land in the hope that ongoing contact can be established with them there.

ARGOBARD. The Archbishop of Lyons, France, who in 840 A.D. condemned the belief of many local peasants in the existence of "ships from the clouds," the inhabitants of which were said to have come from a place called Magonia. The farmers are said to have traded with these beings, and on one occasion to have stoned to death four individuals, three men and one women, who are said to have fallen from a sky "ship."

ARK OF THE COVENANT. A chest built by Moses according to very precise instructions given by God as to size, construction, and covering. The full details are given in chapter 25 of the Book of Genesis.

Inside the chest, Moses was to place the commandments inscribed upon stone which God had given him. The chest itself was treated as a holy object, representing the presence of God. Only divinely appointed persons were permitted to handle it. Immediate death was the punishment for anyone else who dared to touch it.

In chapter 4 of *Chariots of the Gods?*, nebecist Erich von Daniken argues that the ark was in reality a crude radio set used as a communications device between Moses and the extraterrestrial astronauts who had provided the instructions on how to build it. Von Daniken also states that the ark was electrically charged and that Uzzah was killed when he touched it. (See 2 Samuel, chapter 6, for the complete details of this incident.)

In chapter 3 of *Crash Go The Chariots*, Professor Clifford Wilson presents an entirely different explanation for the incident involving Uzzah. He points out that the ark could not have been electrically charged because its manner of construction would have caused an immediate short circuit. He suggests that, upon touching the ark, Uzzah died because of the great shock which he experienced after realizing that he had committed sacrilege. Professor Wilson also disputes von Daniken on other points. Specifically, he notes that, contrary to von Daniken's claim, nowhere does the Bible mention the fact that the ark was surrounded by sparks. Nor, he argues, did the priests have to wear special insulating clothes to handle the supposedly electrically-charged ark, as is claimed by von Daniken.

Professor Wilson also presents an interview with Geoff Peers, an electronics technician, and shows why the ark could not have been used as a radio with which Moses could communicate with the alleged spaceship which von Daniken postulated. As additional proof, he points out that God communicated with Moses prior to the construction of the ark, and that, therefore, the ark served no necessary function as a medium of communication.

A similar critical discussion of von Daniken's theory about the ark appears in *Some Trust in Chariots*, edited by Barry Thiering and Edgar Castle. Entitled "Excuse Me, Ezekiel," the chapter was written by Rev. Dr. R. A. Cole.

ARNOLD, KENNETH. On June 24, 1947, Kenneth Arnold, a businessman and commercial pilot from Boise, Idaho, was flying past Mount Rainier, in Mount Rainier National Park, State of Washington, when he sighted a strange formation of nine luminous saucer-shaped objects. He related this unusual experience to newsmen, and news of the mysterious objects, dubbed "flying saucers," was spread nationwide.

Following Arnold's sighting, numerous people across the country began to report that they had also seen similar objects. The date of Arnold's sighting has become the accepted date ushering in the modern UFO period. After the sighting, Arnold became something of a folk hero in ufology.

ARTIFICIAL EVOLUTION. This refers to the belief that extraterrestrial interference in the evolutionary processes, i.e., artificial evolution, helped create man and possibly other forms of life. Hence, this type of evolution is distinguished from natural evolution.

See: Astro-Evolution; Seeding.

ASHTAR. The self-given name of an entity who has contacted through mental telepathy a great number of mediums and UFO contactees. Ashtar frequently represents himself as a high-ranking member of something called "The United Council of the Universal Brotherhood." He frequently urges the contactees to go out and preach to "save the world." He has an intimate knowledge of the background histories of the contactees and frequently makes predictions, some of which come true, some of which don't.

The name Ashtar is associated with a pagan Canaanite goddess. The existence of Ashtar, and others like him, is frequently cited by some ufologists as an indication of the potentially evil, or Satanic, nature of UFOs.

ASSUMPTION OF MEDIOCRITY. This is a logical exploratory tool of science. Its basic premise is the universality of the laws of nature. Proceeding from this premise, it deduces logical conclusions. The certitude of the deductions is by no means proven. But in the absence of actual scientific experimental verification, these deductions provide temporary working hypotheses. In short, the Assumption of Mediocrity is a useful scientific tool.

The Assumption of Mediocrity was formulated by Sebastian von Hoerner, an astronomer. He believes that if the ancient Greeks had reasoned on the basis of the Assumption of Mediocrity, they could have used the knowledge at their disposal to determine, inter alia, the distances between stars.

Believers in extraterrestrial life have adopted the Assumption of Mediocrity to argue for the existence of extraterrestrial life and to argue that these intelligent beings could have landed on Earth millenniums ago. This argument proceeds from the knowledge about our solar system and extrapolates from this.

The argument would basically develop as follows: Our sun, a Class G star, has planets; therefore, other Class G stars should have planets. One planet (Earth) in our solar system is definitely known to have life; therefore, it should be possible for at least one planet in the planetary system of a Class G star to have life. Intelligent life arose on Earth; therefore, intelligent life could also have arisen on a planet in a planetary system of a Class G star. Earthmen are now reaching out into space and talking about colonizing other planets and traveling to other stars. Intelligent life on a planet in a planetary system of a Class G star older than our sun may have embarked on space exploration and colonization millenniums ago. Therefore, these alien astronauts may have visited Earth in times past and influenced the course of evolution here.

Though by no means conclusive, the Assumption of Mediocrity is convincing and can be used as a supporting tool to argue for extraterrestrial influence on Earth in times past as well as is the present.

See: Astroevolution; Nebecism.

ASTEROID. One of the numerous small celestial bodies orbiting the sun and lying between Mars and Jupiter. One theory has it that asteroids were formed from an exploding planet which was positioned between Mars and Jupiter. If this theory proves to be true, science would then have to determine what caused the explosion. Hopefully, detailed examination of asteroids at some future date will provide more definitive answers as to their origin and nature.

ASTRAL GOD. The word "astral" refers to the stars. According to the nebecian theory, there was nothing supernatural or spiritual about the gods of antiquity. These gods were in reality nothing more than astral gods, i.e., technologically advanced beings who originated from some distant planetary system. Primitive man in his ignorance mistook these aconian astral astronauts for gods, and began to worship them. Some nebecists see this as a possible origin of religion.

See: Befap; Nebecism.

ASTROENGINEERING. One consequence of the rise of learning is the start of engineering activities or projects by man. Engineering is the practical application of the knowledge derived from the pure sciences, such as physics, chemistry, and biology. Bridges, tunnels, skyscrapers are but some of the results. Engineering has permitted man to conquer his environment and to reshape it in such a way as to provide him maximum benefits. Similarly, we now hear of biological engineering; that is, the manipulation of genes in order to achieve optimum biological efficiency.

The advent of the space age has widened man's engineering concepts. As man took his first steps into space, he also began thinking about a new type of engineering. Theoretically, it should be possible for man to conquer the environment of space and to reshape it. The accomplishment of such feats is solely a problem of knowledge. Man must first learn more about the environment of space and then decide what to reshape and how to reshape it.

The possibility of astroengineering (i.e., the reshaping of the environment of space) is not a new idea. It was first suggested by the Greeks. Archimedes, in a somewhat jesting manner, pointed out the laws of physical mechanisms when he stated that if he could position a fulcrum and a lever in a suitable location, he could move the world.

Technologically, astroengineering is already within man's reach. Nuclear energy and lasers are capable of accomplishing some astroengineering projects. Theoretically, it should be possible to dismantle planets, to move planets to other orbits, to create stars, etc. A much to be desired project would be the creation of Dyson spheres, which may hold the answer to the energy shortage. Presently, most of the sun's energy is wasted. Dyson spheres would collect this energy and make it possible for man to use it.

As science and technology advance, man will one day embark upon a systematic organized program of astroengineering in his solar system. Carl Sagan, astrophysicist at Cornell University, has suggested a plan whereby Venus could be made habitable. It would take about five thousand rockets filled with algae. If algae were dumped in a sufficient quantity on Venus, these one-celled plants would be able, through the process of reproduction, photosynthesis, and decay, to transform the environment of the planet. They would dissipate the heavy clouds which hang over the planet. Through photosynthesis and decay, the algae would release oxygen, thus helping create a life-sustaining atmosphere. Once started, this process would create an ongoing chemical change until a suitable environment could be created.

The possibility of astroengineering raises a related question. Assuming that there are befaps somewhere in the Universe, it would be reasonable to postulate that they have also engaged in astroengineering. It may be possible to detect the presence of such befapian civilizations by the discovery of their celestial astroengineering projects, assuming that they undertook and performed the right types of astroengineering projects. One method of searching for these projects would be to look for any possible signs that a celestial phenomenon might be of a non-natural origin. For example, some astrophysicists believe that the unexplained, very high-intensity waves emanating from the center of our galaxy might be signs of befapian presence. However, they are also quick to caution that on the basis of physical laws all astronomical phenomena should be considered natural until and unless proven otherwise.

See: Dyson Sphere; Terraformation; Type II Civilization.

ASTROEVOLUTION. The traditional theory of evolution holds that man arose as a result of natural evolutionary processes on Earth. This theory is rejected by adherents of the extraterrestrial theory of evolution. They argue that natural selection and mutation couldn't have by themselves given rise to man and to certain other species of plants and animals. The proponents of this theory have two main reasons for rejecting natural evolution.

The first is that evolution works too slowly to account for the multitude of species, especially man, which have arisen.

The second reason involves the problem of "missing links." If there were an orderly transition from one species to a new and higher species, there should be fossils showing the gradual, progressive changes as one species evolved into another. In the case of man, there are no fossil records to show a detailed transition from an ape to an ape-man to a man. The theory of natural evolution is also at a loss to explain man's big brain and super intelligence.

However, adherents of the extraterrestrial connection argue that astroevolution, i.e., evolution from space, can solve all the problems which the theory of natural evolution can't. This theory is basically a synthesis of natural evolution and astroevolution. The origin and/or diversity of life on Earth, especially the origin of man, can be satisfactorily explained by the joint, complementary functioning of astroevolution and natural evolution.

In this theory, beings from another planet (befaps) could have landed on Earth and speeded up the natural evolutionary processes, creating man and possibly other species of life. This artificial influence would explain why there are no "missing links"—there simply are no such links.

In this theory, UFOs are viewed as spacecraft from the civilization which gave rise to man. They are presently monitoring the development and progress of mankind.

The theory of Astroevolution was systematically presented and elaborated in depth by Max H. Flindt and Otto O. Binder in *Mankind—Child Of The Stars.*

The theory of extraterrestrial influence of the origin of and evolution of life on Earth can also be found in works of many authors dealing with ufological themes. There are slight variations in the theory as presented by various authors. Basically, the disagreement centers around the time of the arrival of the ancient astronauts, the duration of their stay on Earth, and the degree of their interference.

See: Binder; Evolution; Flindt; Life; Seeding; Sendy.

ASTROLOGY. A study or field of alleged knowledge which believes and claims that heavenly bodies have an influence on human affairs. Astrologers claim the ability to interpret the influence of celestial bodies on human affairs and human events. This is done through their alleged ability to interpret meanings said to be found in a celestial chart called a zodiac. In this chart, the heavens are divided into twelve sections, each of which is represented by an appropriate symbol.

Astrology traces its origins to Babylonian days. It was an early form of the science of astronomy; in particular, the practical application of astronomy. It continues to have a large following despite the fact that many scientists and scholars dispute the claim that heavenly bodies exert any significant effect on human affairs and behavior. To a degree, however, there is an effect. Sunlight, for example, affects life on Earth in a very real and direct manner. On bright sunny days, people are generally more cheerful than on cloudy, rainy days. Another example is the moon, which in western culture has been identified as a romantic symbol.

This influence of the moon and the sun, however, is undeniably psychological. To what extent this influence is natural and to what extent it is culturally conditioned is still another issue. Therefore, though the sun and the moon do appear to exert a limited influence on behavior, distant stars and planets appear to have none at all.

According to scientists and scholars, one of the most damaging arguments against the validity of astrology is the fact that it makes Earth the center of the Universe. Other heavenly bodies are supposed to affect life on Earth and to decide the destinies of men and countries. But if astrology is valid, the astrologers ignore the possibility that Earth may have a corresponding effect on life on other heavenly bodies.

This is important to note because man has already visited another heavenly body. In *The Coming of the Gods,* Jean Sendy poignantly pointed out that when Neil Armstrong stepped onto the surface of the moon, Earth then became a heavenly body which was supposed to affect him. However, in their scheme astrologers had not taken Earth into account as an affecting heavenly body. No doubt, however, as time goes on astrology will be modified to take this into account.

It will be interesting to see how things develop in astrology. In the meantime, unless astrology places itself on a more solid scientific footing, it will continue to remain on the fringes of scientific study and interest.

See: Zodiac.

ASTRONAUT. A person who travels beyond Earth's atmosphere. Literally, the term is a combination of two words, "astro" and "naut," and means a traveler of, in, to, or from the stars. As a general term it can be used to designate all intelligent beings, whether human or aconian, who travel in space. Specifically, however, it applies to spacemen from the United States of

America. Spacemen from the Union of Soviet Socialist Republics are known as cosmonauts.

See: Cosmonaut; Starman.

ASTRONAUT GOD. In the nebecian theory, the gods of antiquity were really supposed to have been astronauts from distant stars. They arrived on Earth and, during their stay, gave an impetus to the evolution of human society. Primitive men mistook these astronauts for gods, and, according to some nebecists, religion developed as a result of their worship of these befapian astronauts.

See: Astral God; Befap; Nebecism.

ASTRONOMY. One of the first and oldest branches of science. Astronomy studies celestial bodies, their physical properties, motions, positions, distances, and magnitude. One of its goals is to search for evidence of intelligent life. On a number of occasions, astronomers had believed that such evidence existed. Among the objects and discoveries thought to have been signs of intelligent origin were the channels (incorrectly rendered into English as canals) on Mars, the Martian moons, and pulsars. However, all of these have been proven to be of natural origin.

Presently, astronomers are looking at another stellar phenomenon as possible evidence of the presence of intelligent life. They are looking at any bright or powerful light sources which might be emanating from a particular star or galaxy in the possibility that such light sources may be attempts by intelligent beings to communicate with other intelligent beings or to make their presence known. Nonnatural radio waves would also be a sign of intelligent life.

Officially, no such radio contact has been established, nor have any intelligible radio waves been intercepted. However, some ufologists, among them Major Donald E. Keyhoe, believe that unreported intelligible radio signals from other stars may have been intercepted and possibly even deciphered.

See: Green Bank Formula; Martian Moons; Project Ozma; Pulsar; Type II Civilization.

ASTROPHOTOGRAPHY. The branch of photography which deals with the photography of stars, planets, and other celestial bodies and objects. Various techniques are used, such as infrared, ultraviolet, and X-ray photography.

ASTROPHYSICS. A branch of astronomy which studies and examines the physical properties and phenomena of celestial bodies, concentrating in particular on the study of the surfaces and interiors of stars via such means as astrophotography and spectrum analysis.

See: Astronomy.

ATLANTIS. An island or continent which was supposed to have existed in the North Atlantic Ocean. Scholars doubt whether the island ever existed. The only primary reference to Atlantis is recorded by Plato in two works, *Timaeus* and *Critias,* but even he admits that he learned of it by hearsay. This makes it an extremely complicated subject to discuss because it is based upon the existence of unverified facts.

Throughout the millenniums, a host of legends, myths, and beliefs have grown up around Atlantis. They are too numerous to list. In fact, over a hundred thousand articles, books, and newspaper accounts have appeared about this "sunken continent." To this day, there exists a group of hard-core believers who maintain that Atlantis did, or still does, or will, exist.

There are six main theories about Atlantis. Each theory will be briefly considered.

One theory holds that Atlantis never existed and that claims about its existence are fantasies and myths.

A second theory maintains that it did exist, but that the Atlanteans were basically no different culturally from the other Grecian city-states. The island of Thera in the Aegean Sea is often cited as a possible location for Atlantis.

A third theory holds that Atlantis was a super-technological state. While the rest of the world's inhabitants worked the ground with plow and hand, and sailed the dangerous oceans in ships of wood, the inhabitants of Atlantis are supposed to have possessed machines capable of flight and of performing other wondrous deeds. Atlanteans were also greatly advanced in the biological and medical fields, and were supposed to have performed various biogenetic experiments on human guinea pigs. Quite appropriately one of the products of these experiments, holds this theory, was the creation of pigs. According to this view, pigs are held to have arisen from mutated humans. If true, this means, of course, that each time people eat pork, they indulge in a form of cannibalism.

A fourth theory holds that Atlantis was located on another

planet. Accordingly, the Atlanteans were befaps. Primitive men who could not comprehend the existence of aerial flight or of space travel misunderstood the Atlanteans when they told men of their place of origin. Primitive men believed it to be from some distant land when in fact the Atlanteans referred to another planet.

A fifth theory holds that Atlantis still exists as a subterranean civilization. It postulates the existence of a subterranean civilization which exists beneath the surface of the planet. According to this theory, UFOs originate from this underground civilization. Likewise, some of the most unfortunate mining accidents are said to have been caused by the inhabitants of this subterranean world who resent the intrusion of the surface dwellers.

A sixth theory maintains that Atlantis was so far advanced technologically that the Atlanteans were able to increase their vibratory rate, and that the entire civilization vanished into a higher frequency level of existence. In this view, Atlantis still exists in a parallel universe. This parallel universe is held to be physically superior to our space-time continuum. Some day, it is maintained, mankind will also vibrate into this higher plane of existence. According to this theory, UFOs originate from this parallel world to monitor man's progress.

All the theories agree that the trident was the symbol of Atlantis, an interesting bit of information because the trident has also been linked to UFOs. Another belief shared by many is that the Atlanteans were literally red-skinned (as opposed to suntanned) people.

Even among those who believe that Atlantis existed there is a great diversity of opinion as to what exactly happened to the island or continent. Those who hold that Atlantis was destroyed claim that such destruction resulted in one of three ways.

Nuclear destruction is held as one possibility. An unexpected natural catastrophe is another explanation. Related to these two, but also separate, is the moral cause. The moral abyss into which the Atlanteans sunk is said to have so affected and perverted their science and technology that their moral corruption was the prime cause of their destruction. Such destruction, according to this view, would have occurred either through nuclear devastation or as a result of the revolt of the subjugated peoples.

Some believe that traces of Atlantis have been found beneath the sea or that remnants of it still exist. The Azores are held to be what remains of the once great and powerful continent of Atlantis. The Basques of the Pyrenees, who are unlike and unrelated to any other European people, have been suggested as possible descendants of Atlanteans.

Atlantis is a fascinating subject. Its existence has been debated for centuries and will no doubt continue to be debated in the future. Those elements in the Atlantis story that relate to UFOs are of particular interest to ufologists. In short, as a subject matter, Atlantis forms a bridge between the historical, the mythological, and the occult. It also touches upon and involves the mysterious UFOs.

See: Mu; Parallel Universe; Trident; UFO.

ATOMIC AGE. The name applied to the period of history ushered in by the development and use of atomic or nuclear energy; in particular, the detonation of the first atomic bomb on July 16, 1945, at Alamogordo, New Mexico. It is an age characterized by the use of nuclear energy for military, political, and industrial purposes. Some scientists, scholars, and writers believe that the dawn of the Atomic Age also ushered in Earth's first contact with UFOs. Adherents of this view believe in the existence of aconins, but doubt that aconins, even if they were aware of Earth's existence, exhibited any interest in Earth prior to the first atomic explosion, perhaps not even being aware of the existence of intelligent life on Earth. However, according to this view, the use of atomic energy, especially the use of atomic bombs, alerted aconins to Earth. Therefore, they began arriving in large numbers to investigate our planet and its inhabitants.

AVRO. In the early 1950s, the U.S. armed services began secretly constructing and experimenting with disc-shaped aircraft. These aircraft were built for the U.S. by the Canadian AVRO Corporation. These AVRO aircraft were a complete failure. One June 24, 1960, the Army officially stated that the AVRO craft could lift only a few feet, that its top speed was a meager 35 mph, and that the craft was difficult to control. The Army, Navy, and Air Force had spent $10 million on the AVRO project before they finally admitted failure and cancelled it.

The AVRO aircraft has an interesting nexus with UFOs. The aircraft first received publicity in 1955. Large-scale UFO sightings had been continuing for a decade. The public was slowly coming to the conclusion that UFOs might be spaceships from other planets or galaxies. The Air Force, officially charged with investigating the UFOs, denied their extraterrestrial origin. It claimed that all sightings could be explained as either natural phenomena or as misidentifications of manmade objects. The remaining cases it labeled as hoaxes. Nevertheless, public pressure kept mounting.

In response to this pressure and in reaction to a scheduled hearing by the House Armed Services Committee, the Air Force, on the day before the hearings, released a photograph of an AVRO aircraft. It further stated that this revolutionary aircraft would be capable of attaining speeds of 1,500 mph. The implication was that such AVRO aircraft had existed for years and that the public had mistaken them for UFOs. The revelation was also an attempt to condition the public into believing that future UFO sightings would in fact be AVRO aircraft.

This brilliant attempt by the Air Force to cover up the UFO phenomenon worked for a while. But the admission by the Army on June 24, 1960, that the AVRO aircraft was a complete failure, officially ended this type of cover-up attempt. Left still unanswered, therefore, was the mystery of the UFOs.

See: Air Force; UFO.

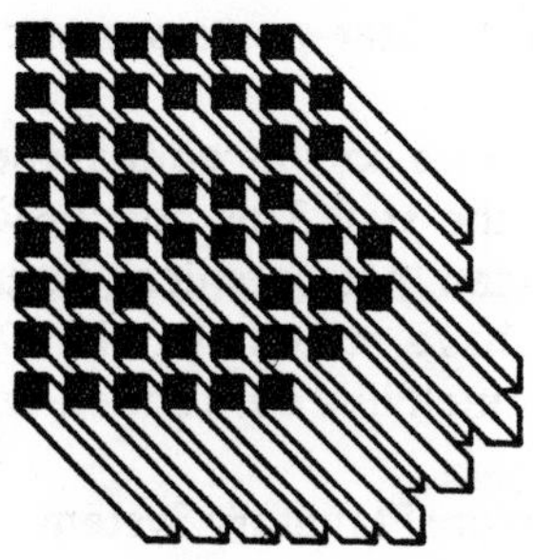

BAALBEK TERRACE. Huge stone platforms found in Baalbek, an ancient ruin located in east Lebanon. The Greeks called the city Heliopolis. In ancient times this city was dedicated to Baal, the Phoenician sun god. When vitrified stones were found there among the ruins, M. Agrest, a Russian ethnologist, proposed in 1959 that the huge stone platforms of the terrace at Baalbek, some weighing many tons, had served as launching pads for alien spaceships. The fiery exhaust from these spaceships, he argued, had vitrified these stones, i.e., had turned them to glass.

Though the vitrification is a mystery, there is, however, no other solid evidence to substantiate this claim.

BALL LIGHTNING. See: Fireball.

BARNARD'S STAR. The name given to a red star located six light years from Earth. The nearest known single star in our galaxy, it was discovered in 1916 by Edward E. Barnard and named after him.

This star is of special interest because scientists are positive that there are a number of planets which revolve around it. This, of course, has tremendous implications for the field of ufology because of the possibility that one of these planets may be inhabited. The beings on such an inhabited planet may be technologically more advanced than humans and may have embarked on a galactic exploratory mission millennia ago.

One way of determing whether a distant star has an orbiting planet would be to find a perceptibly irregular "wobble" in the rotation of the star. This would indicate that the gravitational pull of an invisible body is acting upon the rotation of the star. Interestingly, Barnard's Star possesses such a "wobble" in its rotation.

By 1956 scientists were convinced that there was indeed an orbiting body around the star. This conclusion was confirmed in 1963 by the American Astronomical Society. Since then, researchers at NASA have stated that Barnard's Star may have three giant planets, much like our Jupiter, Saturn, and Uranus, orbiting around it.

See: Dark Companion; Planetary System.

BEFAP. An acronym formed from "Being from Another Planet." This is a general term referring to and identifying all intelligent beings, other than human beings, that may exist in other parts of the Universe.

In the past these beings from points unknown may have visited Earth. It is possible that they may still be visiting Earth if the UFO reports are indeed true and if UFOs originate from outer space rather than from a parallel space-time continuum.

If befaps do indeed exist, the question then arises as to how many different kinds there are. On the basis of man's present knowledge, however, there is no definitive answer to this question. Descriptions provided by witnesses who claim to have seen UFO beings vary greatly with regard to the physical features of these creatures.

See: Aconin; Manadim.

BELIEF. A conviction, based on nonverifiable grounds, about the truth or reality of something. Belief accepts an alleged fact as true or correct without positive knowledge or proof. Many psychological factors enter into the formulation of a belief. A man's fears, hopes, desires, past experiences, incomplete evidence of the discussed subject, opinions of others, and coincidences all enter into the picture.

Belief also enters into the UFO phenomenon. No revealed scientific proof exists of their existence, nor has science explained away the phenomenon. Though proof or knowledge of UFOs is incomplete, this does not deter people from holding an opinion on the subject.

One group of people denies and ridicules their existence. Another group believes that they exist, but disagrees on whether they are from another planet or from a parallel universe, and on whether they are friendly or hostile. A third group takes the middle position. It is willing to admit the possibility of their existence, but remains as yet unconvinced.

BERLITZ, CHARLES. Renowned expert on the area of mysterious disappearances known as the Bermuda or Devil's Triangle. He has conducted extensive research into the disappearances and has written a number of books and articles on the subject, notably *The Bermuda Triangle* and *Without a Trace.*

In the book *Mysteries from Forgotten Worlds,* Berlitz, in effect, challenges the ancient astronaut hypothesis that much of man's achievement in the past was due to intervention by extraterrestrials. Instead, he suggests that there were supercivilizations on Earth in the past which were destroyed by cataclysmic disasters and by nuclear war, and that there are hints about these civilizations, including Atlantis, in the various myths and legends of the world.

BERMUDA TRIANGLE. One of several synonyms for the Devil's Triangle.

See: Devil's Triangle.

BIBLE. The collection of sacred writings of the Jewish and Christian religions. Christians divide the Bible into two parts, the Old Testament and the New Testament. Religious teaching holds that the books of the Bible were inspired by God.

Some nebecists have utilized various parts of the Bible to bolster their argument that befapian astronauts landed on Earth in its remote past, and that they influenced the events recorded in the Bible. However, not one of the nebecists who use the Bible as a source material has yet provided a nebecian explanation for the entire Bible. Rather, each nebecist who relies on the Bible concentrates on only a few sections of it.

Theologians point out that the Bible constitutes one whole complete work which presents a special message of God's relation and revelation to man, and of man's relation to God. Therefore, a critical review of the Bible should focus in on its central meaning—the story of man's transgression of God's law, and of the salvation offered man by God. This message runs throughout the entire Biblical account.

Nebecists have been severely criticized by Bible scholars, who accuse the nebecists of picking out parts from the Bible, of misinterpreting these parts by taking them out of context, and then of using these parts as proof of extraterrestrial visitations to Earth in the past. Bible scholars emphasize that no nebecist who has used the Bible as a source has yet focused on the Bible as one whole complete work. Bible scholars also point out that some nebecists even create their own Biblical facts and then cite these facts as though they were actually found in the Bible.

See: Ark of the Covenant; Eden; Elohim; Enoch; Ezekiel; Nebecism; Yahweh.

BIG BANG THEORY. According to this cosmogony or cosmology, all matter was originally compactd together in one colossal mass. About 12 billion years ago, something triggered an explosion, or big bang, which sent matter hurtling into space in all directions; thus the Universe came into being.

There is a corollary to this theory which has direct consequences to philosophy, religion, and metaphysics. Some scientists believe that space contains more matter than had been originally believed. Matter is held together by gravitational forces, and the Big Bang theory has an important implication in this regard.

Because of the vast amount of matter in space, the mass which was hurled may not have enough energy or momentum to break free from the gravitational pull which each body exerts upon another. For example, if a rocket lacked enough fuel to lift its weight out of Earth's gravitational field into space, it would fall back to Earth. This means that eventually the Universe may stop expanding and collapse into itself. All matter would then again form a giant mass and the process of a Big Bang would start all over again. If this theory is true, the question which then arises is how many times has this happened in the past, and how many times will it happen in the future.

The Big Bang theory does not preclude the existence of God. God may still be necessary to explain the existence of matter and of the natural laws which govern matter.

The Big Bang theory has direct relation to some of the nebecian views. According to one variant of the nebecian theory, God was a befapian astronaut, and the immortality promised by many religions was not a spiritual immortality but a technological one, that is, the know-how and ability to prolong life by eliminating diseases and replacing worn-out vital organs.

However, one difficulty with regard to immortality, whether it be spiritual or physical, is posed by the Big Bang theory: If, as the theory implies, our Universe is finite, how will immortality be possible in a finite universe? The matter which constitutes our Universe may be eternal, but the Universe itself may not be eternal. It also follows that if God is eternal, obviously He could not then depend on or exist in a finite universe. Thus, if immortality is a true promise, such immortality or eternal life has to be in a plane of existence different from the one in our visible and finite universe. The implications are, of course, that an eternal life would have to be in a parallel universe, and that the aconian "gods," if they were sincere in their promise of immortality, would have had to come from such a parallel universe.

See: Space; Steady State Theory; Superspace; Technological Immortality.

BIGFOOT. The American name of the North American version of the Yeti or the Abominable Snowman. Bigfoot refers to a large anthropoid creature, usually 7–9 feet tall and estimated to weigh 500–700 pounds, seen most frequently in the northwestern areas of the U.S. and Canada. Sightings in other areas of the U.S. have also been reported. Investigators are divided on the question of whether Bigfoot, known mostly in Canada as Sasquatch, is an unknown species of ape or whether it is a surviving species of man-ape.

Sightings of Bigfoot are infrequent. Several expeditions have gone in search of Bigfoot but have failed in their attempt to capture one. However, one excellent film clip of Bigfoot exists. It was taken on October 20, 1967, at Bluff Creek, California, by Roger Patterson, who along with Bob Grimlin, was searching for Bigfoot. The genuineness of the film continues to be a source of controversy.

Though sightings of Bigfoot have been relatively infrequent and rare, actual contact cases have been even rarer. However, there have been reported cases of hostility on the part of the Bigfoot creatures.

One unresolved question about Bigfoot is whether these creatures are permanent inhabitants of the areas of sightings. UFOs have frequently been sighted around the Bigfoot sighting areas, and this has led to the theory that there might be a relationship between UFOs and Bigfoot. The Bigfoot creatures may, for example, be pets of the ufonauts. Another even more bizarre possibility is that the Bigfoot creatures may be the actual occupants of at least some of the UFOs.

The case linking Bigfoot and UFOs possesses one strong argument. If Bigfoot were an earthly creature, then sightings of it ought to be more frequent and one should have been captured by now. But if the creature comes from UFOs or is merely a temporary physical entity resulting from the transmogrification of energy, as has been suggested by some researchers, then this would explain why the creature is so elusive.

No conclusive evidence regarding the Bigfoot creature exists at present. Nor has the link between UFOs and Bigfoot, strong as it is, been conclusively established. However, it is inevitable that in time this mystery will be solved.

See: Transmogrification.

BINDER, OTTO O. A believer in the existence of extraterrestrial civilizations, he also believes that man's history has been influenced by beings from space. On the UFO question, he shares the extraterrestrial theory as opposed to the dimensionalistic theory. He has written books on the subject of UFOs and has also authored various works of fiction, including science fiction, and popular scientific works. Perhaps his most ambitious work on the extraterrestrial and UFO theory is a book he co-authored with Max H. Flindt, *Mankind—Child Of The Stars,* in which the theories of Hybrid Man and Earth Colony are explored and systematically developed.

See: Earth Colony; Flindt.

BIOGENESIS. The biological doctrine that living organisms come from other living organisms. Empiricism substantiates this doctrine. But its weakness or vulnerability arises at only one point: It cannot explain the genesis of life, i.e., the creation of the first living organisms from matter or from prebiological molecules.

See: Evolution; Life; Seeding.

BIOLOGY. The branch of science which studies life and living organisms in all their forms. It is divided into two branches, botany and zoology. Presently, biology is limited only to the study of living organisms on Earth. This limitation has prevented the formulation of more universal laws of biology. Some biologists believe that the laws of biology are as universal as the laws of physics or chemistry. They believe that life arises naturally at a certain stage in the development of molecules. Therefore, some biologists believe or at least are willing to admit the possibility that life exists outside of Earth. Their hopes are heightened by the discovery in space of vast amounts of preorganic molecules. All that would be needed is some appropriate stimulus to give the molecules the spark of life. Exobiology, a new branch of biology, is exploring the question of extraterrestrial life.

See: Assumption of Mediocrity; Botany; Exobiology; Life; Zoology.

BIOLUMINESCENCE. One of the most unusual and rarest of biological phenomena is the production of light by living organisms. Such light production is called bioluminescence. Science does not yet understand the process involved. The firefly is perhaps the most widely known example of a living organism capable of bioluminescence. The most fascinating aspect of this process is that all energy is utilized in producing the light. No heat or waste by-product is produced.

If science could learn how to convert all energy into light without simultaneously producing heat, a major step in the utilization and conservation of energy would be found. Presently, science can minimize the production of heat, as in fluorescent lamps, but it cannot eliminate the heat entirely.

Bioluminescence has also been suggested as a possible explanation of some UFOs. Perhaps there are some aerial animals, as yet unidentified, which are bioluminescent and which are mistaken for UFOs. There is, for example, a species of deep ocean fish, called angler fish, which are equipped with built-in light sources to help them survive in the dark, inhospitable depths of the ocean.

One of the most unusual cases of bioluminescence concerns the so-called "wheels of light." This phenomenon has been observed most often in the tropical waters of the Indian Ocean, the Persian Gulf, and the South China Sea. The phenomenon consists of revolving lights which stretch out in a shape similar to the spokes of a wheel. These "spokes" have a definite origin, and this point of origin has been seen to move. Furthermore, these "spokes" of light do not broaden as does the beam of a flashlight, but stretch out in even parallel bands.

The lights may be the result of *Noctiluca miliaris,* a single-celled marine animal found worldwide but most abundant in tropical waters. These creatures light up when stimulated. Though these animals may be the cause of the light, they do not provide self-stimulation. One theory is that an underwater craft, perhaps a UFO, or more properly, a USO, broadcasts waves via radar or sonar which stimulate these creatures.

These wheels of light have been reported by numerous ships passing through the above-noted waters. The experience is eerie, and, not unexpectedly, no one has as yet found the courage to go underwater and investigate. In several cases, these wheels of light passed right under the ship. In other cases, they were spotted as originating at the horizon and then moving closer. These strange wheels of light constitute one of the arguments in favor of the existence of UFOs, especially of the sea-diving ones.

See: USO; Zeroid.

BIONIC. A term popularized by the TV series "Six Million Dollar Man." It refers to an individual who is part organic and part mechanical. On a very rudimentary level bionics already exist. The advance of medical science and technology has made possible the implantation of certain synthetic parts to replace defective organic ones, and the utilization of prosthetic devices to substitute for missing limbs. At other times, a mechanical unit, a pacemaker, for instance, is implanted not to substitute for the heart, but to aid in the proper functioning of a defective heart.

The benefit of artificial parts to either replace or aid organic parts is readily evident. Life is prolonged, and a useful, productive existence is made possible. The continuing advance of medical science and technology should bring further improvements in this area.

The utilization of artificial, mechanical parts also opens up another fascinating possibility. Healthy but vulnerable organic parts could be replaced early in life with durable artificial ones to increase strength and endurance. This could have application to many areas of human endeavor, including use on long space journeys. At present, however, an advanced bionic man is possible only in the realm of science fiction.

An important distinction should be drawn between a man who is part mechanical and part organic, and an aconin who is part mechanical and part organic. Bionic refers only to a human and presupposes a human nature. An aconin, assuming such beings exist, who is part mechanical and part organic is called a cyborg.

Ufologist Major Donald E. Keyhoe, USMC (Ret.), for example, believes that some ufonauts may be cyborgs.

See: Aconin; Cyborg.

BLACK HOLE. At the end of their lifetimes, massive stars, fifty times or more larger than the sun, implode or collapse into themselves. In the formation of neutron stars, nuclear force stops the stars from completely collapsing in on themselves. In the formation of black holes, however, there is nothing to arrest the implosion of the giant stars. Eventually, their matter becomes so compressed and their gravity so strong that nothing can withstand their pull, not even light. Because light cannot escape from their surface, black holes cannot be seen optically. Their presence is established gravitationally. For this reason, such collapsed stars are called black holes.

The term black hole is actually a misnomer because there is no hole present. There is a solid object. Nor is a black hole necessarily black. It may be white-hot and extremely bright, but because of its enormous gravitational pull, this light can never escape from its surface. Scientists believe that a black hole has an extremely smooth surface, and that, because of its tremendous gravitational pull, ripples cannot form on it. Anything that is trapped within its gravitational pull can never escape. It can even suck in other stars. Astronomers believe that there is a black hole, called Cygnus X-1, about eight thousand light-years from Earth, near the star known as HDE 226868, with which it revolves and from which it sucks in clouds of gas.

Because black holes are a recent discovery, very little scientific information is available about them. However, there has been much speculation. One speculative scientific theory states that black holes may be space gates, i.e., short-cuts between different parts of the Universe and possibly between different epochs of time. Carl Sagan, astrophysicist at Cornell University, discusses this possibility in his book *Cosmic Connection.* This hypothesis is based on the theory that, since nothing can escape from it, a black hole seems to be a microuniverse within the Universe.

If this hypothesis is proven to be true, then black holes may indeed be used for interstellar travel. This possibility, therefore, also relates to the question of UFOs. If they originate from distant places in the Universe, then how, considering that the nearest black hole is several thousand light-years from Earth, were they able to travel to Earth even if they did emerge from Cygnus X-1? This is still too great a distance for UFOs to travel, unless they have overcome the problem of conventional propulsion.

Furthermore, it is generally acknowledged that a black hole is a solid object, occupying a particular place in space and existing in a definite time. As such, it is separate from all other spatial bodies. In view of this, it is difficult to see how black holes could be connected with other parts of the Universe. Also, it is difficult to believe that any spacecraft could withstand and escape the enormous gravitational pull of a black hole, when even light, traveling at 186,000 miles per second, cannot acomplish this.

However, not enough concrete information is known about black holes to provide a definitive answer as to whether they could be used as space gates. Hopefully, further study will provide more answers.

See: Absolute Event Horizon; Space Gate; Superspace.

BLACKOUT. The extinguishment of all lights in a given area due to power failure. During a war, blackouts are deliberately produced as precautionary measures on orders from a government or military authority.

Blackouts have also been associated with UFOs, whose ability to interfere with electromagnetic waves has been convincingly argued. UFOs are often sighted near power stations. It is not positively known whether these UFOs are piloted by intelligent beings or whether they are simply unexplained natural phenomena—UAPs. The frequent sightings of UFOs near power stations has led to one theory which holds that UFOs are somehow either caused by or attracted to electromagnetism.

Regardless of whether these UFOs are a natural phenomenon or spaceships, the fact remains that they have been held responsible by ufologists for blackouts of whole cities, sections of cities, and indeed of whole areas. To date, the Great Northeast Blackout of November 1965 is the largest blackout believed by ufologists to have been caused by UFOs. A sudden powerful surge of electromagnetic energy from a UFO is held to have overloaded the system so quickly that the safety controls did not even have time to function.

If UFOs do indeed cause blackouts, the unanswered question is why. Any answer is at best speculative. The only reasonable explanation is that it is either accidental or else some sort of test, for reasons yet unknown. Some ufologists suggest that these blackouts may be tests conducted by UFOs prior to an actual invasion.

See: EM Interference; UAP.

BLISK. A unit of velocity equal to the velocity of light. Light travels at 186,300 miles per second. Blisk 1, therefore, is equal to a speed of 186,300 mps; blisk 2 to a speed of 272,600 mps; blisk 3 to a speed of 558,900 mps; etc.

BLUE BOOK. See: Project Blue Book.

BOGEY. A synonym for a UFO used most often by military pilots and by astronauts.

See: UFO.

BOLIDE. This is a large and brilliant type of meteor, especially one which explores. It is possible that some bolides have been mistaken for UFOs.

BOTANY. The branch of biology which studies plant life. As yet its study has been confined to plant life on Earth. The possibility of plant life existing on other planets in the Universe is most intriguing and would be of immense interest to botany. A specialized branch of botany, exobotany, would then arise.

See: Biology; Exobiology.

BUFF. A person who exhibits great interest and dedication in any field, in this case, that of UFOs. In particular, he believes that UFOs are spacecraft from other planets which are coming to Earth for some purpose not yet adequately or positively ascertained. UFO buffs are split into two large groups. One group feels that the UFO beings are benevolent and would help man. The second group warns against contact with UFO beings. They warn against the possible dangers involved and the evil intentions that these beings might have.

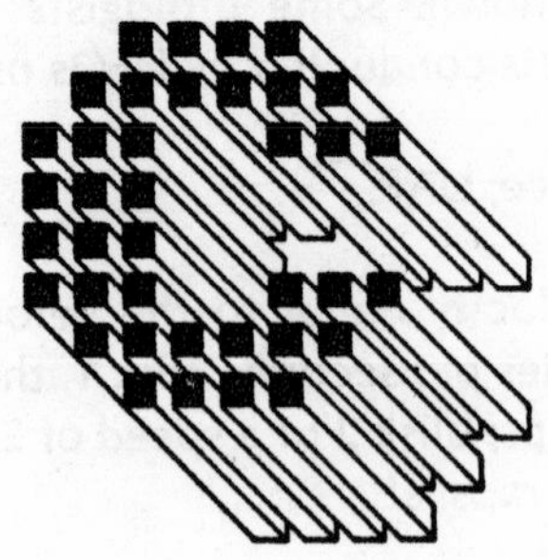

CABALA. A system of esoteric theosophy utilizing the Bible as its source. Theosophy is a form of religious or philosophical thought which claims special insight into the divine nature or to a special divine revelation. Adherents of the cabala claim that the Bible has two levels. The first of these is the obvious covert meaning of the text which is accepted by the major religions as the truth. But the real meaning of the Bible, argue the cabalists, is hidden in the text. And its secrets can be understood only by those who know the keys towards unlocking them. One such key is gematria.

The cabala has a peripheral relationship to the UFO phenonenon. Nebecist Jean Sendy claims that his interpretation of the Bible, utilizing the cabala, revealed to him the secrets of man's past, in which alien astronauts played a major role, and the promises of the future, when man will fulfill his potential.

See: Gematria; Nebecism; Sendy, Jean.

CARBON-14 DATING. See: Radiocarbon Dating.

CARTER, JAMES "JIMMY" EARL. The thirty-ninth president of the United States. Of interest to ufologists is the fact that President Carter is the first president to admit having seen an UFO. The admission first came on September 13, 1973, during an interview in Dublin, Georgia, when he was governor.

His sighting had come in 1970 while campaigning for governor in the small Georgia town of Leary. Carter was to make a speech before the local Lions Club. He and the members were gathered outside when suddenly a blue, disc-shaped object appeared in the sky. The sighting, which lasted nearly ten minutes, was witnessed by everyone present.

It remains to be seen whether President Carter will change the official government policy of secrecy towards UFOs and replace it by open public discussion of the phenomenon.

CELESTIAL. In nebecian philosophy, celestial is one of the general appellations used in referring to the befaps who allegedly arrived on Earth in the remote past and who during their stay influenced the cultural and perhaps biological evolution of man. It is a neutral designation and simply means "those beings who came from the sky, from the visible heavens, or from the stars of heaven."

See: Befap; Nebecism.

CELESTIO-METATHESIS. This term refers to an exchange of matter from one celestial body to another or from both to each other. The term is used by Charles Fort in *The Book of the Damned* to define the process by which such exchange seems to occur with Earth when, hurtling through space previously occupied by other celestial objects, our planet intercepts the path of another object or some debris which may be invisible to the human eye or enveloped in a cloud. From these celestial bodies or forms, objects are drawn to Earth. This might explain some of the strange falls of objects, known as fafrotskies, and might also explain some of the luminous clouds frequently seen preceding earthquakes or the lights seen preceding the recent skyquakes on the east coast of the U.S.

Celestio-metathesis may also explain the dark-outs, the mysterious, localized blackouts of the sun, and the mysterious disappearances of people into what appear to be clouds. Pilots, for instance, have reportedly at times flown into clouds and never emerged. These may have been celestial clouds.

Fort suggests that "visitors" may be torn from these alien bodies and drawn down to Earth and that the opposite may also occur. Fort cites an incident in Lisbon, Portugal, on October 15, 1755, where numerous "meteorites" were seen in the sky and the city was plunged into profound darkness. Some people ran to a nearby quay for refuge. They and the quay mysteriously vanished and not a trace of either the quay or the people was ever found.

See: Fafrotskies.

CENTRAL INTELLIGENCE AGENCY. See: CIA.

CETI. Acronym for Communication with Extraterrestrial Intelligences, the name of the U.S. program to establish contact via radio astronomy with extraterrestrial intelligences by listening to signals which might come in. Presently, the program is known as SETI.

See: Ryle; SETI.

CHARIOT. Ancient works, including also the Bible, mention heavenly chariots as connected with unusual phenomena. Some nebecists see this as proof of befapian presence on Earth during the planet's past. They claim that the ancients described alien spaceships by comparing them to the manmade objects on Earth which were most similar to them, i.e., chariots, often adding the word "fiery" to describe the exhaust or luminescence of the spaceships. Accordingly, nebecists use the term "chariot" as a synonym for a space vehicle or spaceship. Nebecist Erich von Daniken uses the term extensively in his works dealing with the subject of ancient befapian astronauts visiting Earth during its remote past.

See: Daniken, Erich von; Ezekiel; Nebecism.

CHINESE DISCS. Also known as Electric Discs. This refers to a series of over seven hundred granite discs found in 1938 in the Chinese province of Tsing-Hai.

The discs, found in a number of caves whose walls were covered with astronomical paintings, were grooved and contained engraved symbols. The discs were each two and one-half feet in diameter and one inch thick. They were found by Chi Pu Tei, a Chinese archaeologist. Also found in the caves were the skeletal remains of strange light-boned humanoid individuals.

In 1962 Professor Tsun Um Nui of the Peking Academy of Prehistoric Research supposedly succeeded in deciphering some of the previously undecipherable symbols. In combination with local legends he reconstructed a startling story.

About 12,000 years ago a group of hideous-looking extraterrestrial beings landed with their craft in the area. They were so hideous that the local people quickly hunted them down and killed them.

It has been speculated that the granite discs, which have a high cobalt content, may actually be a medium for storing information, much like the magnetic tape used in tape recorders. In *Is Anyone Out There?,* Jack Stoneley and A.T. Lawton calculate that there may be a total of 14 million bits of data recorded on all the discs. This would equal an amount twice that contained in the Bible.

The painted astronomical images found in the caves may indicate the point of origin of the extraterrestrials or, by showing the position of the stars in relation to the sun, the time when they landed on Earth.

Stoneley and Lawton suggest that the full story may be known by Peking. If this is indeed the case, this information has not been released.

CIA. Acronym for Central Intelligence Agency. This secret U.S. government agency was formed in 1947 to collect foreign intelligence, to carry on espionage in foreign countries, to indulge abroad in activities protecting the national interests, and to combat radical organizations and movements in foreign countries. The CIA has also become involved in the UFO phenomenon.

A number of ufologists have written about the CIA's entrance into and involvement with the UFO phenomenon. One of the best analyses of the CIA as the power behind the UFO cover-up is detailed by Major Donald E. Keyhoe in *Aliens from Space.* Major Keyhoe, who bases his research on what he considers to be reliable confidential sources, states that the CIA took over the Air Force investigation of UFOs in 1953. According to him, the CIA was able to accomplish this takeover because it has authority over the intelligence departments of all the military services. He further states that since 1953 the CIA has used its power to guide and support the Air Force deception of Congress, the press and the public.

See: Air Force; MIB.

CIRVIS. Acronym for Communication Instructions for Reporting Vital Intelligence Sightings from Aircraft. This was a secret directive contained in JANAP-146, an order promulgated by the Joint Chiefs of Staff. CIRVIS detailed the procedures which have to be followed in reporting UFO sightings.

In Instruction 102, JANAP-146 emphasizes that CIRVIS reports are to be used only for information of vital importance to the security of the United States. In Instruction 201, JANAP-146 states that UFO reports require immediate transmission, preceded by the international "Urgency Signal," military precedence or emergency. Instruction 206 directs that all CIRVIS reports are to be transmitted to the Air (now Aerospace) Defense Command, the Secretary of Defense, and the nearest U.S. Military Command.

Furthermore, JANAP-146 prohibits the unauthorized transmission or revelation of CIRVIS reports and warns that transgression of this prohibition is punishable under the Espionage Laws. CIRVIS applies to both military and commercial pilots and crews. Passengers aboard commercial flights have also often been pressured by the government personnel into maintaining silence. CIRVIS effectively clamped down a veil of official secrecy on the UFO sightings and reports. It has been most effective in preventing pilots and crews from talking about their experiences.

CIVILIZATION. A highly advanced, highly organized and complex form of human activity. A civilization is identified with culture, but usually encompasses more than a single culture. Diverse cultures which share certain fundamental features are said to share a common civilization. For example, there exists a German culture, an Italian culture, a Belorussian culture, a Swedish culture, an American culture, etc. But all of these cultures are part of Western Civilization. This civilization is characterized, inter alia, by its emphasis on science, learning and technology, and by its faith in progress.

In a similar context, the term "civilization" is also used by nebecists to apply to other possibly highly organized and highly advanced befapian societies or cultures, in particular, to those already capable of space travel. Though the existence of a befapian civilization has not yet been conclusively proven, or if it has, then information about it has not been made public, scientists have already theoretically divided such possible civilizations into three basic types. This classification is based on the amount of energy a technologically advanced civilization possesses and controls. This classification has also been made applicable to Earth.

See: Type I Civilization.

CLAIRVOYANCE. A psychological term describing the ability or power to see objects or events beyond the natural range of vision. Such a power may extend to seeing both current events as well as future events. That some persons possess such powers has been established beyond doubt. However, how the process functions or how these individuals acquired it is unknown.

The ability to see current events is in theory at least explainable. The brain is a complex transmitter and receiver of electrical impulses. Thoughts and consciousness generate psychoelectrical waves. Perhaps a peron with the right type of cerebral electrical circuits can pick up the psychoelectrical waves or thoughts of other people. It is generally accepted that clairvoyance of current events may work along these lines.

An issue more complicated, however, is the clairvoyance of future objects or events. This brings in the complicated concept of determinism and in the process involves UFOs and manadims.

See: Determinism.

CLAWMAN. Among the various UFO beings who have allegedly made contact with humans have been beings with claw-like appendages rather than hands. Clawman refers to and identifies this particular type of UFO being, or aconin, from a point of origin unknown. A further characteristic of clawmen is that in their contact with humans they are frequently reported to have exhibited hostile behavior, often by performing experiments on their human subjects. This has led ufologists to suggest that there may be several kinds of aconins, and that clawmen belong to that group whose friendliness to men is questionable.

CLOSE ENCOUNTER. An expression created by Dr. J. Allen Hynek in his book *The UFO Experience: A Scientific Inquiry* to refer to sightings of, and contacts with, UFOs and/or their occupants.

Dr. Hynek enumerated three types of "close encounters." The first he called "Close Encounters of the First Kind," to refer to those incidents where UFOs are sighted at a close distance. The second type he called "Close Encounters of the Second Kind." This refers to those UFO sightings where physical evidence is discovered to substantiate a UFO's presence. The third type of encounter Dr. Hynek called "Close Encounters of the Third Kind." This refers to those encounters where contact is actually established with the UFO occupants or where, at the very least, the UFO occupants are seen.

The expression "Close Encounters of the Third Kind" served as the title of a Columbia Pictures motion picture released in late 1977. Dr. Hynek served as technical advisor and consultant in the production.

See: Hynek.

COLORADO UNIVERSITY PROJECT. On October 7, 1966, the Air Force announced a UFO study-project which was to be undertaken by a nongovernmental agency or department. Dr. Edward Condon of Colorado University was named as the director of the project. The project, accordingly called the Colorado University Project, was supposed to be a serious, objective, and scientific investigation of the UFO phenomenon.

On October 31, 1968, the CU Project Report was delivered to the Air Force. On January 9, 1969, it was released to the public. In the opening section, Dr. Condon reaffirmed the official AF position on UFOs. He declared that UFOs were nothing but illusions and hoaxes, and stated that there exists no basis to the speculation that UFOs are interplanetary spaceships. He described many UFO witnesses as unreliable. He denied that UFOs pose a threat to national security and also denied that AF secrecy exists relative to UFOs.

Many prominent scientists, major national newspapers, and writers such as Major Donald E. Keyhoe, who had read the project report, called Dr. Condon's conclusions a whitewash. They argued that the project was primarily set up to reaffirm the prior conclusions of the Air Force. Therefore, they demanded a new and truly objective study. To date no new officially sanctioned national study has been approved or undertaken.

Other equally prominent persons agree with Dr. Condon's main conclusions. Professor Wilson, for example, in his book *UFOs and Their Impossible Mission* believes that Dr. Condon was right in his basic assumption that UFOs are of a paraphysical nature rather than actual spaceships. Professor Wilson leans towards the dimensionalist theory of UFOs.

Relying on the official conclusion of the project report, the Air Force announced that Project Blue Book was being terminated. Nevertheless, many ufologists maintain that the AF continues to secretly investigate UFO sightings and reports. The release of the Condon Report also had worldwide significance in debunking the case for UFOs. For example, shortly after the report appeared, UFO research centers in various countries were also officially closed. But in these countries as in the United States, secret investigations into the UFOs presumably continue.

See: Dimensionalism; Nebecism; Transmogrification; UFO.

COMET: A celestial body moving around the sun in an elongated elliptical orbit. The origin of comets has not been established. Many scientists lean towards the theory that they originate in the vicinity of Jupiter. Likewise the celestial orbital behavior of some comets has been erratic. Astronomy has as yet been unable to explain this motion.

A comet consists of a central mass called the nucleus which is surrounded by a misty covering called the coma. The coma extends into a tail which can stretch for millions of miles.

It is possible that some comets may have been mistaken for UFOs. And in ancient records some reports of strange celestial objects may possibly have been observations of comets.

COMMUNICATION INSTRUCTION FOR REPORTING VITAL INTELLIGENCE SIGHTINGS FROM AIRCRAFT. See: CIRVIS.

CONDON REPORT. The Colorado University Project to investigate UFOs was headed by Dr. E.U. Condon. As a result the project is at times called by his name.

See: Colorado University Project.

CONSCIOUSNESS. The faculty or ability of man to be aware of his existence, of his mind, and of his thoughts and feelings. It also involves other mental faculties such as reason. The ability to be aware of one's behavior involves the ability to reflect on it and through reasoning to either continue it or to modify it. It is a quality found in no other living organism on Earth, though some animals, such as chimpanzees, seem able for brief fleeting moments to be aware of their existence. In a basic sense, it is this one essential quality of self-awareness that differentiates man from other animals.

Self-consciousness is a specific variety or evolved attribute or form of consciousness. Its genesis is unknown. Was it developed naturally during the course of evolution or was it a gift to man from God? Religion argues that it was a gift from God and that it is the essence of the soul. Some philosophers identify it with the essence of man and find in this self-consciousness man's immortal being. They argue that once it has developed an identity, self-consciousness can never be destroyed.

Some nebecists hold a different position. According to this theory, self-consciousness may have been a gift from beings from other planets (befaps). Ancient astronauts may have landed on Earth and by genetic manipulation may have given rise to man. This seemingly altruistic befapian behavior is derived from the nebecian concept that there is a moral code which argues for the spreading of intelligent life throughout the Universe.

Whatever its origins, one fact remains clear. Self-consciousness has made man aware of himself, of his existence, of the possible existence of God, and of his relation to nature. It became the impetus to knowledge as man strove to understand himself and the world. His quest for knowledge and truth has given rise to science. This same quest for knowledge and truth has now led him to consider the possibility that there may be other forms of intelligent life in the Universe.

See: Nebecism; Science; Seeding; Soul.

CONSTELLATION. The heavens are replete with stars. Certain relatively bright stars occur in well-marked groups. Such a group of stars is called a constellation. The term is formed from the Latin words "con," meaning "together," and "stella," meaning "star."

CONTACTEE. A person contacted by UFO beings. This presents perhaps the most mysterious and baffling problem associated with UFOs. Two common factors are associated with contactee stories. The method of communication is usually telepathic, though verbal communication is also at times reported. Secondly, the contactee is usually alone at the time of the contact. This invariably tends to cast doubt on contact stories in general. But if their reality is accepted, then the naphologist still encounters problems.

For example, if UFOs originate from other planetary systems light-years away, then why after such a long journey do they not decide to contact a person of importance? Or why do they not make their presence known to a large group of people?

In the past, UFO beings have told contactees many false facts and stories, among which were tales that Venus and Mars were both inhabited. Some contactees even claim that the UFO beings took them aboard their UFO for a trip into outer space. There have also been a large number of apparently senseless and silly contacts. In one case, a UFO landed, a being emerged and approached the waiting human, bid him peace, reentered the spaceship and flew off.

The absurdity of many contacts and the obvious lies told by the UFO beings do not necessarily disprove the existence of the contact. But it does throw serious doubt about the extraterrestrial origin of UFOs. One must assume that a civilization on another planet capable of space travel would possess a certain level of sophistication. Such a civilization would be rational and intelligent. But these UFO beings rarely exhibit such qualities.

One idea which has been suggested is that contact stories are hallucinations. But even this explanation still does not solve the basic problem. A hallucination has to be caused or triggered by something. There have simply been too many contact reports to relegate all of them to the realm of hoaxes and hallucinations. However, a hallucination may also be induced upon unsuspecting victims by outside forces, human or otherwise. This leads to the question as to who does the inducing.

Some psychologists dismiss the reality of contact stories by pointing out that such stories originate mainly from old people and widowed or single women. Contactees also tend to be poor, uneducated and of poor physical health. The majority of cases do indeed fit into this category. However, contactees have also been young, married, and educated. This also emphasizes another fundamental problem. If there are indeed UFO beings, then how and whom do they decide to contact? On the other hand, if all contactee stories are merely hoaxes and hallucinations, then who is it that decides to perpetrate a hoax and for what reason? And if it is a hallucination, then what triggers its occurrence?

There are far too many mysteries and questions associated with contactee stories to be able to provide definitive answers to the many questions which arise. Conclusions and the significance of contact stories may be summarized as follows. Contactee stories tend to argue against the idea that UFOs originate from other planetary systems. However, contact stories do not as such disprove the reality of UFOs. Rather, taken as a whole, contact stories tend to support the dimensionalist theory of UFOs.

However, it must be noted that perhaps both types of phenomena are involved. Some UFOs may perhaps be from other planetary systems, while other types of UFOs may be from parallel dimensions. The little evidence that presently exists can be used to support both theories. Hopefully the accumulation of further data will help eliminate one of the options.

See: Advanced Being; Dimensionalism; Hallucination; Telepathy.

CORIOLIS EFFECT. A geophysical phenomenon relating to the tendency of everything to be pushed to the north and to the right in the northern hemisphere and to the south and to the right in the southern hemisphere. When combined with other geophysical phenomena as whirligigs and magnetic anomalies, the Coriolis Effect may be responsible for explaining the disappearances of some ships, airplanes, and people over certain areas around the world.

It is believed by some naphologists that a specific combination of natural geophysical phenomena might create a vortex, i.e., a gap in our space-time continuum, which could cause natural objects to drop into and out of our space-time continuum.

COSMIC HOAX. This expresses the dimensionalist view that UFOs are not space vehicles from outer space, but the products of some nonhuman intelligence. Through sightings and occasional contacts this nonhuman intelligence desires to make people believe in the extraterrestrial origin and objective reality of UFOs. The belief that UFOs are space vehicles, argue the dimensionalists, is nothing but fiction—a hoax, a great cosmic hoax being perpetrated and perpetuated on unsuspecting, gullible humans. The purpose of this deception or hoax is to divert people's attention from the real danger. And this real danger is, according to the dimensionalists, the fact that there exists a parallel universe inhabited by intelligent beings. These beings are basically malevolent towards humans, and intrude on and influence the course of human affairs for their own ends.

See: Dimensionalism; Manadim.

COSMOGONY. A theory of the genesis of the Universe. The traditional cosmogony provided by religion linked the birth of the Universe with an act of creation by God. With the rise of science, other alternative explanations arose. No scientist can say for certain how the Universe came into being. Presently there are two main scientific theories or cosmogonies of the Universe.

See: Big Bang Theory; Steady State Theory.

COSMOLOGY. The branch of philosophy or science which studies or concerns itself with the origin and general structure of the Universe. Its constituent elements and laws, such as space, time, causality, and freedom, are its (cosmology's) main subjects of interest.

See: Determinism.

COSMONAUT. In the Union of Soviet Socialist Republics, spacemen or astronauts are officially known as cosmonauts. Literally, the term is a combination of two words, "cosmos" and "naut," and means a traveler of, in, to or from some place in the cosmos or universe.

COSMOS. A synonym for space or the Universe. But the word "cosmos" possesses another special meaning. In the philosophical sense the cosmos represents the world or the Universe as an embodiment of order and harmony. On a deeper philosophical-psychological level it represents man's innermost desire to find or to establish an orderly Universe. This is done by categorizing natural phenomena and by attempting to discover the laws which govern them.

This desire to find or to establish harmony and order in nature also explains in part man's quest to find intelligent life on other planets, and his unconscious desire that these intelligent beings be superior to man and benevolent in character. The Universe is vast. Intelligent beings who conquered the vastness of the Universe through space travel would necessarily possess a great knowledge of the natural world, i.e., they would have a high degree of understanding of the natural order in the Universe, and of the relation of intelligent life to this complex system. Such beings would necessarily be symbols of order.

CRICK, FRANCIS. At a joint meeting of the American and the Soviet science academies in 1971, Francis Crick of Cambridge, England, one of the world's most eminent molecular biologists, jointly put forward with Leslie Orgel of the Salk Institute at San Diego, California, the intriguing theory that extraterrestrials had purposely "infected" Earth with life. In 1973 these two renowned scientists published a follow-up on the subject in the prestigious journal *Icarus.*

See: Flindt; Seeding; Terraformation.

CU PROJECT. See: Colorado University Project.

CYBORG. Short for "cybernetic organism." A cyborg would be a hybrid between an organic being and machine. In essence, a man or an aconin would become a semirobot. Chemical "mind changes" would readjust certain mental patterns of thought. Surgery, on the other hand, would replace his heart, kidneys and other vital organs with artificial parts. Such a being would have no need for food, water or sleep. Nor would such a being be emotional. It would be a self-sustaining biological unit.

The purpose of such a being would be to use it on long space journeys which a normal human astronaut would not be able to endure. Some scientists at NASA have suggested the possibility of creating such a being, but no definite plans have as yet been made. In any event, the construction of a cyborg is presently beyond man's technological capabilities.

Such a being would, of course, be readily distinguishable from ordinary humans by his body movements and countenance. Some of the sighted UFO beings are reported to have exhibited rigidity in movement. These movements were reported as being deliberate and conscious, lacking the flexibility and spontaneity of human movements. These beings were also usually reported to be wearing either silvery garments or metallic suits. This has led some ufologists to propose that these beings may in fact be highly sophisticated robots. Another possibility which is offered is that these beings may be befapian cyborgs from some distant part of the Universe. Neither theory has been proven or disproven. But the prospect that these ufonauts could either be robots or cyborgs is potentially frightening.

It should be noted that "cyborg" is a generic appellation for a being who is part biological and part mechanical. As such it can apply to both humans and aconins.

See: Bionic; Robot.

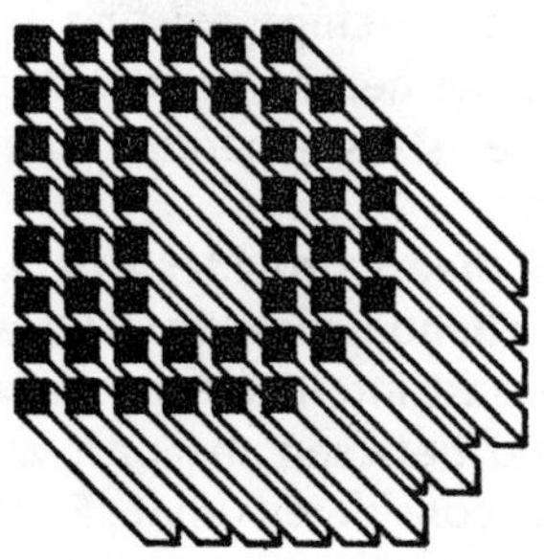

DANIKEN, ERICH VON. Though not the first to propose the nebecian theory, von Daniken has done the most to popularize this theory and is certainly the best known nebecist. In his books, Erich von Daniken does not specifically deal with UFOs as a current phenomenon. His main interest lies in exploring the possibility that in ancient times Earth was visited by astronauts from another planet who during their stay on Earth were mistaken by primitive man for gods and who imparted to man special skills and knowledge.

He finds evidence for befapian presence on Earth in various myths, legends and tales, including the Bible, and in various physical structures and artifacts, such as the pyramids, for instance. Being the most popular of the nebecian proponents, he has been subjected to the most criticism. Critics accuse him of lacking precision and methodology in his research work and of being ignorant of crucial findings in such fields of science as anthropology, archaeology, and Biblical studies.

Whatever the merits of this criticism and whatever the technical shortcomings of his works, von Daniken has, nevertheless, made an important contribution to the field of science and learning by helping to raise and to propagate a certain concept.

First, he has raised and popularized the nebecian theory that Earth may have been visited in ancient times by befapian astronauts and that the course of man's evolution may have been affected by them. This theory can neither be proven nor disproven, and is, therefore, one of the options scientists and scholars must consider if they want to be thorough.

Second, he has focused attention on the Universe and on the possibility of intelligent beings existing somewhere in outer space. By so doing he has helped fire the imagination of humans to try to reach the stars—thereby helping engender the philosophy of starism.

Third, his nebecian theory provides a background explanation for the current UFO phenomenon. If UFOs are under intelligent control and if in the past intelligent beings also visited Earth, a link is thereby forged between the past and present, and the possibility must be considered that Earth has been under surveillance of an alien intelligence since time immemorial.

See: Archaeology; Bible; Nebecism; Pyramid; Starism.

DARK COMPANION. One of the major goals of astronomy has been to determine if other stars possess planetary systems. This has been a difficult task due to the fact that planets emit no light and thus cannot be detected optically (this does not apply to the planets within our solar system, however, which can be detected optically because of their proximity to Earth). An irregular "wobble" in the rotation of a star, however, would indicate the presence of a nearby heavenly body, probably a planet. On this basis, the American Astronomical Society confirmed in 1963 that Barnard's Star possesses an orbiting body. Since then, researchers at NASA have stated that it may have three orbiting bodies. Such an orbiting body is called a dark companion because of the fact that it cannot be seen but its presence can be detected. These dark companions are most probably planets, but scientists are still cautious about employing this designation.

See: Barnard's Star.

DARK-OUT. An inexplicable darkness during the daytime which is not caused by an eclipse or any known visible phenomena. Quite frequently it is a very localized phenomenon, lasting for only a short period of time. The darkness is usually so intense that sight is virtually impossible and light devices are relatively useless.

Quite a few occasions of such dark-outs are reported to have occurred. The darkness described in the Bible (Exodus 10:21-23) as one of the plagues visited upon the Egyptians, may have been of such a nature. It lasted three days.

As to cause, it has been suggested that some celestial object, perhaps a cosmic cloud, comes between Earth and the sun at a localized spot. During such periods of darkness, people are reported to have disappeared. The disappearances may be the result of celestio-metathesis. There are indications that UFOs may somehow be responsible for at least some of these dark-outs.

See: Celestio-metathesis.

DAUGHTERS OF MEN. See: Sons of God.

DEBUNKER. Officially, the Air Force does not acknowledge the possibility that UFOs may be spacecraft from distant planets in other stellar systems. It maintains that UFO sightings can be explained as misidentifications of manmade objects, as natural phenomena, or as hoaxes and hallucinations. Specially trained AF officers, called debunkers by ufologists, are assigned to investigate and report on all UFO sightings which are of significance. When the eyewitness insists on the objective reality of what he saw, his report is then publicly dismissed by the Air Force. Often these debunkers will ridicule a person who insists on the truth of his story.

According to ufologists, in the UFO phenomenon the Air Force is confronted with something which it can neither control nor explain. Rather than publicly admit its lack of knowledge, and thus expose itself to criticism, it debunks all UFO stories. The desire to maintain secrecy is also responsible for the debunking. Undoubtedly, the Air Force would like to capture a UFO and learn the secret of its flight. In addition, it is possible, ufologists claim, that the AF has accumulated much secret information about UFOs. The AF may feel that the facts would be so disconcerting that it is better to protect the public from the truth. Therefore, debunkers have to deny and ridicule all reports of UFO sightings.

See: Air Force: CIA.

DEIMOS. See: Martian Moons.

DEMON. In the Jewish and the Christian religions, demon is one of the several names for an evil spirit or devil.

See: Devil; Evil Spirit.

DETERMINISM. A philosophical theory or system of belief which holds that the Universe has been so ordered that everything has been programmed in advance. In this complex intricate feedback system of cause and effect, nature becomes a mere actor, playing out its prearranged or preprogrammed role. Men also are victims of this preprogrammed evolution and they merely act out their roles. Free will or free choice is merely an illusion in this scheme and even when an individual believes that he is acting freely his actions are merely the fulfillment or the playing out of the cosmic plan.

Determinism is a self-contained and complete system. Taken to its extreme it can lead to a sense of futility and despair. If everything is predetermined, then what is the rationale of human effort to change, when such change is merely an expression of the prearranged cosmic plan? However, if determinism is indeed the law of the Universe, then the fact that acknowledgment of this would have a depressing effect on the human spirit is no valid philosophical or scientific argument to reject it.

Interestingly, however, whether or not men believe in determinism, men have always behaved as if they indeed possessed free will and free choice. They act in their political and social intercourse as if what they do was an act of free choice and in the realization that they have to bear the consequences of these acts.

The reality of determinism versus freedom is more complex, however, and involves in its periphery the problem of UFOs.

Determinism is what makes possible or would substantiate the claims of prophets, clairvoyants, soothsayers, fortunetellers, and other persons who claim to be able to foretell the future. That there is some validity to their claims is undeniable. But the manner in which this ability works is debatable. Persons claiming to know the future are divided into two groups. One group claims that this gift is of natural origin. The second group claims that the future was revealed to them by nonhuman entities. In actuality, in both instances the prophecies of future events have been both correct and in error.

The validity of predicting the future is a complex problem. Furthermore, even if the future is accurately predicted this does not necessarily prove determinism. A person who accurately predicts the future may simply be very astute. Human social behavior as well as individual behavior is subject to certain universal patterns or laws. A thorough understanding of these laws would make it possible to accurately predict certain consequences or future events.

Another possible natural explanation involves mental functions and processes. The brain operates on electrical energy. There also seems to be another energy force in the brain which is presently unverified. As a gigantic system, the brain both sends out and receives electrical impulses. It has been established that some people have more powerful systems than others. They are able to sense, unconsciously perhaps, what others are thinking. Or they can project their thoughts onto others, thereby influencing their behavior. The processes involved are complex and still in the rudimentary stages of understanding.

However, since time immemorial some men have also claimed knowledge of the future as a result of revelation by beings. These beings have been variously identified as angels, gods, and demons. In more recent times, contactees have reported that UFO beings make predictions. Not all such predictions have come true, however, but some have. The fact that some predictions have proved true does not substantiate determinism. Conversely, neither does it prove freedom.

The UFO beings who make predictions hold special interest for naphologists because their foretelling of the future raises the question of determinism. Can these beings transcend time and look into the future to see man's destiny? Time is relative, so perhaps a hypothetical case can be made for this. But this raises the question of the nature of these beings. Are they so kind and concerned about man that they would warn him about future disasters? Another possible explanation exists: These beings know natural laws so well that their predictions are in fact merely high probabilities which come true. This is certainly a real possibility.

The fact that they do make predictions has led some ufologists to question whether these beings are in fact befaps. From a strictly rational perspective, it makes no sense that befaps would travel trillions of miles just to arrive on Earth and then not to establish any official contact. Instead, they warn ordinary men about future disasters if mankind does not change its ways. At other times, they foretell the future, and sometimes their predictions come true. This does not sound like the type of behavior that beings from other planets would exhibit.

It is primarily because of this type of irrational behavior that one group of ufologists looks to the dimensionalist rather than to the nebecian theory for an explanation. Those naphologists who adhere to the dimensionalist school advance the theory that those beings who make predictions are not befaps but beings from another dimension. According to them, these beings (manadims) are evil and mischievous, and whatever their intention is, it is not motivated by any genuine concern for man's welfare.

Dimensionalists explain the workings of spiritism, black magic, possession, reincarnation, etc., as due to the activities of these other dimensional beings (manadims). But the essence of this argument is that manadims influence human events, i.e., they can make a prediction and then attempt to influence human events in such a manner as to make it seem that the event predicted occurred naturally and that they spoke truthfully. At other times, ridiculous predictions are made purely as jokes with no intention or attempt ever being made to bring them to realization. The manner in which manadims can act upon or influence events are several. Followers of certain occult groups can be used as agents or manadims can possibly act by direct intervention.

The whole intellectual and scholarly problem of determinism is very complex. It touches upon many areas and facets of reality. Hopefully, the advance of science and learning in general will provide some answers or at least it will provide a better perspective in which to view the problem.

See: Dimensionalism; Manadim; Transmogrification.

DEVIL. In the Jewish and the Christian religions, the term devil is one of the several terms used to denote an evil spirit. At times devil (capitalized) is used as a synonym for Satan, the supreme spirit of evil.

See: Demon, and Evil Spirit.

DEVIL'S TRIANGLE. The most famous of the vile vortices is the Devil's Triangle. It has been known by several names, including: Bermuda Triangle, Limbo of the Lost, Devil's Sea and Sargasso Sea. A misconception has developed that this area is triangular in shape. In actuality, this area is not triangular and is not in any way dependent upon Bermuda as the misnomer "Bermuda Triangle" implies. The area is lozenge-shaped and extends all the way from the Gulf of Mexico to the Azores.

See: Vortex.

DIMENSION. In naphology, dimension refers to a plane or a level of existence. There may in fact be several dimensions or planes of existence. So far, however, only one plane of existence, i.e., the Universe, is known for certain to exist. The Universe exists in time and its existence is verifiable by measurement.

The concept of other dimensions is not an idea peculiar only to naphology. The concept of heaven is a basic element of religion. If heaven exists then it must exist somewhere. The place of its existence must be a different dimension or plane of existence. Occultists also claim there exists a world beyond the senses, i.e., they believe in another dimension or level of existence beyond the corporeal one in which man exists.

The concept of parallel dimensions is a very complex one and raises many fundamental questions about Nature.

See: Dimensionalism; Nature; Space-Time Continuum; Universe.

DIMENSIONALISM. The branch of naphology which believes in the existence of one or more parallel universes. These parallel universes or different (parallel) space-time continuums are believed to be inhabited. Beings from these parallel dimensions are said to be able to enter our space-time continuum. This process of entering and leaving our space-time continuum is not fully understood by dimensionalists. Electromagnetic forces may play a part. Volition evidently also plays a part. For example, spiritualists and black magicians claim the power to summon these beings. Dimensionalists believe that most of the beings or manadims from these parallel worlds are evil, mischievous and notorious liars. Their aim seems to be to deceive man, to play pranks on him and to do him harm. Dimensionalists explain UFOs as creations, illusionary or actual, of these beings. They also claim that in the past these beings created fairies, elves and other creatures. The type of phenomena they create is contingent upon the cultural level of the society they wish to mislead.

See: Manadim; Parallel Universe; Parapsychic; Parapsychology; Superspace.

DIMENSIONALIST. Of or pertaining to dimensionalism. The term also designates an adherent of dimensionalism.

See: Dimensionalism.

DIONE, R.L. Though a nebecist on the UFO question, Dione parts company with other ufologists on certain points. His is a theory that is a synthesis of Biblical teachings, theogony, science and ufology. His basic premise is that there is a physical world subject to physical laws. There is no room in his system for the supernatural. Everything can be explained according to natural physical laws if only these laws can be discovered. By definition there are no such phenomena as miracles or mysteries; there are only events or phenomena which may be the result of laws which man does not yet understand.

The crux of his theory centers around the view of God. According to Dione, God is not supernatural but supertechnological. God is a physical entity who knows everything there is to know and who via technology, i.e., knowledge of the laws of Nature, is immortal. Dione's theory is vague on the relationship between God and Nature, i.e., did God create Nature or did Nature create God—or are both God and Nature simultaneous?

According to Dione, the Bible reveals God's code to man and as such should be obeyed, for it is good and just. God has the power to punish transgressors. Dione does not dispute Biblical "miracles"; he explains them by physical laws, and by superior technology. For example, in Dione's scheme, UFOs are agents of God, and it was a UFO that was responsible for the parting of the Red Sea.

Earth, according to Dione, is still at a primitive stage of development and for this reason is quarantined from contact with other intelligent civilizations. Because of this quarantine UFOs can visit Earth, but cannot establish permanent or direct contact. On the question of Armaggadon, Dione is an optimist. Mankind has, he believes, at least 2,000 years more before the end-time. That is, man had 2,000 years of infancy, 2,000 years of puberty, and now has entered into the third and last cycle—adulthood.

See: Nebecism; Technological Immortality.

DIRTY ICEBERG. The nucleus of a comet is at times referred to as a "dirty iceberg." The term is by extension also at times used as a synonym for comet. The name refers to the fact that a comet's solid mass is believed to be composed of ices made up of frozen water, ammonia, methane, and carbon, in addition to particles of dust, silicates, and various other gases and metals.

See: Comet.

DYSON SPHERE. Much of the energy presently emitted by the

sun is wasted. Mathematician Freeman Dyson of the Institute for Advanced Study offered a mind-boggling astroengineering project to eliminate this waste. Jupiter would be dismantled piece by piece and then transported to the distance of Earth from the sun. There the pieces would be reconstructed into a spherical shell—a system of separate units revolving around the sun. These fragments would capture the sunlight which could then be used for various technological projects. Some of these fragments might even be suitable for habitation.

However, the construction of a Dyson sphere, whether from a dismantled Jupiter or from artificial units made of metal, is presently beyond man's technological ability. The proposal is made by some scientists as a possible project for the distant future, not as a serious project for the present.

A Dyson sphere would absorb the visible light from the star around which it revolved. The sphere would not, however, be able to indefinitely absorb energy without also radiating some of this energy, in the form of infrared radiation, back into space. This infrared radiation or flux could then be detected by other civilizations.

Carl Sagan, astrophysicist at Cornell University, points out that large infrared objects of temperatures less than 1,000 degrees Fahrenheit have been detected in space. Scientists state that this does not prove that there are Dyson civilizations. The infrared radiation may merely be from dust clouds surrounding nascent stars. However, if the source of these infrared radiation emissions were determined to be of a nonnatural origin, the theory that other civilizations exist in the Universe would be confirmed. This in turn would give a big boost to the argument that astronauts from other planets (befaps) visited Earth in its remote past and that they may still be visiting our planet at the present time.

See: Astroengineering.

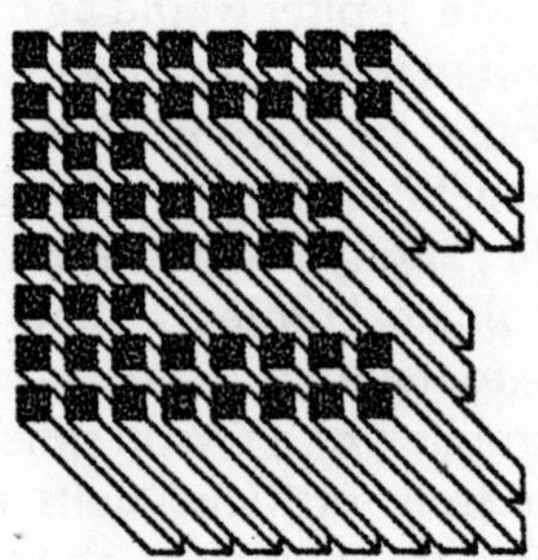

EARTH. The third planet from the sun at a distance of about 93,000,000 miles. It is the home planet of man.

EARTH COLONY. In the extraterrestrial theory expounded by Max H. Flindt and Otto O. Binder, Earth is a colony. Man is a hybrid being, a cross between terrestrial hominids and starmen. An intelligent human society was created on Earth by beings from another planet. Earth is thus a colony created and established by starmen who, it is assumed, desired to spread intelligent life throughout the Universe. Accordingly, UFOs are presently engaged in a continuing surveillance of their colony, Earth, monitoring human progress.

See: Astroevolution; Binder; Flindt; Hybrid Man.

EARTHLING. A general appellation referring to a human inhabitant of Earth.

EARTHMAN. A general appellation designating and applicable to any individual human inhabitant of Earth. It can also be used to identify an intelligent being originating from Earth as opposed to one who might originate from other planets or galaxies.

EASTER ISLAND. An island lying 2,350 miles off the coast of Chile. The island contains numerous colossal statues primitively fashioned from volcanic rock, many of which are only partly finished. In chapter 8 of *Chariots of the Gods?,* nebecist Erich von Daniken argues that the remains point to the influence of astronauts from other planets.

However, some nebecists do not share von Daniken's views on Easter Island. For this reason and because the various points presented by him are too involved and lengthy, it would serve no useful purpose to discuss it in depth. Interested persons can consult the chapter directly.

Critics of Erich von Daniken have presented scholarly opposing views on the supposed mysteries of Easter Island. In chapter 2 of *Crash Go the Chariots,* Prof. Clifford Wilson presents a detailed discussion on Easter Island. In this chapter he provides answers to some of the questions raised by von Daniken, including the manner in which the colossal statues were raised and moved. A similar critical review is presented by Gordon Whittaker in a chapter entitled "The Spaceman in the Tree," appearing in *Some Trust in Chariots,* a book edited by Barry Thiering and Edgar Castle.

EDEN. In the Bible, Eden was the name of the place where God planted a garden into which He placed man before his (man's) downfall. After man violated God's commandment not to eat of the forbidden tree, man was expelled from the Garden of Eden. Those adhering to the Biblical view have long speculated on the location of Eden. The consensus is that it was located somewhere in the Middle East, probably around Mesopotamia. The Bible itself states that the garden was located "eastward in Eden" on a river which passed through the garden and then branched out into four rivers: Pison, Gihon, Hiddekal, and Euphrates.

According to exponents of the extraterrestrial theory who rely on the Bible as a source, Eden was the name given to the base used by ancient astronauts who landed on Earth in its remote past. It was at this base, it is maintained, that the ancient astronauts conducted their biological experiments, including ones carried out on man. They expelled man from Eden after man learned something he was not supposed to know, i.e., he "ate" of the forbidden fruit. Afterwards, the ancient astronauts supposedly blew up Eden so that no trace of it would remain and then left Earth. Their experiment on Earth had been a failure.

EDWARDS, FRANK. Late journalist and radio commentator, who died in 1967. His interests spanned the entire field of unusual, mysterious, unexplained phenomena. In *Stranger than Science, Strangest of All,* and *Strange World,* Edwards presented numerous such incidents and events. He presented the facts as best he could reconstruct or establish them. These books are an excellent general introduction into the field of unexplained and mysterious phenomena that science has not been able to explain.

In *Flying Saucers—Serious Business* and then in *Flying Saucers—Here and Now!,* Edwards presented in depth his views on the UFO phenomenon. He is an adherent of the extraterrestrial theory with regard to the origin of UFOs and discounts the authenticity of contactee cases.

ELECTROMAGNETIC INTERFERENCE. See: EM Interference.

ELECTROMAGNETISM. The phenomenon which results from and depends upon the relation between electricity and magnetism. It is of immense interest to science and has multifarious applications, forming the basis of the electrical industry.

Ufologists believe that electromagnetism may be one of the key elements in the propulsion system of UFOs.

See: Electricity; EM Interference; Magnetism.

ELEMENTAL. A term used by John A. Keel to refer to those beings who are supposed to inhabit the parallel universe.

See: Dimensionalism; UT.

ELEPHANTINE. An island in the Nile. Von Daniken and other adherents of the extraterrestrial theory claim that the island resembles an elephant in shape and that, since there is no hill in the vicinity from which this shape could have been ascertained, it must have been viewed from the air. Since the Greeks did not have flying machines, the only other explanation for the knowledge of the island's shape is that it was received from ancient astronauts who had visited Earth in the remote past and who had viewed the island's shape from the air.

History scholars, however, take issue with this extraterrestrial position. They point out that: 1) the island does not in any manner resemble an elephant in shape, and 2) that the Greek word elephantinos, from which the name of the island comes, does not mean elephant but ivory, and that the Greek name is a direct translation of the original and still older Egyptian name for the island, Yeb, which means ivory.

ELOHIM. The Hebrew word for God, often used in the Hebrew text of the Old Testament. The curious feature of this word is that it is the proper plural of Eloi, the word for God in the singular case. Bible scholars claim that Elohim is used in the singular sense in the Bible. English translations have rendered Elohim as "God."

A contrary view is presented by the nebecists. They argue that the Book of Genesis in reality describes the arrival to Earth of astronaut-gods. In the nebecist philosophy propounded by Jean Sendy, it is argued that Elohim is actually the name of the group of astronaut-gods who landed on Earth and who, after restoring the biological and geological equilibrium of Earth after the onslaught of the Ice Age, began biological experimentations on man and other forms of life. Their experiment on man turned out to be a failure because man learned something which he was not supposed to know. These astronaut-gods subsequently left Earth.

There were several of them, perhaps as many as a dozen or two. But because they acted in unison, they were regarded as one by man. However, despite their departure, their story was recorded and preserved in the Bible and in other corrupted and less reliable sources.

Sendy argues that his theory of several astronaut-gods would explain why, in Genesis, God frequently refers to Himself in the plural: "Let us make man in our image, after our likeness." (Genesis 1:26); "Behold, the man is become as one of us . . ." (Genesis 3:22). These lines from Genesis imply that there were several Elohim. Sendy further argues that by reading Elohim as "God," a deliberate attempt was made to cover up the truth. According to him, Elohim should have been translated as "gods."

If true, Sendy's theory is interesting for two reasons. First, it provides a nebecian explanation for the Garden of Eden story. Second, it provides a name of these aconins, a name which has not been recently concocted, but one which has existed for millenia. In addition to providing the group name of these aconins, Jean Sendy argues that the Bible also provides the specific names of some of the individual Elohim; namely, Adonai, Shaddai, and Yahweh.

This nebecian theory is directly opposed to the religious philosophy of the Jewish and of the Christian religions. On the point of the plural form "Elohim," theologians argue that the plural is often used as a sign of deference and respect, and that it is not to be taken literally. According to the religious view, the Book of Genesis relates the act of creation by God. It describes how man was expelled from the Garden of Eden because of his disobedience and how he was forced to eke out a living by the sweat of his brow. Man would henceforth know pain, sorrow, and death. According to the religious view, however, the Bible is more than just the story of man's fall and the events which followed; it is also the story of God's effort to reach man and to offer him salvation.

See: Bible; Eden; Nebecism; Sendy, Jean; Yahweh.

EM. Acronym for electromagnetism.

EM INTERFERENCE. There exists a large body of data which indicates that UFOs have the ability to interfere with electrical circuits. The most probable way they accomplish this is by controlling and directing electromagnetic waves. UFOs have been held responsible for the failure of headlights on cars, interference with radio and television transmissions, and interference with electrical equipment aboard aircraft, creating a potentially dangerous situation. However, the blackouts over certain cities and areas have been, to date, the most widespread and serious cases of EM Interference which have been attributed by ufologists to UFOs.

See: Blackout.

ENERGY. In the metaphysical sense, energy is one of the two separate distinct expressions or forms of reality. In practical application, energy describes the dispersion of power. Some forms of energy, like electrical, which can be generated by a rotating flywheel, are readily controllable; other forms, such as light, are not. Heat is the lowest form of energy, i.e., heat is wasted energy. Energy has great utility, especially when converted for mechanical purposes. It is then able to power a variety of machines, tools, cars, etc., all of which are useful to man. Energy is convertible to matter and vice versa.

See: Law of the Conservation of Matter and Energy; Matter; Transmogrification.

ENOCH. In the Bible, Enoch was the son of Jared and the father of Methuselah (Genesis 5:18-24). In chapter 4 of *Chariots of the Gods?,* Erich von Daniken claims that Enoch forewarned Methuselah of the coming great flood. Subsequently, Enoch is supposed to have been taken by a fiery heavenly chariot and to have left Earth forever.

However, Prof. Clifford Wilson, in *Crash Go the Chariots,* criticizes von Daniken by pointing out that the Bible makes no mention of the contention, and in no way supports the UFO theory, that Enoch was taken into space by a fiery chariot. The sole Biblical mention of Enoch in the Old Testament is contained in verse 24 of chapter 5 of the Book of Genesis: "And Enoch walked with God; and he was not; for God took him."

It should be added, however, that the Old Testament Book of Sirach, accepted by Catholics, also makes two references to Enoch: "Enoch pleased the Lord, and was taken up." (Sirach 44:16); and, "But upon the earth was no man created like Enoch; for he was taken from the earth." (Sirach 49:14).

A reference to Enoch is also made in St. Paul's Epistle to the Hebrews: "By faith Enoch was taken up that he should not see death; and he was not found, because God had taken him up: for before he was taken up he had this testimony, that he pleased God." (Hebrews 11:5).

The Bible does make it quite clear that Enoch did not die but was taken up bodily by God. Nowhere, however, does it mention a fiery chariot when speaking of Enoch. How he was taken up bodily and to where he was taken is not clear. And it is this ambiguity which can be used to support the argument that UFOs were involved.

ENTITY. An entity is something that exists. It can either refer to a nonintelligent creature or to an intelligent being. The term is used at times by dimensionalists to describe the beings from other space-time continuums. It is a neutral term and evokes no special emotional response. However, its very neutrality as a descriptive term creates some uneasiness, for if there are other beings, then they must necessarily possess certain characteristics. To refer to them as simply "entities," however, is to shroud them in mystery. If there are indeed parallel universes and if these universes are inhabited by some kinds of beings, it is doubtful whether man at his present stage of scientific knowledge could know very much about them.

See: Dimensionalism; Manadim; UFO; UT.

EPIC OF GILGAMESH. A Babylonian epic describing the adventures of Gilgamesh. The origins and significance of this epic are disputed. Some nebecists have used it to support their arguments about befapian influence on Earth in ancient times. See chapter

5 of Erich von Daniken's *Chariots of the Gods?* for a further treatment of this view.

Curiously, several parts of the epic parallel parts of the Bible, as in the account of the flood. The main argument therefore centers on the epic's relation to the Bible; specifically, whether it was based on it. Biblical scholars, among them Prof. Clifford Wilson, deny the historical significance of the Epic of Gilgamesh and maintain that the Bible predated it.

EPSILON ERIDANI. One of the two stars which Project Ozma, organized to search for intelligent life in the Universe, examined in 1961 for intelligible radio signals.

See: Project Ozma.

ESP. Acronym for Extrasensory Perception. This term refers to the type of perception or communication which is outside of normal sensory activity. It includes clairvoyance and telepathy.

That ESP exists is beyond doubt, but the manner in which it functions is unknown to science. The reality of ESP, however, raises fundamental philosophical problems about the nature of the Universe. Specifically, it raises the question about the validity of determinism.

Scientists lean towards the theory that ESP probably works on the principle of some sort of psychoelectric energy. All persons possess the ability for ESP, but some are more sensitive than others. It is possible that the brain structure of some people is more sensitive and is thus able to pick up psychoelectric waves. This would explain how some people can know what others are thinking.

Animals seem better attuned to electromagnetic or psychoelectric impulses than man. In particular, horses, dogs, and cats seem able to pick up impulses which escape man and which might be classified by man as psychic or parapsychological phenomena.

This type of extrasensory phenomena may also be involved with UFOs. Animals seem to be aware of UFOs and other phenomena before man senses them. Also, UFO contactees often report that communication with them was established via ESP; specifically, via telepathy. In other cases dealing with paranormal phenomena, contactees seem to be possessed by some alien beings or life forms. Phenomena such as these have led some naphologists to question whether UFOs originate from other planets. They lean towards the dimensionalist theory and see UFOs as merely another manifestation of the psychic and parapsychological phenomena which have plagued man for millenniums.

See: Determinism; Dimensionalism; Telepathy.

ESTIMATE OF THE SITUATION. In general this is the term applied to any report made by intelligence units in reference to any vital problem. In ufology, the term has a narrower, more specific meaning. It refers to a specific report made by the Air Technical Intelligence Center (ATIC) in mid-1948 on the UFO phenomenon. The report, stamped TOP SECRET, contained only analyses of UFO reports from highly reliable, credible witnesses: scientists, pilots, etc. The report's assessment—UFOs were interplanetary craft.

This ATIC estimate was rebuked and rejected by Gen. Hoyt S. Vandenberg, the Chief of Staff of the Air Force, in early 1949.Vandenberg refused to believe the extraterrestrial explanation. The estimate was declassified and ordered destroyed, but a few copies managed to survive. This rejection of the estimate was soon to produce a profound effect on the Air Force's attitude towards UFOs.

See: Project Grudge; Project Sign.

ETI. Acronym for Extraterrestrial Intelligence. This is one of several terms used by scientists and ufologists to refer to intelligent beings who may live in other parts of the Universe. The term literally means "intelligence from beyond Earth."

EUROPA. The second largest of Jupiter's moons. It is four-fifths the diameter of our moon.

Europa is of interest because of the claim of American researchers that they had detected ice caps on its surface. This, of course, leads to the possibility that there may presently be life on that satellite, or that there may have been life there at one time in the past.

Though it is doubtful whether intelligent beings exist there presently, it is possible that they may have done so in the past. The possibility also exists that such beings may have developed a technological capability to have visited Earth in the past.

EVOLUTION. A biological theory referring to the seemingly continuous adaptation of life to the environment by the interrelated mediums of natural selection, hybridization, inbreeding, and mutation. Currently, evolution is the most popular scientific theory to explain the large diversity of life. It should be stressed, however, that evolution does not seek to explain the origin of life as such, but only the large diversity of life forms. However, even scientists admit that evolution is still only a theory. It is not universally accepted.

Evolution leaves several fundamental problems unresolved. It does not provide an answer for the internal mechanism which causes change in a species and gives rise to a new species. Nor does evolution answer the fundamental questions of why every possible type of environment on Earth is inhabited and why every species is adapted to its environment. Another major problem is that evolution requires an endless series of missing links to explain the transition between species.

Evolution cannot be directly proven. It is a scientific way of answering the question of how the present-day variety of animals came into being.

There are four main arguments for evolution. These are: a) the anatomical argument, b) the physiological argument, c) the historical or paleontological argument, and d) the embryological argument. For example, in the historical argument, fossils provide a great mass of material regarding the successive appearances of different species. In other words, mammals are found above the aves, and the aves are found nearer the surface in fossil pits than are reptiles. This indicates that each type preceded the other.

Though the exact mechanisms of evolution are still not fully understood, scientists maintain that evolution is a continuous though slow process. All higher complex forms of life are supposed to have evolved from simple one-celled animals. Man is supposed to have arisen from a now-extinct species of ape. According to the theory of evolution, evolution is still at work even now.

Another major problem with regard to evolution arises with the existence of intelligence. With his vast, ever-increasing scientific knowledge, man is now able to influence and affect evolution, including his own. The significance of this must be stressed. For millions of years, evolution was nature's way of preserving life by adapting it to the changes in the environment. It was a slow trial-and-error process. Now, with his intelligence, man can control the environment. He reigns supreme on Earth. He can destroy whole species of animals. And with radiation he can now manipulate genetic development.

This ability to control some of the basic life processes raises moral as well as scientific questions about man's competence to affect evolutionary development.

The possibility and realization that man can now affect the course of evolution leads to another interesting possibility. Nebecists maintain that befapian astronauts landed on Earth during its remote past (the time given is usually between 20,000 B.C. and 12,000 B.C.) and influenced the evolutionary development of life on Earth. It was during this time that these aconins helped to firmly establish intelligent life on Earth. Another major nebecian theory holds that befaps directly influenced the course of evolution on Earth by seeding certain species, among which may have also been man.

The whole subject of the origin of life and of evolution is an extremely complex one. Far too little is known about either life or evolution. Presently, man has only the species of animals on Earth to study. This is why space exploration is important. Exploration of other planets and of other planetary systems may lead to the discovery of life there. The study of these life forms would provide invaluable knowledge about the general laws governing evolution and the origin of life.

See: Biology; Life; Nebecism; Seeding.

EVIL SPIRIT. In the Jewish and the Christian religions, an evil spirit is a spiritual being who opposed and rebelled against God. Religion maintains that an evil spirit is a real being and not just an imaginary one. It is capable of possessing man and of afflicting him with bodily disease and spiritual corruption. These evil spiritual beings hate and despise man and attempt to deceive him about the true nature of God and reality. Devil or demon are two words synonymous with evil spirit. Satan, or Lucifer, is the supreme evil spirit.

These degenerate beings are supposed to live in and to rule over Hell. However, Christian religion never explicitly identified the location of Hell, except by stating that it is in a spiritual world.

However, if these beings are able to influence man, then it follows that they must be able to exist in our world, at least temporarily. The unanswered question is, how do they enter our world or space-time continuum? According to Christian religion, one way is when man summons them. This is why both the Jewish and the Christian faiths have always opposed spiritualism, fortune-telling, divining, etc.

The religious concept of evil spirits has many parallels with the dimensionalist theory about the existence of beings in other space-time continuums. These manadims exhibit patterns of behavior similar to those attributed to the evil beings, so that, in effect,there exists no basic difference between them,

See: Dimensionalism; Elemental; Invisible; Manadim; Satan; UT.

EXOBIOLOGY. The branch of biology which is interested in, and which deals with and studies, life which exists beyond Earth. To date, except for prebiological molecules, no life forms have been discovered either in space or on those celestial bodies which manned and unmanned vehicles have visited. Some writers, however, have hinted at the idea that the government may have discovered such life forms or that it may know details about it, but does not want to reveal this information.

However, though no extraterrestrial forms of life have been officially acknowledged, scientists have discovered and have admitted to the existence of numerous examples of preorganic molecules in space.

Though exobiology is still in its infancy, various theories have already been offered as to what qualities life in other parts of the Universe, if indeed such life exists, might exhibit.

See: Biology; Life.

EXTRASENSORY PERCEPTION. See: ESP.

EXTRATERRESTRIAL INTELLIGENCE. A general descriptive term referring and applying to any intelligent beings which may inhabit other parts of the Universe.

EZEKIEL. Some nebecists, notably Erich von Daniken, have seized upon the Biblical Book of Ezekiel as one of the proofs that Earth was visited in ancient times by befapian astronauts. There are several parts in the Book of Ezekiel which, maintain the nebecists, support their argument. For example, verse 17 of chapter 1 describes what seems to be a spacecraft. The beings in this spaceship or UFO are then said to have communicated with

Ezekiel (chapter 2). Nebecists who rely on the Book of Ezekiel as one of their sources contend that Ezekiel was not able to understand the phenomenon he was witnessing and so mistook the UFO and the UFO beings for agents sent by God.

This nebecian interpretation of the Book of Ezekiel has been severely criticized by Biblical scholars. In his book, *Crash Go the Chariots,* Clifford Wilson, Ph.D., maintains that the Book of Ezekiel can by no stretch of the imagination support the UFO theory. He points out that Ezekiel explicitly states that he was having a vision. The first time the vision occurred (Ezekiel 1:1), Ezekiel was by the river Chebar with other exiles. Professor Wilson maintains that the Book of Ezekiel supports a religious experience and substantiates the Biblical contention that the Bible is the word of God. Furthermore, Professor Wilson argues that Ezekiel was being symbolic in his descriptions, telling us that he was in contact with Almighty God.

A third major alternative interpretation of the Book of Ezekiel is offered by R.L. Dione in *God Drives a Flying Saucer.* He agrees that Ezekiel did in fact have a vision but believes that the experience was caused by a UFO. He argues that a UFO did not literally appear to Ezekiel, but that it did affect his mental processes in such a manner so as to give him a vision of what it wanted to tell him. Dione takes a middle position, and his hypothesis that the experience was caused by an induced hallucination cannot be proved or disproved.

Dione also shares a view of many other nebecists. This is the belief in the existence of benevolent UFO beings whose main purpose is to watch over the moral development of man. This supposed benevolent purpose forms the foundation of Dione's theory and explains why the UFO beings bother to give man moral instructions via either direct contact or dreams and visions.

However, not all ufologists share a belief in the existence of benevolent UFO beings. In fact, a good case can be made for just the opposite conclusion, that whatever may be the primary interest of these UFO beings, man's welfare does not seem to be it.

See: Nebecism; Philosophy.

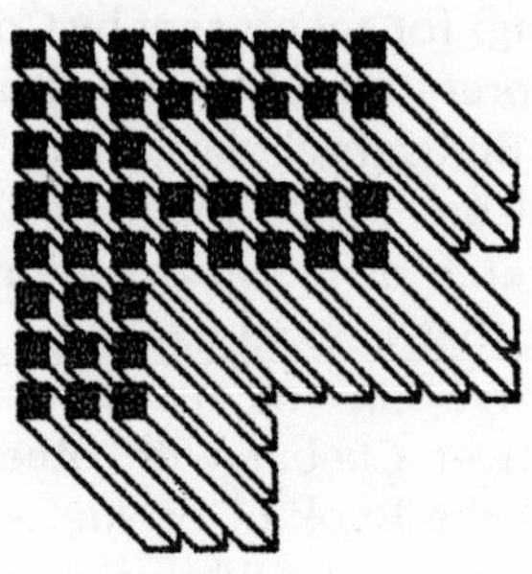

FAFROTSKIES. An acronym for the strange things that have been seen to "fa(ll) fro(m) t(he) skies." The term was coined by the late Ivan Sanderson, a well-known biologist and ufologist.

Through the ages many unlikely objects have fallen from the sky. These objects can be divided into two categories: organic and inorganic. Among the organic items to fall have been: fish, frogs, eels, toads, snakes, worms, ants, animal flesh, and fresh mammalian blood, usually of ungulates, such as sheep, goats and cattle.

The inorganic items are of two types: manufactured and natural. These inorganic items have included the following: bricks, coal, foil, bullets, metal pellets, nails, mud, bluish-green phosphorescent snow, and angels' hair.

There is no logical, rational explanation for these fafrotskies, and orthodox science simply ignores them or tries to explain their occurrence as the results of tornadoes or hurricanes. Sometimes these fafrotskies fall with rain, other times alone from perfectly clear skies. An extensive listing of fafrotskies is provided in Appendix B of Ivan Sanderson's *Investigating the Unexplained* (Prentice-Hall, Inc., Englewood Cliffs, N.J., 1972).

Some ufologists have suggested that fafrotskies are dropped by UFOs as refuse. With regard to the showers of blood and flesh, it has been suggested that this is the fate that befalls the animals, and perhaps humans, that are abducted by UFOs or that mysteriously vanish from the face of the earth.

See: Angels' Hair.

FATIMA. In 1917, this small village in Portugal was the scene of what is generally maintained to have been a religious experience. An angel and, subsequently, the Virgin Mary are said to have appeared to three small children. During one of the appearances, on October 13, 1917, the miracle of the dancing sun was witnessed by thousands of people.

After the dawn of the modern UFO era, following Kenneth Arnold's 1947 sighting, the Fatima experience began to interest ufologists. Investigative ufologists noticed similarities between the miracle at Fatima and the behavior of UFOs. Ufologists who have studied the Fatima phenomenon believe that there is a connection between the orbs of lights seen at Fatima and the strange aerial lights presently known as UFOs. They question the religious nature of the experience.

FERTILE CRESCENT. A once-fertile area in the Middle East in which scholars believe that man first discovered and practiced agriculture.

FIREBALL. Though the process is not yet understood by science, lightning can at times form into the shape of a ball. Such a ball of lightning, or fireball, as this type of spherical lightning is called, exhibits unusual behavior, including the ability to bounce around like a gas-filled balloon. Fireballs have frightened people who have suddenly come upon them. They are usually described as making a sizzling noise and invariably as exhibiting strange movements. Sometimes they either fade away without a sound or else silently disappear from the observer's proximity, after which they are believed to also vanish without a sound. At other times, they vanish with a thunderous explosion.

It is clear that fireballs are a rare phenomenon which occur during storms. But why they behave as they do, science does not yet know. In fact, it is a violation of the laws of physics, as man presently understands them, for lightning to assume a spherical shape. Comparing the odd behavior of fireballs with the behavior of UFOs, there seems to be some similarity and correlation. It is therefore possible that some UFOs might be explained as misidentified fireballs.

See: UAP.

FIRST CIVILIZATION. Every ancient society possessed a story of its origin. These creation stories can be divided into several main types. One type relates how the people descended from animals. Another type traces man's origin to plants. Other types, known as the First Civilization stories, maintain a bond between man and the sky. Though their historical origins are lost in time, these First Civilizations left accounts about their origins, and much of what we know about them is from these stories.

These stories all follow the same basic pattern. They tell of how gods, physically similar to man, arrived from the sky and influenced man's development by introducing him to technology and agriculture. Due to failure or disappointment, the gods subsequently returned to the sky. By the time they left, however, they had given a spurt to civilization. Some of the knowledge left by them survived and was guarded by the priestly class. These priests, according to the nebecian theory, did not always know the full significance of their teachings, but they always stressed that they had acquired their knowledge from their ancient forebears, who had personally known the gods. The visitation of these gods was retained in legends, myths, and stories, albeit often in distorted forms.

Nebecists argue that these First Civilizations constitute one of the proofs that befapian astronauts landed on Earth in man's prehistoric past. The time of their arrival is usually placed between 20,000 B.C. and 12,000 B.C.

FLAP. A time during which there occurs a large amount of UFO activity and a large number of UFO sightings within both a specific area and a short period of time.

FLAP AREA. See: Flap.

FLINDT, MAX H. Dissatisfied with the theory of evolution as a viable explanation for the origin of man and other species of life, Flindt began to investigate the possibility of extraterrestrial influence as an alternative. In 1962, he privately published a pamphlet, *On Tiptoe Beyond Darwin,* which examined the extraterrestrial alternative to natural evolution. His continued interest and research into this theory led to the publication in 1974 of *Mankind—Child Of The Stars,* which utilized the twin concepts of Hybrid Man and Earth Colony. This book, which he coauthored with Otto O. Binder, sought to show via a comprehensive approach, based on scientific grounds wherever possible, that the theory of extraterrestrial influence is the only viable explanation for the rise of man. UFOs in this view are spacecraft of the starmen which are monitoring the progress of Earth and mankind. It is argued in this book that open contact will one day be established with the starmen.

See: Astroevolution; Earth Colony; Hybrid Man.

FLYING SAUCER. On June 24, 1947, while flying past Mount Rainier, Kenneth Arnold spotted a formation of nine brightly-lit, disc-shaped objects. When he described his experience to a newsman after he landed, the newsman on the basis of Arnold's description promptly labeled the phenomenon as "flying saucers."

The name caught on and spread rapidly throughout the world. Many foreign countries now bear the same type of name in their own native languages. The Air Force subsequently began to investigate the phenomenon. It found the term "flying saucer" inadequate. Therefore, it coined the term "Unidentified Flying Object," UFO for short, to describe this phenomenon. UFO is currently the official designation. Nevertheless, the term "flying saucer" continues in use as a popular and widely-used, but unofficial, name for these brightly-illuminated, mysterious flying objects.

See: UFO.

FLYING SAUCER REVIEW. This British-based publication is recognized by most professional ufologists as the world's foremost UFO journal. It has published for over twenty years and features contributions by leading scientists and ufologists. It does not limit the coverage to UFOs, however. Other related phenomena are also covered.

FOO FIGHTER. In the winter of 1944–45, Allied airmen flying missions over Nazi-occupied Europe encountered flying discs and spheres which they nicknamed "foo fighters." At times, only one foo fighter was encountered, while at other times, a formation of foo fighters was observed. Military intelligence personnel believed that these objects were either secret German flying machines or possibly new kinds of weapons. However, there was never a reported attack, even though these objects did pace

Allied airplanes. In one case, a B-24 bomber was followed by a formation of fifteen such discs. Later, similar objects were also encountered by B-29 crews on bombing raids over Japan.

After the war ended and the victorious Allies had a chance to study enemy documents, the mystery of the objects deepened. Allied military officers discovered that the Germans and the Japanese were also puzzled by these objects, believing them to be either Allied aircraft or weapons of unknown purpose. At that time terms like "flying saucer" or "UFO" had still not come into use. The space age was still over a decade away, and the possibility of interplanetary or interstellar space visitors did not even seriously occur to anyone. Faced with unexplainable sightings, military intelligence had blamed them on pilot fatigue, hoaxes, and illusions. This explanation stretched plausibility to the limit because it is highly improbable that such a large number of pilots on both sides could have been so similarly affected or that they had acted independently of each other to perpetuate the same kind of hoax. Scattered sightings of foo fighters continued to occur throughout 1946.

It has never been determined what these objects were or from where they originated. It is clear, though, that they were some sort of UFOs. The description of these objects is very similar to that of objects being sighted right up to the present time. But the reason as to how and why they were attracted to Earth during World War II remains a mystery, though some explanations have been offered. One of these holds that the extensive military bombing raids attracted their attention.

See: UFO.

FORT, CHARLES. Born Charles Hoy Fort on August 9, 1874, in Albany, New York, he died on May 3, 1932, in the Bronx, New York. Fort was one of the earliest compilers of all manner of strange and seemingly unexplainable phenomena. Fort did his research and authored his books in the early part of the twentieth century. He realized that there were phenomena beyond human comprehension occurring around the world. These phenomena presented a challenge which science, unable to adequately explain, chose to ignore or exclude. These excluded phenomena Fort called the "damned," and titled his first book into this field *The Book of the Damned.*

His research and work provided part of the foundation on which subsequent research into unexplained and mysterious phenomena would expand. His name has entered the field as a synonym for out-of-place, inexplicable phenomena.

See: Fortean Event.

FORT ITAIPU. A fort in Brazil which, according to Maj. Donald E. Keyhoe, USMC (Ret.), was the scene of a seemingly unprovoked UFO attack on November 4, 1957. At 2:00 A.M.on that day, two sentries on guard duty spotted a brilliant light above them which they mistook at first for a star. But when it started to descend they took alarm. The UFO, which was described as circular and about 100 feet in diameter, stopped about 150 feet above the fort and cast an orange glow on the compound and astounded sentries. A steady hum accompanied the strange glow. Suddenly, a blistering blast of heat struck the two soliders. Their cries of anguish woke up the garrison. Afterwards the UFO streaked away. The two sentries were found to have burns. The Brazilian authorities were baffled by the unprovoked incident and referred the matter to the U.S. government. Investigators from the U.S. Army and Air Force were equally baffled and also could not provide a definitive explanation for the occurrence.

See: Heat; Walesville.

FORTEAN EVENT. Any event or occurrence which defies rational, scientific explanation. Coined after the name of Charles Fort, a late investigator and compiler of out-of-the-ordinary things. An example of a Fortean event are the fafrotskies—organic and inorganic objects that have been recorded as falling from the skies. These include: rocks, chunks of ice, frogs, fish, blood, pieces of meat, etc.

See: Fafrotskies; Angels' Hair.

FOURTH DIMENSION. The fourth dimension is time. The Universe or reality is composed or length, width, depth, and time. And it can be scientifically measured.

See: Time.

FREE WILL. One of the basic concepts of natural law philosophy and religion is that man possesses consciousness and reason. One consequence of this ability to think, judge, and analyze is that man can make free choices: in other words, he has free will. This means that he can make rational and intelligent decisions which can be motivated though not compelled by external influences. Because man possesses this freedom, natural law philosophers state that man is therefore morally responsible for his actions. Free will does not directly enter into the UFO phenomenon. It is involved with the phenomenon only indirectly as the alternative to determinism.

See: Determinism.

FUSION. In physics, fusion is a thermonuclear reaction in which the nuclei of light atoms join to form nuclei of heavier atoms. In the process there is a tremendous release of energy. The energy released in a fusion reaction is many times the energy released in a fission reaction. Man has not yet learned how to produce a controlled fusion reaction. Such a discovery would produce vast amounts of energy which could be used to produce electricity. If applied in a practical manner to the space program, controlled fusion could provide sufficient energy for high-speed interplanetary journeys in our solar system, thereby making it possible to travel even to the most distant planets in a matter of a few days. It could also be used for interstellar journeys.

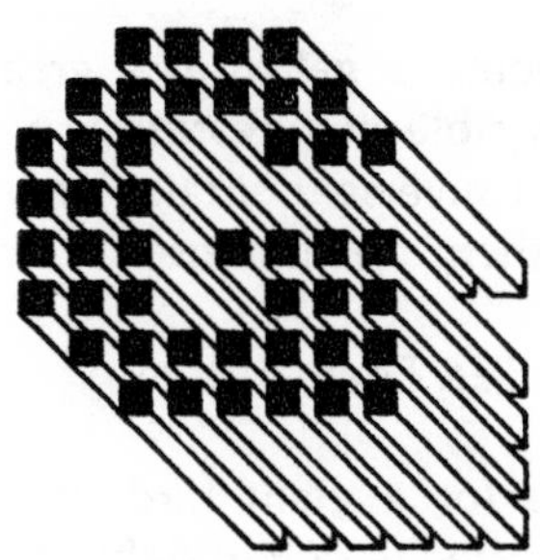

GALAXIAN. This is a generic name referring to and identifying all intelligent beings who may inhabit or originate from a particular galaxy. It is a most interesting appellation because it forces man to see reality in better perspective. The befaps who are reported to have visited Earth, and who, the ufologists believe, still are visiting Earth, cannot exclusively be called Galaxians. Such a designation would neglect one important fact; that is, that men are also Galaxians. As inhabitants of the Milky Way Galaxy, human beings can also rightly refer to themselves as Galaxians. Therefore, if the befaps are from our galaxy, both they and we are Galaxians of the Milky Way Galaxy. Practically speaking, however, it will be a long time before man begins calling himself by such a name.

The existence of this term illustrates one salient fact. The space age is influencing and changing civilization on Earth. In particular, it is changing man's view of himself, of his relation to the Universe, and of his place in the Universe. It is forcing man to broaden his intellectual and philosophical scope. It has begun the slow process of educating man about deeper and broader concepts concerning himself and the Universe. For the first time in history, man is at least being exposed to the idea that before he is a member of any one nationality, he is first and foremost an Earthman. He is also being exposed to the idea that as an inhabitant of the Milky Way Galaxy he is also a Galaxian. In addition, he is also being made aware of the fact that if befaps exist in our galaxy, they too are Galaxians. The Space Age has forced upon man an intellectual and philosophical revolution unlike any which the world has ever seen.

GALAXY. In astronomy, a galaxy is a great stellar system. The Milky Way is the visible manifestation of the galaxy in which humans live. The Universe contains many galaxies, and the distances between them are immense.

GARDEN OF EDEN. See: Eden.

GARUDA. A name for a giant bird. In areas where unusual phenomena are reported to occur, sightings of gigantic birds also occur from time to time. The birds are so huge as to be biological impossibilities. The existence of such giant birds has not been conclusively proven, but if they do actually exist, science would be faced with a major challenge in trying to explain them. John A. Keel devotes significant attention to sightings of garudas in *The Mothman Prophecies.*

See: Mothman; Transmogrification.

GEMATRIA. One of the elements of the cabala based on the characteristics of the Hebrew alphabet. This alphabet contains twenty-two letters. The first nine letters represent units, the next nine represent tens and the last four represent hundreds. As a result each word written in Hebrew also represents a number. The search for an esoteric meaning in the Biblical text, expressed in figures through words, constitutes gematria.

See: Cabala.

GHOST ROCKET. The name applied to a series of UFO sightings which plagued Europe and parts of Asia Minor (Turkey) and North Africa during the period between 1946 and 1948. The ghost rockets were first seen during the summer of 1946. They were usually seen at night, were always traveling at extremely high speeds, varied in color, and were described as round or projectile-shaped.

The Swedish defense staff is said to have conducted a comprehensive study of the sightings and to have concluded that the ghost rockets were all explainable, natural astronomical phenomena. It is strange, however, that such easily explainable natural phenomena caused so much confusion and required a comprehensive study before they could be explained.

GIANT. Ancient sources contain scattered references to giants. Some nebecists have seized on this as proof of befapian presence on Earth in man's remote past. They argue that these giants were either befaps or else the progeny of a union between befaps and earthlings. In such cases, the befaps were usually male, while the earthlings were female humans.

The factual basis for such an argument is rather weak, though. For this reason, many nebecists avoid relying too heavily on references to giants to substantiate their theories.

Critics have rightly pointed out that measurement of size is relative. In ancient times men were usually shorter than they are today. Therefore, any tall people that these Biblical people would have encountered would have been classified as giants. Furthermore, critics of the nebecian theory argue that the term "giant" was often applied by ancient people to men of great stature who performed great feats. Analogously, the term "giant" was also applied to one's enemies. When a leader overestimated and overpraised his enemy, and then defeated him in battle, the honor and praise which he received as the victor was greater than if his enemy had been downgraded and derided as insignificant.

GOLDEN AGE. In the nebecian view, the name given to the time in man's remote past when befapian astronauts were on Earth. With their supertechnology, these astronauts helped man to arise from an ape. Their purpose in doing so is not clear. The reasons given by nebecists vary. The most widely accepted reason is that the befaps were responding to the moral code which necessitated the spreading of intelligent life throughout the Universe. There is a consensus among nebecists that these befaps, whatever their original motives, affected man's evolution and gave him the spurt to acquire knowledge and cultural advancement.

Once this was done, the astronauts left. Nebecists are not agreed as to the reason for their departure. Perhaps their experiment with man was a success or perhaps they left because they were disappointed with man. In any event, according to the nebecists, man was then left to his own resources. Legends, myths, and traditions have survived which record the arrival, presence, and influence of these befapian astronauts.

The passage of time distorted and embellished these accounts. Though ancient man had these accounts, he did not fully comprehend their meaning and significance. According to the nebecists, before the befapian astronauts left, they promised man that one day he would equal them. By the use of sophisticated computer technology, they predicted that the "renewed Golden Age" for man would occur in the sign of Aquarius, which started in 1954. This promise, maintain the nebecists, can be found recorded in ancient texts if one knows how to interpret them. The "renewed Golden Age" refers to the time when man, having achieved a sophisticated space technology, will be capable of exploring neighboring star systems and of even implanting intelligent life on other planets. The conquest of space will also mean that man will have advanced scientifically to such a degree that he will be able to control diseases and bodily infirmities, thereby making possible a longer, better, and richer life. Then and only then will man realize his true origin and the true meaning of many ancient texts.

The zodiac, it is claimed, is a major substantiation of this variant of the nebecian theory as proposed by Jean Sendy. Some nebecists claim that through the ages religions have adopted and followed the signs of the zodiac. They see significance in this because, according to them, the origin of the zodiac can be traced back to the time of the original Golden Age when the celestials originally drew up a chart of the heavens.

See: Aquarius; Nebecism; Zodiac.

GRAVITATION. A concept in physics referring to that force of attraction which exists between all particles or bodies. It is a universal law governing the motions of all material bodies.

Ufologists are in general agreement that UFOs use a propulsion system which neutralizes gravitation. However, this is merely a reasonable conclusion and no proof exists of this.

Development of antigravitation machines would have far-reaching implications for space travel. Such machines, however, are presently beyond man's technological knowledge. First, science would have to better understand the nature of gravitation.

However, if it would be possible for man to one day neutralize gravitation and to construct a flying machine based on an antigravitation propulsion system, this would strengthen the argument for the existence of UFOs. Man would then have to admit the possibility that there may be aconian civilizations which invented antigravitation flying machines millennia ago. This would make possible a new and more serious reappraisal of UFO reports.

GRAVITATION II. See: Gravity II.

GRAVITY. The force of attraction by which bodies or objects tend to fall toward the center of Earth and, by extension, towards the center of other celestial bodies, if they were to be there.

GRAVITY II. Dr. John Carstoiu has formulated a mathematical presentation of a theory that there exists a second gravitational force alongside the ordinary gravitational field. The theory may hold the key to explaining some of the hitherto unexplained phenomena on Earth. The theory proposes certain effects on our planet's surface, in particular over some maritime regions, as a result of Gravity II.

In *Invisible Residents,* Ivan T. Sanderson posed the question of whether Gravity II may play a part in the mysterious disappearances of airplanes, boats, and people in certain areas of the world.

It is purely speculative as to whether any other effects and possibilities, such as interdimensional or interstellar travel, can be connected with Gravity II. Further research into this theory should prove fascinating and should provide man with a better understanding of the physical world.

See: Superspace.

GREAT LAKES TRIANGLE. A vile vortex similar to the Bermuda Triangle, located in the Great Lakes region. Under certain conditions not precisely understood, aircraft and ships are destroyed with devastating speed. Aircraft are reported to simply fragment and crash. Reports also indicate that disappearances of ships can be instantaneous. UFOs or some related mysterious phenomena or energy force are believed responsible for these occurrences. The mystery of this area is discussed in depth by Jay Gourley in *The Great Lakes Triangle.*

See: Devil's Triangle; Vortex.

GREAT RED SPOT. The name of the mysterious reddish-orange blemish which is visible on the southern hemisphere of Jupiter. It is elliptical in shape and is larger in size than Earth's surface.

Curiously, it is not a stationary phenomenon but floats along the planet's surface. One scientific theory suggested that it was a phenomenon caused by either a depression or a high spot on the surface of Jupiter.

One ufological theory maintained that the Red Spot was in reality a giant spaceship orbiting Jupiter and waiting for man to reach the point of annihilating himself. When this moment comes, holds the theory, this colossal spacecraft would come and rescue mankind, acting as a sort of modern-day Noah's Ark.

However, the Pioneer 10 space probe sent back information indicating that it is an 18,000-mile wide vortex over the planet. As a result of this finding, the ufological theory about its being a gigantic spaceship or an observation station has been laid to rest. The current scientific explanation that it is a storm seems to be conclusive.

GREEN BANK FORMULA. In November 1961 a top-level scientific meeting was held at Green Bank, West Virginia. The purpose of the meeting was to estimate the number of advanced planets that might exist in the Universe. Basing their conclusion on a variety of factors, the scientists concluded that there may be as many as 50,000,000 inhabited planets in the Milky Way Galaxy which possess at least our level of technology and which are capable of communicating with Earth.

The fact that Dr. Otto Struve headed this meeting gives it its real significance. Just a short half-year earlier, Dr. Struve had announced the termination of Project Ozma and had ridiculed attempts to establish contact with befapian civilizations.

Major Donald E. Keyhoe is one of the more prominent ufologists who see a connection between Project Ozma and the Green Bank Formula. He believes that the scientists may have intercepted intelligent messages during the initial operation of Project Ozma, and that they may have even deciphered them. The interception of such messages could have led to the hasty and panicky decision to officially terminate Project Ozma. However, it is maintained that Project Ozma is still in operation, though now as a secret project. If true, this would add additional support to the possibility that radio communications may have been intercepted.

If such contact was indeed established, it would support the reality of UFOs. If there are indeed advanced civilizations in other parts of the Universe, as on the planetary systems of Tau

Ceti and Epsilon Eridani, the two stars which were the objects of study by Project Ozma, then it is entirely possible that some of these befapian civilizations have in the past undertaken intersellar journeys to Earth.

GREEN FIREBALLS. The term used to describe a series of aerial phenomena, or UFOs, which first gained prominence in late November 1948. People around Albuquerque, New Mexico, began to report sightings of strange green lights in the sky. In time, these reports became more frequent and the lights became bigger and brighter.

An official Air Force investigation was launched into the mystery. It was first believed that they were meteorites. But an intensive search failed to produce any fragments. Meanwhile, the phenomenon continued. It was apparently limited to the skies over New Mexico and continued all during December 1948 and January 1949.

Dr. Lincoln La Paz, head of the University of New Mexico's Institute of Meteorites and a world-renowned authority on meteorites, conducted a thorough investigation of the green fireballs. His conclusion: they were not natural phenomena.

A special project was created to try and determine what the green fireballs actually were, but it proved a dismal failure. When the green fireballs disappeared, interest in them died.

See: Project Twinkle.

GREMLIN. A number of airplane pilots during World War II complained about mischievous beings who landed on their airborne planes and caused engine trouble and mechanical difficulities. Army Intelligence discounted reports of these beings or gremlins, as they were called. It was claimed that these beings were imaginary. Stress, tension, and flight fatigue were held responsible for producing what was called an hallucination. During the war, many pilots on both the Allied and Axis sides also encountered phenomena termed "foo fighters." These were also dismissed by intelligence officers as imaginary. It is possible that there was a nexus between these reports. Perhaps these gremlins came from the foo fighters.

Both types of sightings occurred at a time when the UFO phenomenon was publicly unknown and the possibility that beings from other planetary systems were visiting Earth was not even seriously entertained. With the dissemination of UFO reports after Kenneth Arnold's sighting in June of 1947, reports of gremlins and foo fighters during World War II began to acquire a different perspective.

See: Foo Fighter.

GROUND SAUCER WATCH. A civilian research organization which performs computer analysis of UFO photographs to assess their authenticity.

GRUDGE REPORT. The popular name of an official Air Force report titled "Unidentified Flying Objects—Project Grudge," Technical Report No. 102-AC-49/15-100.

On December 27, 1949, it was officially announced that Project Grudge was being terminated on the recommendation of a special report which was soon to be issued. This was the Grudge Report.

The Grudge Report, a massive, 600-page document, contained the official discussions, conclusions, and recommendations about UFOs. Out of 237 of the best UFO reports, studied by Dr. J. Allen Hynek and his staff, 32 percent were explained as astronomical phenomena. Another 12 percent were explained as balloons. Thirty-three percent were explained as misidentified objects, hoaxes, or as too vague. This still left 23 percent in the "unknown" category.

Even so, the report provided untenable explanations for these admittedly "unexplainable" reports. Ufologists were unconvinced and more certain than ever that a cover-up was being perpetrated.

The Grudge Report recommended that Project Grudge be "reduced in scope." And, indeed, Project Grudge was terminated, at least officially.

See: Estimate of the Situation; Project Grudge; Project Sign.

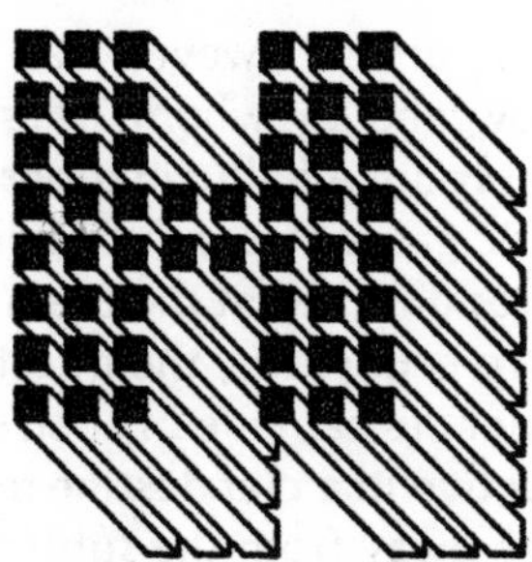

HALLUCINATION. A sensory experience despite the absence of external objects to stimulate the senses. Hallucination should be distinguished from an illusion. In an illusion, a person may actually see something which, however, he misidentifies. In an hallucination, a person sees something which is not there, but which exists only in his mind. Hallucinations occur in certain mental disorders, such as schizophrenia. They can be induced by physical or emotional deprivation. Extreme hunger, thirst, fear, guilt, and loneliness can also cause hallucinations. An hallucination is unquestionably subjective, i.e., the object exists only in the mind of the person.

The mental mechanisms which trigger hallucinations are still insufficiently understood. What is basically involved, however, is that, under certain conditions, thoughts are abstracted, and the mind views itself. In so doing, the mind, which contains a memory bank, can recreate past images or combine these past images to create new ones. The process may be unconsciously set in motion, and the images may be so vivid that a person actually believes he sees a real object.

This hallucinatory process has application to both ufology, and consciousness expansion. In consciousness expansion, the initiates claim to have a vision of the supersensible or spiritual world. The question which arises, however, is whether perhaps their minds are simply hallucinating and no real experience has occurred.

In connection with the UFO phenomenon, scientists and the

Air Force argue that certain sightings of UFOs may merely be hallucinatory in nature. No doubt some UFOs may be explained in this manner.

Other questions also arise, however. Can UFO sightings be induced and, if so, how and by whom? It is known that certain drugs and gases can produce hallucinations. Can a combination of certain atmospheric gases also induce hallucinations, and can electromagnetic waves directed at the brain also induce them? If the second alternative is possible, the question then arises as to who might have a machine capable of such stimulation. For such a machine to be effective in a clandestine manner, it would have to be quite a distance away from the subject. Such a machine is presently beyond man's technological know-how.

The problem of hallucinations raises another related problem. Admittedly, some people do hallucinate UFOs. But it stretches credibility to believe that a large number of people, at different times and at different places, could experience similar hallucinations. Futhermore, UFOs have often been sighted and reported by people who did not believe in them. Why, therefore, should people who are aware of but who do not believe in UFOs have hallucinations of them? Similarly, why should people who have never heard about UFOs also have hallucinations of them? By definition, such hallucinations would be either most unlikely or impossible.

This leads to the conclusion that something is actually sighted in the sky. The suggestion that all or most UFOs are merely hallucinatory is almost impossible to accept.

The subject of hallucinations is undoubtedly a complex one. It involves many factors and processes which are still too poorly understood. Most directly, it involves the mind, which is involved in the accumulation of all sense data and sense experience. But the nature, structure, and processes of the mind still pose too many unanswered questions.

See: Illusion.

HEAT. UFOs have occasionally been reported to generate a tremendous, furnacelike heat which was used as a weapon against humans. The use of heat seems to have been for both defensive and offensive purposes. Heat is only one of the weapons associated with UFOs. Attacks by lasers, and sonic guns have also been reported.

See: Fort Itaipu; Laser; Sound; Walesville.

HEAVEN. In the traditional religious view, heaven is the dwelling place of God and His angels. Among some Christian denominations, heaven is the place where the souls of good people go when they die. Heaven in this view is held to be a nonphysical place, a place beyond the reach of the senses. Heaven is regarded as separate from the physical world.

The advent of the space age, the rise of modern science, and the sightings of UFOs have put a new perspective on the nature of heaven.

One possibility is that heaven may be another dimension, i.e., a space-time continuum. There is a belief among some scientists that inherent in Einstein's theory of relativity is the existence of a parallel universe, i.e., Superspace. Time supposedly doesn't exist in Superspace. The absence of time suggests the possibility of eternity or immortality, a concept inherent in Christian theology about heaven.

Another view holds that heaven may simply be the name of a planet somewhere out in space or perhaps the name of an entire galaxy. This view is popular among adherents of the extraterrestrial theory. The Bible, for instance, mentions that Enoch was taken up bodily by the Lord (Genesis 5:24, Sirach 44:16, Sirach 49:14, Hebrews 11:5). Presumably, he was taken to another planet.

There is at present no scientific basis upon which to prove or to disprove any of these theories about heaven.

See: Enoch; Superspace.

HILL. One of the most famous and spectacular UFO contact- abduction cases involves the UFO encounter of Barney and Betty Hill on the evening of September 19, 1961.

The incident, dramatized in a TV movie, started after the Hills left Colebrook, New Hampshire at about 10 P.M. They first spotted the UFO at about 11 P.M. The UFO followed them for about thirty miles, then positioned itself over the highway and stopped in midair. The UFO continued to follow them as they turned off Route 3, then from Route 175 onto a side road. There they were captured and reportedly taken aboard the UFO. They were allegedly aboard the UFO for two hours, between midnight and 2 A.M.

The beings who captured them were described as humanoid, though with widely spaced slanted eyes and bridgeless noses. Betty Hill remembers that there were eleven ufonauts.

Aboard the UFO the Hills were subjected to a thorough physical examination. Their memory of the encounter was erased, and it was only later, through hypnosis, that their encounter with the ufonauts was revealed.

The Hill encounter continues to be a source of controversy. Ufologists who ascribe to the extraterrestrial theory tend to accept the encounter as genuine. Other ufologists believe that the experience was a paranormal one. The possibility that real extraterrestrial beings abducted the Hills is incredible to this group of ufologists. The UFO debunkers explain away the Hill experience as either an hallucination or a dream experience.

See: Abductee; Contactee; Zeta Reticuli.

HOLOGRAM. A three-dimensional projection of an image. This is accomplished by splitting laser beams which bounce from an object, thus creating length, width, and depth. Scientists have already mastered the initial techniques of producing holograms.

One group of ufologists believes that many UFOs may be holograms. They point out that UFOs usually have a disclike shape which is similar to the shape of our galaxy. In their opinion, many UFOs are simply hologramic messages being beamed to Earth from points in space. According to these ufologists, man has not recognized this very obvious meaning of UFOs.

The source of these UFO-holograms could be befaps who directly beam them to Earth from their home planet. Another possibility is that these UFO-holograms are beamed to Earth from a machine located somewhere in space. According to this second theory, the machine was placed by the befaps somewhere in space—the moon has been suggested as a likely possibility—and was then triggered by certain activities on Earth. After the initial triggering, the machine would operate automatically and intermittently. The detonation of nuclear weapons would indicate to the befaps that civilization on Earth had matured technologically. It may have been these explosions, hold the proponents of this theory, that triggered the mechanism to set the hologram-producing machine into motion. As a substantiation of their theory, they are quick to point out that UFOs were first definitely sighted around the time of the first atomic explosions during World War II.

Indeed, ever since World War II, UFOs have appeared cyclically in large numbers. If such a hologram-producing machine does indeed exist, no theory has yet been suggested which would explain its method of functioning; specifically, which set of stimuli causes it to project another series of UFO-holograms to Earth. Nor is there an explanation as to how and when such broadcasting is to cease.

The UFO-hologram theory is one of many explanations offered by ufologists to account for UFOs. However, most ufologists do not seriously consider this theory as a viable explanation.

HOMINID. A term designating a being which resembles a human but which is not because it lacks the necessary mental characteristics of a human, such as self-consciousness and high intelligence. Hominid should be distinguished from humanoid.

See: Humanoid.

HOMO SAPIENS. The scientific name for modern man. It literally means the knowing or wise (sapiens) man (homo).

HUMANOID. A term designating a being which, though it resembles a human in physical appearance and in such essential mental qualities as self-consciousness and high intelligence, is not actually human, i.e., is not a *Homo sapiens.* There have been many varying reports from contactees on the appearance of UFO beings. Curiously enough, some of these reports describe them as humanoid in appearance and behavior. If true, this raises several interesting questions.

Is there a direct connection between man and these humanoid beings? If there is a connection, does this mean that the origin of man is somehow linked to these beings? In other words, are some of the befaps also *Homo sapiens*? Such a possibility touches upon the nebecian philosophy; in particular, on its concept of seeding. If there is no direct connection between man and these humanoids, does this mean that the laws of biology are as universal as the laws of physics and chemistry, and that similar intelligent beings can, therefore, arise in different parts of the Universe as a result of parallel evolution? Such a possibility would indicate a similarity of environment and would then raise interesting questions about the nature of evolution.

This whole area of discussion is a fascinating one. Unfortunately, at present too little information is available for more definitive answers.

See: Assumption of Mediocrity; *Homo sapiens;* Nebecism; Seeding.

HYBRID MAN. The belief that man isn't solely a product of natural evolutionary processes has led to the theory of Hybrid Man. In this view, man has progenitors in the stars. Humans are supposed to be hybrids, a cross between the apes, or the man-apes, of earthly evolution and intelligent beings from space. According to this theory, starmen, through the use of advanced genetic engineering, implanted their superior genes into earthly hominid species, creating as the end result the human race. Humans thus have a biological bond with the extraterrestrial intelligences.

The theory of extraterrestrial influence on human evolution is shared by many researchers. The term "Hybrid Man" is used by Max H. Flindt and Otto O. Binder in *Mankind—Child Of The Stars,* where they develop in detail the basis for such a theory.

See: Astroevolution.

HYNEK, JOSEPH ALLEN. One of the most prominent ufologists. He was associated with the official Air Force investigation of UFOs, and in March 1966, as the Air Force's top scientific advisor on UFOs, he issued the controversial "swamp gas" explanation for UFO sightings near Ann Arbor, Michigan, for which he was much criticized. After his association with the Air Force, Dr. Hynek decided to pursue UFO research as a private citizen. He is director of the Center for UFO Studies.

Undoubtedly one of Dr. Hynek's lasting contributions to ufology will be the creation in his book *The UFO Experience: A Scientific Inquiry* of the expression "Close Encounters of the Third Kind" to refer to those UFO contact cases where the occupants of UFOs are seen and actual physical contact is sometimes made. The expression was used as the title of the successful Columbia Pictures motion picture released in 1977, for which Dr. Hynek served as technical advisor and consultant.

HYPERSPACE. See: Superspace.

HYPNOSIS. Hypnosis refers to a psychological condition, which can be artificially produced, in which a person's mind is controlled to a great degree by the hypnotist who induces such a state. A person in such a condition is markedly susceptible to suggestion and may subsequently act on the basis of such a suggestion. Such a condition is also characterized by a marked loss of willpower and of sensation. The mind and willpower of a person in such a condition is, to a large degree, under the control of the hypnotist.

Some persons who have sighted UFOs seem to have been under hypnosis during the experience, whatever the actual experience may have been. This is especially true of those persons who claim to have come into direct contact with UFOs. Other contactees seem to have been under a posthypnotic suggestion to forget the experience. Not enough cases exist to form a general conclusion, but from those cases available, a tentative conclusion can be reached; that is, that hypnosis is used only by those beings who, it is claimed, are hideous looking. Contactees who describe humanoid-type aconins rarely exhibit symptoms of hypnosis.

The Hill experience in New Hampshire is a classic case of the sort of experience in which contactees were hypnotized during the encounter. The memory of such an experience cannot be entirely erased, however. Contactees sometimes remember their experience, especially when asleep. It may be a source of nightmares and an unknown source of emotional problems. The internal turmoil and stress in such cases is so great that the contactees so affected waste away in tension and worry, and die prematurely.

See: Posthypnotic Suggestion.

HYPNOTISM. The branch of science which deals with and studies hypnosis, its inducement, its effects, and its possible medical applications.

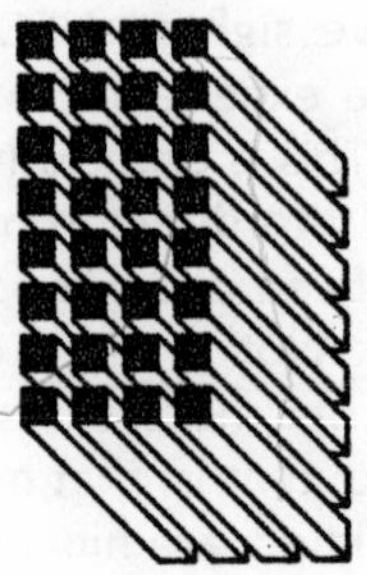

ILLUSION. An illusion is usually a misidentification of a real object. Such a visual deception can be caused by poor light, too great a distance between the object and the observer, the psychological preconceptions of the observer, etc. Illusion should be distinguished from hallucination. In an hallucination, a person believes to see something which does not really exist. In an illusion, a person may actually see something, but wrongly interprets what he sees.

The Air Force, scientists, writers, and other persons who discount the reality of UFOs, often claim that many UFO sightings are nothing but illusions. That is to say, the person reporting the sighting misidentified a natural phenomenon or manmade object for an UFO. This, of course, is a complicated area, for unless photographic evidence exists, the observer cannot prove what he really saw nor can the Air Force positively explain what he saw.

Admittedly, some UFOs may in fact be illusions. This is especially true when sightings occur in poor light, as at dawn or dusk. When the object is very far away, it is also easy to misidentify it. However, when the object is sighted at close range and the witness is reliable, or when a number of credible witnesses are involved, then credence must be given to the sighting.

See: Hallucination.

IMMORTALITY. The capability or ability to have eternal life. Many religions have promised that men who live righteous and good lives shall never know death but shall continue to live forever in a spiritual existence or as a corporeal being in a resurrected body.

See: Soul; Technological Immortality.

INCREDIBLE DECADE. The term applied by M. K. Jessup, a pioneer ufologist, to the decade between 1877 and 1887. During this period of time there was, in the words of Jessup, a "greater and more representative" concentration of UFO-related phenomena than during any other equivalent period prior to 1947, when the modern UFO age was ushered in by Kenneth Arnold's sighting near Mount Rainier.

INFRASONIC SOUND WAVES. See: Sound.

INSTANT TRANSFERENCE. See: Teleportation.

INTELLIGENCE. Intelligence is a term describing a particular type of mental ability. It enables those living organisms which possess it to learn about the outside world. Once remembered, this experience forms a pool of knowledge which is then used for specific purposes. Practically speaking, intelligence is basically the ability to learn from experience and then to apply this knowledge for one's own benefit or for the benefit of others. The existence of intelligence presupposes the existence of such other mental capabilities as memory, analysis, synthesis, deduction, and logic. Both man and animals possess intelligence, but man surpasses animals in the level of intelligence.

Intelligence has permitted man to conquer his environment and to begin modifying it for his own needs. Intelligence is an innate factor, common to all men. However, some men and nations have exhibited more intelligence than others. This is due to various factors, among which is the degree to which culture and religion permit the use of intelligence.

On a larger cosmic scale, intelligence is tied in with the question of life. If life exists in other parts of the Universe, then it follows that intelligent life should also probably exist. The search for such intelligent beings in the Universe is among man's prime goals. Such intelligent beings need not necessarily be more intelligent than man. Even the UFO beings need not necessarily be more intelligent than man, though they definitely are more technologically advanced.

If the space program continues, the future should hopefully provide more definitive answers as to whether or not there exists intelligent life in the Universe and, if so, whether these aconian beings are more intelligent than man or less so.

INTERCALACTIC. A term pertaining or relating to the space which lies between or among the galaxies, and to the ability to come from, or to travel to or through this space. Among the problems facing ufologists is the need to determine the celestial location from which UFOs originate, assuming that they originate from space and not from a parallel universe. UFOs are probably not from our solar system, but ufologists are still undecided as to whether they originate from our galaxy or from a neighboring galaxy.

INVISIBLE. In dimensionalism, invisible is a term describing the world or reality which, though part of our space-time continuum, is beyond the ability of the senses to perceive. The term is also used to refer to beings from this reality. According to some dimensionalists, as, for example, Ivan Sanderson, there may be an invisible world existing alongside our sense-world. This world is held to be inhabited by beings who are capable of either entering into our sense-world or of making their presence felt in our sense-world.

There is an overlap between the dimensionalistic idea of an invisible world and the dimensionalistic theory of the existence of a parallel universe or other space-time continuum. There is also an overlap between the religious concept of evil spirits and the dimensionalistic concept of invisible beings. The beings in both these beliefs exhibit similar behavioral characteristics in relation to man. According to dimensionalists, only the existence of either a parallel world or an invisible world can explain some of the phenomena on Earth. The dimensionalist branch of naphology further believes that UFOs may also originate from a parallel universe.

Science has not yet been able to resolve the basic question of whether such a world exists. However, it has discovered that certain phenomena which were once assigned to supernatural origin are in fact caused by psychokinetic energy emanating from the mind. Science has thus at least been able to put some of the problems into better focus.

See: Aconin; Parallel Universe; Reality; Supersensible; UFO; UT.

ITF. See: Instant Transference.

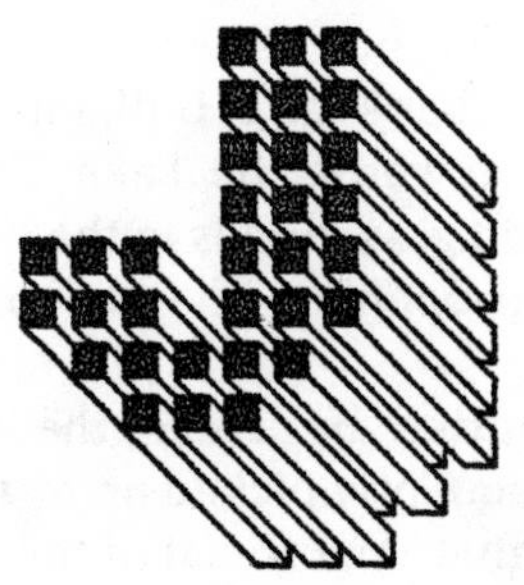

JANAP-146. This designation identifies an order promulgated by the Joint Chiefs of Staff, titled Communications Instruction for Reporting Vital Intelligence Sightings from Aircraft (CIRVIS). Among its provisions were orders on how to deal with UFO sightings. The directive applied to both military personnel and to airline pilots and crews. It labeled UFO sightings as being of vital importance and required their immediate transmission to appropriate military and government departments; specifically, to the Air (now Aerospace) Defense Command, the Secretary of Defense, and the nearest U.S. Military Command. The orders also warned that unauthorized release of CIRVIS reports was in violation of the Espionage Law. The order has been quite effective in preventing pilots, both military and commercial, from making public their UFO sightings.

Publicly, the Air Force denies the objective reality of UFOs and denigrates the idea that they could be alien spacecraft from another planet. However, if the government and military really believed their own statements, there would be no need then for any secrecy on the UFO question. The very formulation of an order such as JANAP-146 presumes the objective reality of UFOs.

JEHOVAH. The name of God in the Old Testament. It is an erroneous rendition of the letters JHVH which should correctly be pronounced as "Yahweh."

See: Elohim; Yahweh.

JELLYFISH. On Tuesday, September 22, 1977 at 4 A.M. a gigantic mass of light brightened the skies of Petrozavodsk in Karelia, USSR, about 130 miles from the Finnish border. The light assumed the shape of a jellyfish and hovered over the city. The phenomenon resembled a torrential rain of light as it emitted forth a multitude of fine beams. After the glow subsided, the jellyfish assumed the shape of a brilliant semicircle and continued its movement towards the Lake Onega region. Subsequently, there appeared gray clouds in the center of which was a bright red semicircular opening. The phenomenon lasted about ten to twelve minutes.

The story was reported by TASS, the official USSR news agency, and was subsequently picked up by the wire services and flashed around the planet. An official of the Petrozavodsk observatory was unable to provide a scientific explanation for the jellyfish phenomenon.

The aerial jellyfish is another in the long line of aerial, marine, and terrestrial mysteries, apparently linked to UFOs, which have awed observers and baffled scientists.

See: UAP; UFO.

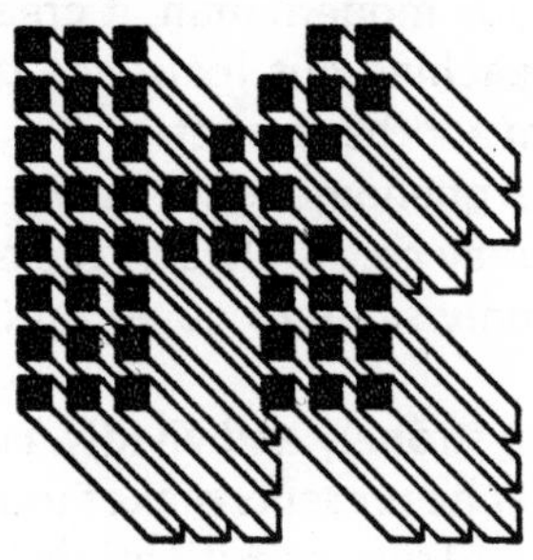

KABALA. See: Cabala.

KEEL, JOHN A. Undeniably one of the deans of ufology, Keel developed and expounded his UFO theory during the course of many years. He views UFOs as part of a larger phenomenon, which includes or involves: spiritism, reincarnation, religion, magic, etc.

In his view, there is a phenomenon which, while managing to conceal its real identity, has throughout the millenniums been manipulating humans for its own ends.

An important element in Keel's theory lies in energy. Energy and matter are interrelated and one can be transformed into the other. The human mind can only perceive part of the electromagnetic spectrum. That portion of the EM spectrum invisible to man may constitute another parallel dimension or universe. There is a phenomenon out there, a conscious energy force, which can manipulate the EM spectrum. By controlling the EM spectrum, the phenomenon can create various effects in our dimension. This theory of the all-powerful phenomenon or superspectrum is developed in his work *The Eight Tower.*

The phenomenon delights in interfering in human affairs and in deceiving humans. The level of its hoaxes, he argues, is tailored to individual cultures and levels of technology. In the Middle Ages, the phenomenon created fairies and elves because the cultural level of man at that time could accept these concoctions as real. In his work *Our Haunted Planet,* he refers to the beings of this phenomenon as ultraterrestrials (UTs) or elementals.

As science and knowledge progressed, its means of deception also changed. To delude modern man, it created UFOs, knowing full well that man, reaching out for space travel, could accept UFOs as vehicles from another planet.

He argues that the phenomenon is using people for its own purpose, whatever it may be. As always, the overt manifestations of the phenomenon only serve to cover up its true identity and purpose.

He presents his case strongly and vividly. His accounts are well written, and the matter he presents makes interesting reading.

See: Dimensionalism; Transmogrification; Ultraterrestrial.

KEYHOE, DONALD E. A firm believer in the objective existence of UFOs. He is one of the leading exponents of the extraterrestrial theory as a viable explanation for UFOs, a pioneer in the field of ufology, and a former director of NICAP. He was among the first to commit himself to studying the phenomenon. The author of numerous books and articles on UFOs, he argues that UFOs should be given serious consideration. In his works, he presents detailed case studies, and his general conclusion is that the government is covering up many crucial facts about UFOs. The failure to tell the public the truth about UFOs can be potentially disconcerting and deleterious, he claims. Had the government told the people the truth about UFOs, the people would have over a period of time accepted the existence of UFOs as normal. But because their existence has been debunked, a new series of sensational sightings or contacts might leave the public unprepared for the confrontation with an alien intelligence, and this could result in panic. Keyhoe argues that there should be an end to all censorship about UFOs and that a new, serious, officially sanctioned investigation into UFOs should be launched.

See: Colorado University Project; Nebecism; NICAP.

KILLER UFO. A designation applied to a UFO which either causes death to humans or permanently abducts humans who come into contact with it.

See: UFO.

KLASS, PHILIP J. One of the foremost debunkers of UFOs. In two books, *UFO Identified* and *UFOs Explained,* Klass provides non-UFO interpretations of, and explanations for, some of the most classic UFO cases. Klass has also authored articles and appeared on talk shows debunking UFOs.

Klass contends that all UFOs can be explained as hoaxes or as misidentified or misinterpreted natural phenomena.

See: Debunker.

KORENDOR. The name of one of the planets from which some of the UFO beings claim to originate in their alleged conversations with contactees. John A. Keel dismisses this as a mere mythical planet. He maintains that the beings who identify themselves as Korendorians are merely UTs.

See: Contactee; Dimensionalism; Manadim; UT.

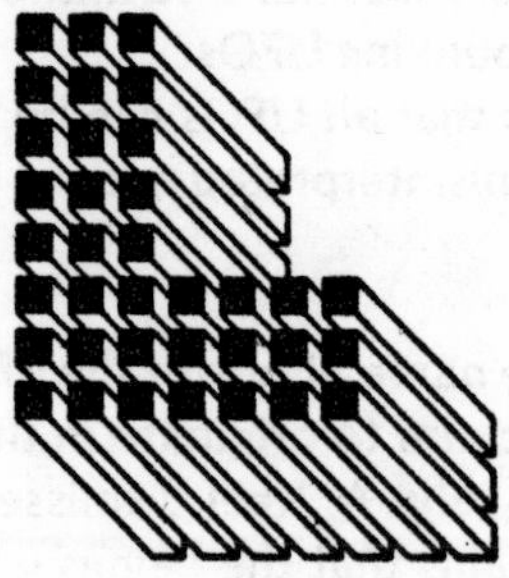

LAGRANGE ORBIT. This refers to an orbit, also known as the Trojan Orbit, around Earth which is the same distance as the Moon, i.e., aproximately 240,000 miles. There the gravitational pull of Earth and the moon would be more or less evenly balanced. An extraterrestrial space probe in such an orbit would be able to monitor Earth a long time before drifting out of orbit.

It is known that the Skylab missions photographed the Lagrange areas, but it is not known if anything was found.

In *Is Anyone Out There?,* Jack Stoneley and A.T. Lawton suggest that radio signals be directed at these Lagrange or Trojan areas to determine if there is indeed an extraterrestrial space probe there.

LASER. Acronym for "light amplification by stimulated emission of radiation." A laser is a type of maser that amplifies visible light radiations. Ordinary light diffuses and spreads out from its source. A laser concentrates all light into one narrow beam.

Such a concentrated light beam or laser beam possesses great power. It has practical medical application, as in delicate eye surgery. It can also be used for communication purposes. But its most frightening use is as a deadly weapon. There would be virtually no defense against such a weapon. Laser beams can cut through any metal no matter what the thickness. Scientists are proceeding with experiments to produce ever more powerful and sophisticated lasers. The ultimate achievement would be to have lasers capable of shooting down missiles. Work is also in progress to create portable laser-guns.

If the reports of a number of persons who have seen UFOs are to be believed, then the evidence indicates that UFOs are also armed with laser weapons. There have been several recorded cases of persons who were shot unconscious by a light beam, presumably by some sort of sophisticated laser beam, after they had ventured too close to a UFO. In other cases, pilots reported seeing beams of light shooting past their airplanes. Barring a natural explanation for this type of phenomenon, the conjecture is that these beams originated from UFOs.

LAW. In science a law is a statement of a relation of a phenomenon or behavior in nature which is immutable and invariable under the same type of conditions. The advance of science has discovered a number of natural laws, as, for example, the Law of Momentum, and the Law of the Conservation of Matter and Energy. Scientists are in agreement that the basic laws of physics and chemistry are universal, i.e., the same throughout the Universe. Still unanswered, however, is the question of the universality of the laws of biology.

See: Assumption of Mediocrity; Biology.

LAW OF THE CONSERVATION OF ENERGY. See: Law of the Conservation of Matter and Energy.

LAW OF THE CONSERVATION OF MATTER. See: Law of the Conservation of Matter and Energy.

LAW OF THE CONSERVATION OF MATTER AND ENERGY. Scientists had long believed that reality or existence was composed of two separate and distinct entities or forms, i.e., energy and matter. It was incorrectly believed that the amount of energy and matter remained constant in the Universe, and that therefore neither matter nor energy could be increased or decreased in amount. This belief led to the formulation of two separate laws, i.e., The Law of the Conservation of Matter and The Law of the Conservation of Energy.

The advance of nuclear physics modified their theory. As a result of nuclear explosions, scientists discovered the interconvertibility of matter and energy. Though the amount of reality or existence, i.e., of matter and energy, remains constant and immutable, one form of reality can be changed to the other; that is, if one form of reality is destroyed a corresponding increase in the other form of reality will occur. Therefore, scientists have combined the two separate conservation laws into one unified law, i.e., The Law of the Conservation of Matter and Energy.

See: Superspace; Transmogrification.

LEM. Acronym for Lunar Excursion Module (LEM). A three-legged type of space vehicle, the LEM was used by American astronauts to descend to the surface of the moon. It carried two astronauts and was separated from the Apollo command module for the lunar landing mission. The LEM was the first manned vehicle to land on the surface of another heavenly body. The knowledge gained by the operation of this vehicle has aided scientists in designing future crafts. It probably will be the prototype of future vehicles which one day will land humans on other planets.

LEMURIA. The name given to a sunken continent said to have existed in the past in the Indian Ocean. It was supposed to have been destroyed in a great cataclysm. Other writers place Lemuria in the Pacific Ocean and use the name interchangeably with Mu. The distinction between the two, if any, is blurry, and the use of one name over the other seems to depend solely upon the inclinations of the individual writer.

Much the same has been postulated with regard to Lemuria as has been with Atlantis and Mu, including the suggestion that UFOs may originate from an underwater colony of Lemuria which survived the cataclysm.

See: Atlantis; Mu; USO.

LIFE. Things, objects or bodies which exist can be divided into two broad categories, the inanimate and the animate. The inanimate preceded the animate and made possible the animate. Scientists are uncertain as to how matter came into being. However, what is certain and indisputable is that living organisms are based on matter. And when death comes, the elements constituting life return to matter.

There are three possible theories as to how life initially arose on Earth: 1) by divine intervention, 2) through a natural interaction of elements, and 3) through the conscious effort of other intelligent life forms.

There are two general steps in the transformation of matter (the inanimate) into life (the animate). The first step is the creation of prebiological molecules; the second step is the combination of prebiological molecules to form biological molecules.

Scientists have discovered the existence of prebiological molecules in space. This has led to the conclusion that under suitable conditions matter can combine into prebiological molecules. But while it is significant that prebiological molecules are formed naturally, the formation of biological molecules from a combination of prebiological molecules must be either a very rare phenomenon or an impossibility.

But once biological molecules are formed, by whatever means, evolution takes over. Evolution seems to be one of the laws of nature and it leads to ever more complex life forms, eventually giving rise, if conditions are suitable, to intelligent life forms.

The crucial question is this: did life arise in different parts of the Universe when conditions were suitable, or did it arise only on Earth? The Assumption of Mediocrity argues that life should have arisen on planets revolving around stars similar to, but older than, the sun. Nebecists share the theory of the universality of the laws of biology, and believe that life starts whenever and wherever conditions are suitable.

If life does arise naturally when conditions are suitable and then evolves into more complex life forms, the question about the origin of life on Earth is answered, as is the question of whether life exists elsewhere in the Universe.

If one assumes that life originated and exists only on Earth, then man stands alone in the vast Universe as an intelligent being. The reported existence of UFOs, however, suggests that there are other intelligent life forms and that these UFO beings, considering their advanced technology, arose earlier than man. The existence of such beings leads to the possibility that they may have influenced the course of evolution of life on Earth.

Indeed, it is a fundamental concept of nebecism that the course of evolution of life on Earth was influenced by astronauts from another planet. One group of nebecists believes that life on Earth arose as a result of befapian intervention. Another group believes that life already existed on Earth, but that its evolution was influenced by befaps.

The degree of intervention with respect to man is disputed among the nebecists. Some argue that these space beings (befaps) created man and possibly other forms of life, too. Other nebecists argue that man already existed and that the befaps merely refined him and speeded up his evolution, and that they possibly enhanced his chances of survival by destroying competitive lines of man such as Neanderthal Man.

This question of befapian intervention itself engenders still other questions. For example, did life arise naturally on their planets or was it formed by divine intervention or through the intervention of still other befaps? Also, are they the end products of natural evolution on their planet or was their evolution influenced by other befaps? Needless to say, such questions cannot be presently answered.

Questions about the origin of life on Earth, about the possibility of life in other parts of the Universe, about the evolution of life, about possible divine or aconian intervention to influence the course of evolution of life, and about the possible means of dispersion of life through the Universe, are extremely complex and mind-boggling. These are questions for which man has no certain, scientifically verifiable answers and for which he may never possess such answers. But the very act of thinking about such questions forces man to ponder his place in the Universe and makes him wonder if there is a higher reality and other intelligent beings in the Universe.

Answers, however tentative, to such questions are significant because fundamental concepts of human society are involved. Ultimately, the organization and values of human society are dependent upon the answers people provide to such questions. Definitive answers are not presently available, but as man reaches out into space and continues advanced biological research, the answers will perhaps be found.

See: Assumption of Mediocrity; Biology; Biogenesis; Evolution; Nebecism; Seeding; Soul; Technological Immortality; Terraformation.

LIGHT. A type of radiation which ranges in wavelength from 4,000 to 7,700 angstrom units and which travels at a speed of 186,300 miles per second. It is the agency responsible for making things or objects visible. Light also possesses a biological function, as in photosynthesis, which requires light in order to function. Light is a necessary condition for the existence of most forms of life. For many higher forms of life, light also provides an indispensable psychological aid. Humans, for example, feel more at ease and relaxed in the daytime than at night. Human eyes do not adequately fulfill their seeing function in darkness. The inability to see properly creates a sense of apprehension. Curiously, many of the occult phenomena occur only at night or in darkness. Light is a panacea for many kinds of fears and horrors.

Light can also be manipulated so as to create a laser. A laser is light which has been amplified and directed in one concentrated beam. Laser beams can be used for man's benefit as when they are used in delicate eye surgery or they can be used as terrible weapons of destruction.

Light is also intimately associated with the UFO phenomenon, specifically with the UAPs. Most UFOs are essentially various types of light manifestations. The source of such lights, whether they are natural or whether they are produced by a spacecraft, is one of the crucial questions yet to be answered about UFOs.

See: Laser; UAP; UFO.

LIGHT-SPEED. Light-speed refers to a unit of velocity (a measurement of velocity) utilizing the velocity of light as the standard unit. The velocity of light is 186,300 miles per second. Light-speed is measured in units of this. The speed of light is equal to 1 blisk.

See: Blisk.

LIGHT-YEAR. In astronomical measurement a light-year is the distance traversed by light in one year. It is used as a unit of measuring distances between stars. Light travels at 186,300 miles per second. At this speed, it can cover about 5,880,000,000,000 miles in one year. The distances involved are immense and mind-boggling.

See: Blisk; Natural Quarantine; Space Gate; Superspace; Tachyon; Theory of Relativity.

LIGHTNING. A flash of light, invariably occurring during a storm, caused by the discharge of atmospheric electricity. Lightning can cause great damage if it strikes vulnerable areas. It has also been responsible for killing humans and animals. At one time it was believed that airplanes were immune from being struck by lightning. A steady accumulation of evidence, though, has proven otherwise. Airplanes have been hit and damaged, and, at times, destroyed by lightning. If an airplane traveling over the ocean were to be struck in a vulnerable area by lightning, it might break into thousands of pieces which would be scattered over a wide stretch of water. The pieces would sink, leaving no trace of the airplane.

There is a strong possibility that lightning may be responsible for the mysterious disappearances of some airplanes, especially in the vile vortices, the most famous of which is the Devil's Triangle. During the winter, storms may arise suddenly and unexpectedly in these areas of the world. The pilot may not even have a chance to take precautionary measures or to radio a distress signal before a disaster strikes. Some of the disappearances which ufologists have classified as suspicious, hinting that either UFOs or occult forces were involved, may possibly be explained by natural means. Lightning or some other natural phenomenon may have been responsible for the disappearances.

LIMBO OF THE LOST. One of the many synonyms for the Devil's Triangle.

See: Devil's Triangle; Vile Vortex.

LORENZEN, CORAL and JIM. Among the most prominent ufologists are Jim and Coral Lorenzen. They are the authors of several books on UFOs. One of their major contributions to ufology was the establishment of the Aerial Phenomena Research Organization, the first major UFO research organization to be founded, which they still head.

They investigated the case of George Adamski, one of the most celebrated contactee cases. In their judgment, this particular contact report was a fake.

In their ufological perspective, they take the extraterrestrial position. The possibility that UFOs may be dimensional craft is scientifically untenable to them. They don't look askance at contact reports and believe that there may be several different groups of extraterrestrials visiting Earth.

Generally, they have a positive attitude towards UFOs and do not consider them to be inherently hostile to human civilization. They believe that the ufonauts will in time establish open contact with mankind.

See: Adamski; Aerial Phenomena Research Organization.

LUBBOCK LIGHTS. A classic UFO case, involving the sightings of strange bluish-green lights in the sky over Lubbock, Texas. The first reported sighting was on the night of August 25, 1951, at about 9:20 P.M., by four scientists who were also college professors. The sightings continued for over two weeks.

The lights first appeared in a semicircular formation, but afterwards they appeared in apparently random formations. One of the possible explanations offered was that the lights were reflections of street lamps off the bodies of plovers, water birds. However, this did not explain how the lights were seen in areas where there were no street lamps. In his book *Flying Saucers,* Donald Menzel of Harvard concluded that the lights were merely refracted city lights.

Five photographs were exposed of the lights by Carl Hart, Jr. Four of the negatives were examined by experts at the Photo Reconnaissance Laboratory at Wright Field. The official conclusion, with regard to the photos, issued by Edward J. Ruppelt, head of Project Blue Book, to the press was that the photos could neither be confirmed as a hoax nor as genuine.

Apparently related to the bluish-green Lubbock Lights was another sighting in Albuquerque on the same evening. On the evening of August 25, 1951, a reliable witness and his wife saw a huge craft fly silently over their home. The craft was V-shaped and described as one and one-half times the size of a B-36. They couldn't see its color, but did note that on the edge of the wings were six to eight pairs of soft, glowing, bluish lights.

A check was quickly made and it was discovered that there were no airplanes in the vicinity at the time. The sighting was later confirmed to Ruppelt by another individual whose wife had seen a similar object in Lubbock. As information about the Albuquerque sighting had not been made public, there was no way she could have known about it.

Ruppelt did a thorough writeup of these UFOs in chapter 8 of *The Report on Unidentified Flying Objects.* He states in the book that no conclusive explanation could be reached about the V-shaped objects. Ruppelt injects into this chapter a rather cryptic section about a certain "group" who had access to the Project Blue Book files and who turned their attention to the Lubbock Lights. This unnamed group was composed of rocket experts, nuclear physicists, and intelligence experts. They were convinced that some UFO sightings were genuine and were convinced that the Lubbock Lights, and the V-shaped crafts, were genuine sightings of extraterrestrial craft.

Despite his objective presentation of the Lubbock Lights controversy, Ruppelt closes out the chapter with a cop-out of sorts. He admits that officially the Lubbock Lights are unknowns, but then states that the lights which the professors saw can be identified as very common, easily explainable natural phenomena. He covers up by saying that he was shown to his satisfaction that this was so by an unnamed scientist who spent months tracking down the answer, but who wished to remain anonymous. Ruppelt also refrains from explaining how the common phenomenon was even discovered, for this, he says, would identify the man to whom he had promised complete anonymity. Ruppelt did not identify the phenomenon nor did he explain why, if it were such a common, easily identifiable phenomenon, the scientists were not able to identify it as such.

LUCIFER. In the Jewish and Christian religions, Lucifer is the vain, haughty, rebellious archangel who was punished by God and expelled from Heaven. Literally, Lucifer means "one who brings light." The term is ironic, however. Lucifer is identified with Satan, the archenemy of good and God. His role is a deceitful one, that of bringing man false light (knowledge) or incomplete light (knowledge) in order to deceive man about the true nature of the world and of God, and thus to keep man from the truth and from God. Some dimensionalists, as Prof. Clifford Wilson, for example, believe that evil forces created UFOs in order to deceive man.

See: Dimensionalism; Satan.

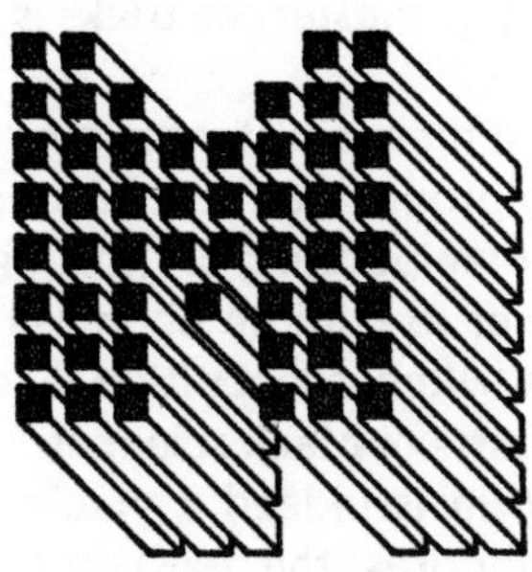

MacARTHUR, DOUGLAS. During World War II, Gen. Douglas MacArthur was the supreme commander in the Pacific theater of war. Under his leadership, the Allies achieved victory over Japan. It was during the war that he learned about and became interested in UFOs. Reports of these mysterious aerial objects began to come in from various pilots, ships, and soldiers. General MacArthur set up an intelligence unit to study these reports. On the basis of these intelligence reports, he became convinced that UFOs were of extraterrestrial origin and that their intentions were hostile to mankind.

His interest in UFOs continued after his retirement from the military. *The New York Times* of October 8, 1955, carried an item about General MacArthur which reported his belief that the nations of the world would have to unite one day to meet a threat from outer space. MacArthur firmly believed that one day Earth would have to battle invaders from space.

MACH. A unit of velocity equal to the velocity of sound in the air. It is named after Ernst Mach (1838–1916), an Austrian physicist. At sea level, sound travels through the air at a speed of about 730 miles per hour. Mach 1 is the term used to designate a speed of 730 mph; Mach 2 that of 1,460 mph; Mach 3 that of 2,190 mph; etc.

MAGIC. In its innocuous form, magic or sleight of hand is a form of trickery based on optical illusions. An artist, called a magician, is able to perform various tricks by diverting the attention of those for whom he performs. Magic in this form involves no real secret. The ability to master the tricks is open to anyone willing to learn.

There is, however, a more sinister form of magic. This involves the alleged ability to produce effects beyond the natural human powers by means of manipulating or utilizing supernatural or occult forces. This power to conjure up invisible forces is claimed by wizards, warlocks, witches, occultists, and various other practitioners of the black arts or black sciences.

If magic in this form is indeed a viable phenomenon in the black arts, it presupposes the existence of some causality; specifically, the existence of forces or beings beyond man's senses. In this manner it also involves UFOs. Some alleged UFO manifestations have involved or touched upon the black arts.

See: Dimensionalism; Occult; Supersensible; Transmogrification.

MAGNETISM. This refers to the ability or property of one substance or body, as a piece of iron, to attract certain other substances. A magnet may be natural or artificial, permanent or temporary. The application of an electric current to iron can, if done in the proper manner, induce magnetism, creating an electromagnet. Magnets and electromagnets have a wide range of application in industrial, military, navigational, and commercial fields. The propulsion system of UFOs may, it has been postulated, involve the use of electromagnetism.

See: Electricity; Electromagnetism; EM Interference.

MAGONIA. In ufological lore, this was the place of origin of the mysterious people with the "ships from the clouds" who visited villages in France in the ninth century A.D.

See: Argobard.

MAN. A term referring to an individual of the genus *Homo,* family Hominidae, class Mammalia. Man is at the highest level of animal development on Earth. He is characterized by distinctive physical and mental attributes. Among his mental qualities are: high intelligence, imagination, self-consciousness, foresight, and reason.

The question as to the origin of man is a complex one. No one has to date conclusively shown how man originated. Most scientists lean toward the theory that man evolved from a species of ape long since extinct.

The question of evolution also involves the question of whether some outside force intervened, i.e., nebecism argues that man's evolution was influenced by befapian astronauts.

According to the religious view, held by many theologians, scientists, and laymen, only direct creation by God can explain the origin of man.

See: Evolution; Nebecism.

MANADIM. Short for MAN(ifestation from) A(nother) DIM(ension). This is a general term referring to and identifying all types of malicious, malevolent intelligent beings which, according to the dimensionalist theory, are believed to inhabit parallel space-time continuums. Dimensionalists believe that by manipulating electromagnetic energy, manadims are able to temporarily assume any form, including a human form. Most dimensionalists equate manadims with that group of beings referred to by religion as demons.

See: Aconin; Dimensionalism; Transmogrification.

MANIMAL. The term is used to refer to those creatures or entities which are apparently related to the UFO phenomenon in some manner not yet conclusively established. They resemble animals in general appearance, but have some manlike qualities, especially in the eyes and expressions, hence the term "man animal." The term has most specifically been used in reference to Bigfoot.

See: Bigfoot.

MANTELL INCIDENT. A classic UFO incident involving the alleged pursuit by Capt. Thomas Mantell, USAF, of a UFO on January 7, 1948, and his death as a result of that chase.

The incident began shortly after noon of that day when some people sighted a UFO near Louisville, Kentucky. Shortly afterwards, other reports came in. A check with nearby Air Force bases showed no flights in the area. The object was spotted visually by tower operators at Goodman AFB at 1:45 P.M. The object proved unidentifiable, even to the base commander.

At 2:30 P.M., four F-51's approached the base. Their flight leader, Capt. Thomas Mantell, was asked to identify the object. One F-51, low on fuel, landed, while the other three took after the UFO.

At 2:45 P.M., above 10,000 feet, Mantell reported that he saw something ahead of him and that he was still climbing. What happened after that is a mystery and a matter of dispute. Ufologists claim that he described the object as appearing metallic and tremendous in size, and reported that he was giving pursuit. He then said it was above him and he was going to 20,000 feet. Everyone in the tower later agreed that he said he was going to 20,000 feet, but disagreed on whether he said he saw the object.

This was the last heard from Captain Mantell. His two wing men leveled off at 15,000 feet and, because they lacked oxygen masks, dared not go higher. They tried to contact Mantell but had no success. They finally landed.

At 3:50 P.M., the tower lost sight of the UFO. A few minutes later word was received that Mantell had crashed and was dead.

The immediately offered explanation was that Mantell had spotted and had been chasing Venus. A year later the official Air Force report on the incident stated that the object pursued might have been either Venus or a balloon, but was probably Venus.

Knowledgeable persons disputed this conclusion, pointing out that Venus would have been too dim to be seen that afternoon, and, if seen, would have only been a point of light. The object Mantell pursued had been described by everyone who saw it as gigantic.

Edward J. Ruppelt reinvestigated the incident again when he was in charge of the Air Force's Project Blue Book and reported in his book *The Report on Unidentified Flying Objects* that Mantell had been pursuing a 100-foot large skyhook balloon. Ruppelt does not agree with the conclusion that Mantell's plane was shot down by an UFO. Mantell apparently blacked out due to a lack of oxygen at the high elevation and plummeted back to Earth. Ruppelt also states that, contrary to rumor, Mantell's plane was not radioactive or magnetized.

Ufologists are not convinced by the official explanations. They are convinced that his death was UFO-related.

MARS. In H.G. Wells's *The War of the Worlds,* invaders from Mars launch an invasion against Earth but fail in their attempt at conquest. With the widespread publicity given UFOs after the Arnold sighting of June 1947, Mars was considered as one of the prime planets from which UFOs might possibly originate.

Preliminary investigations of Mars by U.S. and USSR spaceprobes failed to find any obvious signs of intelligent life. In 1976, two U.S. Viking spaceprobes landed on Mars. One of their primary purposes was to search for life. The tests proved inconclusive. Scientists have therefore not excluded the possibility that life exists or that it may have existed in the past on Mars.

Perhaps the most spectacular accomplishment of the Viking lander was the transmission back to Earth of a photograph of a rock with what was apparently the letter "B" on it. This was indeed a shocking discovery. NASA promptly explained the letter as the result of shadowing, a not altogether convincing explanation.

The possibility that the letter was indeed a genuine inscription is most intriguing because it would be tangible proof that intelligent beings were, or still are, on Mars.

Mars warrants further exploration. Indubitably, it may contain other mysteries.

MARTIAN MOONS. Mars has two moons, Phobos and Deimos (the former name denotes fear, the latter denotes terror). Phobos is the larger of the two moons, its diameter being about ten miles across. In 1944 at the U.S. Naval Observatory, B.P. Sharpless made an in-depth study of the two moons and found an unexpected fact. Phobos had a secular acceleration. This means that its orbit was slowly declining, and that in time Phobos would crash to Mars. Sharpless could not explain this unusual occurrence.

These two moons acquired a temporary spotlight in the nebecian and ufological theories when in 1960 Russian astrophysicist I.S. Shklovsky, after examining the secular acceleration of Phobos, found that no known celestial forces could account for it. However, he found that their orbital behavior paralleled that of the artificial Earth satellites. Therefore, he concluded that Phobos was an artificial satellite produced and launched by an advanced, but now extinct, Martian civilization.

Such a statement from a prominent astrophysicist electrified the imagination of the scientific and ufological worlds. So confident were the nebecists and ufologists that the moons were artificial, that some of them constructed elaborate theories on the origin of these artificial Martian satellites. Others merely cited this as proof of their arguments that Earth was or still is being visited by extraterrestrial beings.

All these theories and the speculations they engendered collapsed abruptly when Mariner 9 sent photographs of Phobos back to Earth. The moons were found to be pockmarked with craters and of natural origin. Their unusual orbits were explained by their dimensions and irregular sizes.

This example stands out as one mystery which has been explained and dispensed with about eleven years after the theory of the moons' artificial origin was first proposed. No one will be able to argue any longer than Phobos and Deimos were the handiwork of aconins.

MASCON. The term is short for "mas(s) con(centration)." It refers to those large circular areas on the moon where the density is so much greater than that of the surrounding areas that these regions produce gravitational anomalies.

See: Negative Mascon.

MASER. An acronyn for "microwave amplification by stimulated emission of radiation." A maser is a device for amplifying electrical impulses by stimulated emission of radiation. A laser is a special type of maser.

See: Laser.

MASS. Mass is the quantity of matter in a body to which inertia is ascribed. It is supposed to be a constant property of a body, unchangeable no matter where in the Universe the body may be situated. The mass of a body differs from the weight of a body. Weight is dependent on the gravitational attraction between one body and another. Therefore, a man or spaceship would weigh more on Earth than on the moon. However, their mass would be constant in both places.

Some ufologists have suggested the revolutionary concept that perhaps even mass is variable. This theory suggests that mass varies but that such variation is so minuscule that man presently lacks sophisticated instruments to measure it. They maintain that it may be possible to reduce a body's mass if man were only able to learn and then control the physical laws which govern mass. If true, the implications are revolutionary.

This theory may also hold the key to traveling at the speed of light. If it does, it would have a direct application to the UFO phenomenon because it would make it possible to attain or surpass the speed of light, an accomplishment which would strengthen the case for interstellar journeys.

The theory of relativity states that the speed of light cannot be attained by a body because as the body would approach the speed of light its mass would increase. To continue accelerating the body would require more energy. This in turn would increase the mass.

However, the theory of relativity only states that a body cannot accelerate to the speed of light. But if a body travels at the speed of light from its first moment, the theory of relativity would not apply. Likewise, if the apparent mass of a body can increase, perhaps the opposite can also occur. Perhaps apparent mass can also decrease under the right circumstances or through the proper manipulations. This is certainly a reasonable possibility. Therefore, if the apparent mass can be decreased to the point where an object would have no mass but would still be present, such a body would then functionally be light and would be able to travel at light-speeds.

The question of the ability to travel at the speed of light is the prime question in discussing the reality of UFOs. UFOs must originate from either a parallel dimension or from a distant star. If the nebecian position is adhered to, then only by proving, at least in theory, that either blisk speeds are possible or that space gates exist, can the UFO argument begin to have genuine scientific validity.

See: Momentum; Tachyon.

MATTER. One of the two expressions of reality. In basic physical terms, matter is any collection of atoms. It is also a word applied to anything perceived or known to occupy space. Matter is convertible to energy, and energy is convertible to matter.

See: Energy; The Law of the Conservation of Matter and Energy; Transmogrification.

McLAUGHLIN, COMMANDER R.B. In the March 1950 issue of *True,* McLaughlin, a regular Navy officer, had published an article entitled "How Scientists Tracked Flying Saucers." The mysterious part about this episode is that the story had been cleared by the military and was an about-face on every press release made by the military in the previous two years. In the article, McLaughlin expressed his belief that UFOs were extraterrestrial craft piloted by intelligent beings.

MEN IN BLACK. See: MIB.

MENTAL TELEPATHY. See: Telepathy.

MESMERISM. Synonym for hypnotism.
See: Hypnotism.

MESON. A particle in the nucleus of an atom. Its mass is 30 to 300 times the mass of an electron, and its charge may be either positive, negative, or neutral. Physicists believe that it possesses the attractive force necessary to bind neutron and proton. It is a short-lived particle and disintegrates into electrons and other atomic particles when it is freed from the nucleus.

Physicists are interested in mesons because they believe that the meson is responsible for holding together the nucleus of an atom. If proven to be true, the cracking of this secret would make possible the release of tremendous amounts of energy. Such energy could then be used for a variety of practical needs, as, for example, solving the energy crisis on Earth, and as a possible source of power for undertaking long space voyages.

METAPHYSICS. The branch of philosophy or science which studies the first principles. Its main constituents are: ontology, the science of being; cosmology, the study of the origin and structure of the Universe; and epistemology, the study of the origin, nature, methods, and limits of human knowledge.

METEOR. A meteor is a meteoroid which is captured by Earth's gravity and which enters its atmosphere. As the meteor passes through the atmosphere, it turns into a transient fiery streak in the sky. It is possible that some meteors are mistaken for UFOs.
See: Bolide; Meteoroid.

METEORITE. Any of the various masses of stone or metal which travel through space, and which, when encountering Earth's atmosphere, are heated to luminosity, thus becoming meteors.
See: Meteor.

MIB. Acronym for Men In Black. MIBs represent one of the most mysterious aspects, and definitely the most frightening, of the UFO phenomenon. It is not known exactly who or what they are, or where they come from.

MIBs are usually described as slight, dark-complexioned men, usually with Oriental features, who appear on the scene after a UFO sighting. They are usually dressed in black suits, wear sunglasses, and identify themselves as CIA men. Their other usual dress and identity is that of Air Force officers.

They are almost always reported to come in a group of three. Persons who have sighted UFOs are reported to have been contacted by these MIBs, investigated, and then warned to remain silent. Those persons who, after being warned, still persisted in talking about their experiences or still continued to investigate UFOs, frequently vanished or else fell victim to fatal and suspicious accidents.

The first modern MIB report occurred on June 21, 1947. Harold Dahl was warned by them not to discuss his UFO sighting. Since UFOs were still publicly unknown on June 21, as Kenneth Arnold was not to make his sighting over Mt. Rainier until three days later, Mr. Dahl dismissed the warning. He vanished soon afterwards.

MIBs remain a persistent factor in the UFO phenomenon. Some ufologists believe that they may indeed be CIA men or genuine AF men. The CIA has, in fact, been secretly involved in investigating UFOs and, as Donald E. Keyhoe establishes in *Aliens from Space,* it has been intimately involved in the UFO cover-up. Other ufologists are skeptical about the existence of MIBs. They point out that CIA men would not identify themselves as CIA men. They also point out that some AF men have also died in mysterious accidents while investigating UFOs. Therefore, they hold, if the AF and CIA were working together on the investigation of UFOs, it would make no sense to suggest that the CIA arranged the deaths of the AF men.

John A. Keel discusses these MIBs in Chapter 9 of his book. *Our Haunted Planet.* Albert K. Bender's *Flying Saucers and the Three Men* and Gray Barker's *They Knew Too Much About Flying Saucers* also deal with the MIB phenomenon. In chapter 5 of *Invisible Residents,* Ivan T. Sanderson hints at the existence of MIBs, but dimisses as without basis the report concerning them that he was sent to investigate.

Julien Weverbergh and Ion Hobana, in *UFOs from Behind the Iron Curtain,* also mention an MIB report from Rumania. However, they dismiss it as a mere rumor. What is significant about this report is the fact that it occurred in Rumania, a communist state. Authorities in the communist states investigate all reports of strange phenomena. Publicity and get-rich schemes are not motivating or permissible factors in communist states. People who fabricate stories would be severely punished. Thus the question is raised of why people in a communist state would lie about MIBs.

The MIB sighting in Rumania also shows that these reports are not confined to America. Such a large-scale operation also rules out the possibility of fraud or fabrication. Of course, it is possible that there exists an earthly explanation for MIBs. Certainly, governments as rich as the United States and the Soviet Union would be capable of conducting a worldwide UFO investigation. Perhaps MIBs are agents of one or the other. There is no definite proof of this, however. All that is certain is that MIB reports continue to come in.

At the present time, there is no way of knowing for certain who or what MIBs are, or from where they come. That they are connected with the UFO phenomenon is clear. Hopefully, one day an answer will be found to this intriguing, mysterious, and sometimes frightening problem.

MILKY WAY. The luminous band spanning the heavens. Our solar system is situated within the Milky Way and is located 26,000 light-years from its center. The galaxy of which the Milky Way is the visible part from Earth is estimated to contain between 100 billion and 200 billion stars.

MIRACLE. An effect produced in the natural (physical) world which seemingly violates natural (physical) laws and which is ascribed to a supernatural agency.

Nebecists suggest that perhaps some of the miracles recorded in ancient times were not supernatural but supertechnological in origin and nature. That is, UFO beings, with their superior technology, performed feats which man mistook for miracles. As support for this theory, they rely on argument by analogy. They point out that even in the nineteenth century, and in many instances in the twentieth century, Western man with his advanced technology was able to impress primitive peoples.

From the philosophical and scientific viewpoints, the idea of a miracle as a violation of natural law is impossible. Reality is one and it is governed by laws. Accordingly, anything that occurs in the physical world is governed by laws. A miracle is not a question of supernatural power but of knowledge. The more scientific knowledge man possesses, the more he can do.

The concept of a miracle is relative to the person who

witnesses it or on whom it is performed. Even God, strictly speaking, cannot perform a miracle. As the Master of all laws, God, in order to perform an act, need simply act through the laws which He Himself originally established.

The idea of a miracle arises when an ignorant person lacks sufficient and basic knowledge about the world. This ignorance may be due to his own lack of an education or to the backwardness of his society. Thus, more educated and scientifically advanced people have been able to impress less educated and primitive people with their ability to perform "miracles."

It is also possible that one species of intelligent beings, assuming there are indeed aconins in the Universe, may have been inherently more intelligent than another group of intelligent beings. These more intelligent beings were able to understand and grasp certain physical laws and concepts which would have eluded the less intelligent beings. By mastering these laws, the more intelligent species would be able to perform technological wonders which would be viewed by the technologically inferior beings as miracles. On the other hand, it is doubtful whether a technologically advanced civilization could accept the idea that any feat performed by another group of beings was a miracle, i.e., a violation of natural law.

That is, let us assume that the nebecian theory is correct, and that ancient befapian astronauts landed on Earth millenniums ago and impressed primitive man with their ability to perform miracles, i.e., technological wonders. At that time the difference in technology between man and the aconins was vast, and primitive man may very well have worshipped these beings as gods. Presently, however, the gap in technological and scientific knowledge has narrowed to the point that if such beings landed on Earth today, they would be regarded as just that, another species of intelligent life. They would be objects of wonder and not of worship and veneration.

The concept of a miracle also has many parallels with the idea of magic. In fact, there may be no difference between the two. However, man has always associated a miracle with good forces. Magic, on the other hand, has usually been the domain of evil. As such, magic involves something more than just scientific knowledge. Here naphology enters into the domain of dimensionalism, and the concepts of both magic and miracles take on different meanings.

In the nebecian theory, reality is composed of the visible

Universe. There is no room for magic or miracles in such a universe. Any miracle or act of magic is merely due to the application of superior technology.

However, in the dimensionalist theory, there exists the concept of a parallel universe. In such a parallel universe there may exist cosmic laws of which man has no knowledge and of which he may possibly never have any knowledge. Here naphology enters into the realm of the spiritual or mystical. In this scheme it is at least admitted in theory that beings from a parallel universe have the ability to perform in our space-time continuum acts which seem to be miracles or acts of magic. Any such acts which seemingly violate natural laws are, however, subject to question and examination.

See: Dimensionalism; Magic; Naphology; Naturalia; Occult.

MOMENTUM. The quantity of motion in a moving body. Momentum is equal to the product of a body's mass and velocity. The scientific concept of momentum is one of the main arguments against the objective existence of UFOs. UFOs have been reported to make very sharp turns at high speeds or to stop abruptly after traveling at very high speeds. Scientists have pointed out that if such space vehicles were occupied by living creatures, these creatures would not be able to survive because the momentum would crush them. For example, if the brakes are suddenly applied to a car traveling at 60 mph, the car will begin to stop, but the passengers, if unrestrained, will be thrown forward and will suffer an injury.

Though ufologists believe that UFOs exist and that they are capable of executing such sharp turns and abrupt stops when traveling at high speeds, they rarely offer an explanation for this seemingly incontrovertible violation of the law of momentum.

However, ufologist R. L. Dione has suggested one possible answer. He did not dismiss the reports of witnesses simply because the facts seemed to have violated the law of momentum. He assumed that the witnesses reported the true facts as they had observed them. Therefore, he sought an explanation for it which would be consistent with the laws of physics.

His theory is based on the following arguments and hypotheses. It is known that momentum is equal to the product of its mass and velocity. Suppose, however, that the mass of an object or body is reduced to zero or to a very small quantity. If the mass of an object would be reduced to zero, the law of momentum would then not apply to such a body, i.e., such a body would have no momentum. It would thus be capable of traveling at high speeds without any momentum. If it should prove impossible to reduce mass to absolute zero, then it may be possible to reduce mass to a very small quantity. In this case, the law of momentum would apply, but it would have no appreciable effect on the occupant. Therefore, if the theory that mass can be totally or mostly elimated is found to be valid, it would then be possible, within the laws of physics as presently understood, for UFOs to travel at high speeds and to be occupied.

This theory is only speculative, based on what is only theoretically possible in physics. It has been neither proved nor disproved. It is a reasonable and plausible theory and is offered by some ufologists as a possible explanation for the flight behavior of UFOs. The key consideration here is whether it is possible to reduce the mass of an object or body.

See: Mass.

MOMO. Short for Missouri Monster. This designation refers to the mephitic Bigfoot-type of creature, the sighting of which in and around the town of Louisiana, Missouri, during the second half of 1972, caused a storm of publicity throughout the country. The appearance of the creature was usually preceded by the appearance of several spheres of light in the sky, thus arguing strongly for a UFO connection.

See: Bigfoot.

MOON. A natural satellite which revolves around a planet. No natural laws dictate the number of moons a planet should or can have. Some planets have no moons, others have several. Nor do any natural laws dictate the size of the moons. Some moons measure only several miles in diameter, other moons can be as large as some planets.

Earth has one moon. Its mean distance from Earth is 238,857 miles, and it is about 2,160 miles in diameter. It has a desolate, crater-marked surface. Initial exploration has discovered no life on its surface. Among the biggest mysteries associated with the moon is its synchronous rotation, i.e., one side always faces Earth.

No accepted scientific explanation exists for this behavior. But nebecist Jean Sendy, who uses the Bible as his primary source, does offer one explanation. According to him, this synchronous rotation is one of the proofs that befapian atsronauts visited Earth in remote times. He believes they stabilized the moon's rotation in order to be better able to monitor and terraform Earth. He also believes that they left a visible sign of their presence on the moon, i.e., the bow of the covenant promised to Noah in the Bible (Genesis 9:13). When man discovers this sign (a launching pad among other things), he will at last know the secrets of his origin, and the ambiguous meanings of many ancient texts and passages will become clear.

It should be pointed out, however, that Mariner 9 showed that both Deimos and Phobos, the two moons of Mars, also rotate in such a manner that only one side is visible to their planet. Synchronous rotation may therefore be a natural pattern of behavior. This would tend to dispute Sendy's claim that Earth's moon was stabilized by artificial means.

See: Nebecism; Negative Mascon.

MOONBUGGY. A vehicle used by American astronauts to ride on the lunar surface. The knowledge gained from the use of this vehicle should prove invaluable. It will probably be the prototype of future vehicles which will roam on the surfaces of other planets and their moons.

MOTHER SHIP. A giant carrier UFO, usually described as a cylindrical cigar-shaped craft, though colossal circular ships have also been reported. The small-size UFOs are believed to be launched from these giant carriers or mother ships in much the same manner that naval aircraft are carried on and launched from aircraft carriers. If true, this suggests that the small-size UFOs may not be capable of making long interstellar journeys. The possibility exists that UFOs originate from stars so distant from the sun that mother ships are the best and safest way to transport a fleet of UFOs to Earth.

Assuming that UFOs exist, the next most difficult task in unraveling the UFO mystery is to determine whether they originate from other planets or from a parallel universe. A good case can be made for their stellar origin, but an equally good case can be made for their dimensionalist origin.

Barry H. Downing, for example, argues that the so-called mother ships are not really ships but space warps, i.e., they are holes or gaps in the space-time continuum which permit UFOs to enter and to depart from our dimension. People mistake these gaps for actual ships. According to Downing, when people report that these mother ships fly away at incredible speeds, they are actually misinterpreting the occurrence. The space-time gap is merely closing, but from a distance it creates the optical illusion of flight.

The problem of the origins of UFOs becomes even more confusing if a third alternative is considered. This third possible explanation combines elements of both the interplanetary and interdimensional theories. This theory accepts the possibility that mother ships may be space gates, but still maintains that UFOs are crafts from distant stars. This is explainable by the theory which states that it may be possible to contract space and time. Therefore, if space gaps or space gates exist, they may be shortcuts between distant parts of the Universe rather than entrances from another dimension into our space-time continuum.

This debate on the nature of the mysterious mother ships illustrates that there are still too few solid facts with which ufologists can deal. The accumulation of data about UFOs is a slow, painstaking effort. Only the gathering of more facts and the development of adequate scientific tools of research and inquiry can make it possible to provide answers to the most fundamental questions associated with UFOs.

See: Space Gate; Superspace; UFO.

MOTHMAN. A strange, eerie creature combining humanoid features with those of a bat. It reportedly inhabited the Ohio River Valley in 1966–67. It was described as gray-featured, over seven feet tall, with a wingspan of about ten feet, and possessing the ability to take off vertically and fly without flapping its wings. On its face were two gigantic, protruding, glowing eyes. In *Mothman Prophecies,* John A. Keel reports the strange incidents occurring, and the creatures (including Mothman) seen, in the Ohio River Valley during 1966–67.

See: Garuda.

MOUNT RAINIER. A dormant volcano in Mount Rainier National Park, located in the state of Washington. On June 24, 1947, Kenneth Arnold was flying past the mountain when he sighted a formation of UFOs. Mt. Rainier and June 24, 1947, have each respectively become the accepted site and date ushering in the modern UFO period. This is only an arbitrary data and place, however, because in actuality UFOs were sighted in different parts of the world before this date, as, for example, the numerous sightings of foo fighters during World War II.

See: Flying Saucer; Foo Fighter; UFO.

MU. The name given to a supercontinent which is said to have existed in a vast area now occupied by the Pacific Ocean. One of the main proponents of the existence of this land has been James Churchward, who has written a number of books on the subject. According to him, Mu was the motherland of all mankind and of all nations. It was there, he claims, that mankind first appeared. Mu was the Garden of Eden, and it was there that man developed an advanced culture which was then spread throughout the world.

Remains of this culture, it is maintained, can be found in the Middle East, on the Asian and American continents, and on islands scattered throughout the Pacific. The giant statues on Easter Island off the coast of Chile are said to have been built by the colonizers or by the descendants of the colonizers from Mu.

The original Egyptian and Mayan priests were supposed to have been sent from Mu to educate the other primitive nations. Mu is supposed to have sunk into the ocean over 50,000 years ago as a result of a series of cataclysmic earthquakes which tore the continent asunder. After the disaster, the priests and their initiates passed on as best as they could the knowledge of Mu. Unfortunately, much of this knowledge was lost or became distorted. For example, it is claimed that the story of the sinking of Mu was distorted into the Biblical story of the Flood and into similar stories from other cultures and parts of the world.

One theory on the origins of UFOs maintains that some of the inhabitants of Mu survived and built a great underwater civilization. UFOs, or more precisely, USOs, are held to originate from this underwater civilization. It should be noted that similar theories have been applied to both Atlantis and Lemuria. Most ufologists do not consider this theory to be a viable explanation for the origins of UFOs.

See: Atlantis; Lemuria; USO.

MUONS. These are nuclear particles, also known as mu mesons, which are produced when atoms are smashed by cosmic rays. Earth is constantly being bombarded by muons which speed into our atmosphere at velocities near the speed of light. Muons are of special interest to naphologists because they substantiate Einstein's special theory of relativity, which deals with the principle of time dilation; that is, as an object approaches the speed of light time would pass more slowly for it.

It is known that the lifetime of a laboratory-produced muon is only 2.2 millionths of a second. These particles are generated naturally only in Earth's outer atmosphere, about ten miles up. Traveling from that distance, they should disintegrate after only about half a mile. Yet, as pointed out by Jack Stoneley and A.T. Lawton in *Is Anyone Out There?,* muons survive long enough to reach Earth. This is known because the track of one muon has been captured on special film. This extension of the particle's life, it is argued, can only be due to the fact that time was dilated because the particle was traveling at near the speed of light.

Some scientists further speculate that if the time dilation principle works for muons, it should also work for other forms of matter, including living creatures. If true, this means that it would be possible to undertake long interstellar journeys. The time dilation principle helps bolster the nebecian theory. Assuming that befaps exist and that milleniums ago they had constructed spaceships capable of speeds at or near the speed of light, it would have been possible for them to have reached Earth from planetary systems thousands of light-years away.

MUTILATIONS. A series of strange animal mutilations began to appear in the northeastern sections of the United States in the early 1960s. These incidents were first isolated. They involved the apparently senseless slaughter and dissection, or perhaps vivisection, of domesticated animals, mostly cattle, and the frequent removal of some of their organs. These mutilations intensified during the 1970s.

The official explanation has been that this slaughter has been the work of predators, vandals, or cult members of Satanic groups who use the animal parts in black rituals. Though this may indeed explain some of the slaughters and mutilations, the extent of the *situation,* plus the concurrent sightings of strange aerial lights, militates against such a conclusion.

A frightening pattern began to emerge as the number of mutilations mounted. Strange aerial lights, i.e., UFOs, were frequently seen at the sites before or after the mutilated animals were found. This has led to serious speculation that the mutilations may be the work of ufonauts. One some occasions, the mutilated bodies of human beings have also been found in these areas.

Perhaps the most bizarre incident of mutilation occurred sometime in early 1977 on the 450-acre grounds of "Jungle Habitat," a wildlife preserve in West Milford, New Jersey. The carcasses of thirty animals were discovered on Monday night, April 4, 1977, by reporters from the *Passaic Herald News.* The animals were mutilated and six were disemboweled and decapitated. One of these was a full-grown elephant whose head had been removed.

Officials of the park at first denied that there were any dead animals. Later they stated that the animals had died of "natural" causes and that the mutilations were due to autopsies. The decapitated heads were blamed on big game trophy hunters.

What purpose such senseless slaughter serves is a matter of speculation. To researchers investigating strange phenomena, this is another in a long line of mysteries related to the UFO phenomenon.

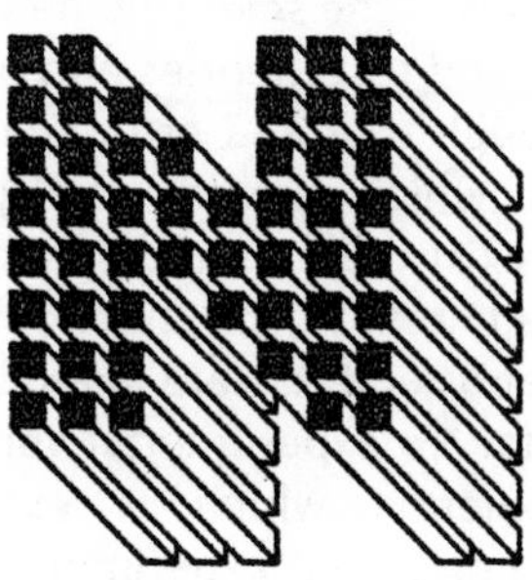

NAPHOLOGIST. A person committed to a serious objective study and investigation of the field of naphology.
See: Naphology.

NAPHOLOGY. A branch of science or a field of study which deals with and examines all manner of phenomena and events which are reported to exist or to have happened, but for which there exists no scientific explanation. It includes such diverse fields as: astrology, occultism, ufology, superstition, spiritism, and reincarnation. The goal of naphology is to find answers to these phenomena and to ascertain how and in what manner they affect human life. Some of the areas of interest to naphologists are also being studied by other branches of science. Parapsychology, a new branch of psychology, is probing the nature and effects of psychic phenomena and psychokinetic energy. These areas touch on spiritism and ufology. Advances in parapsychology will have direct application to ufology. Conversely, the accumulation of data by ufology may be of interest to parapsychology.

By definition, the field of interest which naphology encompasses declines as other branches of science increase their knowledge. Many natural phenomena, events, and occurrences which at one time were mysteries and were a source of fright and awe to man have already been scientifically explained. Lightning and thunder, for example, were once thought by men to be caused by angry gods. With the advance of science, however, man learned that lightning and thunder are natural phenomena. No extraordinary significance is now attached to either lightning or thunder.

Naphology fills in the vacuum left by the lack of scientific knowledge. The essence of the scientific method is experimentation. Scientists devise and test theories and hypotheses. Through experimentation, through trial and error, scientists discover the laws and principles which govern the physical world. In naphology there also exist theories and hypotheses which seek to explain the observed reality of phenomena. However, in naphology only the reported facts are available. Conclusions are drawn from these data. No experimental verification is possible because the phenomenon which is examined cannot be recreated at will in a controlled experiment from which a scientist might learn what caused it and how it functions.

Naphology is a science which lacks the tools of science. Like other branches of science, it approaches its subject matter in a rational, organized and systematic manner. By filling in the gaps left by other branches of science, it performs a useful function. By providing tentative hypotheses, possible explanations and theories for scientifically unexplained phenomena, events and occurrences, naphology focuses public and scientific attention on a problem, i.e., on a reported natural phenomenon for which there is no generally accepted explanation. By emphasizing that a gap exists in man's knowledge of some field of study, naphology strives to develop scientific tools to deal with the problems and to come up with scientific explanations for them.

See: Dimensionalism; Nebecism; UFO.

NASA. Acronym for National Aeronautics and Space Administration. This is the agency which is responsible for America's space program. Many of America's space probes, space satellites, and manned space vehicles were surveyed by UFOs. NASA has released some photos of UFOs in space. Among the most publicized photos is the one taken by Astronaut McDivitt on June 4, 1965, during the flight of Gemini 4.

NASA does not deny the reality of the UFO phenomenon nor does it present an official explanation for it. It does not affirm or deny the possibility that UFOs may be spacecraft from another planetary system. It simply states that UFOs are an unexplained aerial phenomena, a statement that encompasses many possibilities, including that they are misidentified manmade craft.

NATIONAL AERONAUTICS AND SPACE ADMINISTRATION. *See:* NASA.

NATIONAL INVESTIGATIONS COMMITTEE ON AERIAL PHENOMENA. *See:* NICAP.

NATURAL QUARANTINE. Distances between the stars are very great. They are so great, in fact, that they are measured in light-years, i.e., the distance that light travels in one year. Stars are unevenly dispersed throughout the Universe. Some are close to each other, others are separated by great distances. Alpha Centauri, the nearest star to our sun, is four light-years away.

Because of the very great distances involved, space travel from one star to another would be very difficult and in some cases impossible. Even if such travel were possible, contact would probably be very limited. This immense distance between the stars constitutes in effect a natural quarantine—a natural isolation created by the immense distances—against interstellar travel and possible contact with other intelligent beings.

Travel at or near the speed of light would be necessary if there is to be any chance of reaching the stars. Travel at such speed, however, would involve another problem. According to the theory of relativity, the principle of time dilation would become operative as an object approached the speed of light. That is, time would pass more slowly for the occupant of a spaceship traveling near the speed of light than it would for the inhabitants of the planet left behind.

Scientists and ufologists who believe that the limitations imposed by natural quarantine are irreconcilable do not believe that UFOs are spacecraft from other planetary systems. They also tend to discount the idea that Earth was visited in the past by intelligent beings from other planets. They do not discount the possibility that intelligent life may exist somewhere in the Universe and that one day contact may be established with such a befapian civilization. However, they believe that such contact will most probably be by radio only. Even here, however, two-way communication may be difficult. The radio signals which Earth stations may pick up in the future may have been sent by a civilization long since decayed or destroyed.

See: Black Hole; Light-Year; Tachyon.

NATURALIA. A general term encompassing all manner of

reported but unexplained natural phenomena. It would include such diverse phenomena as: astrology, witchcraft, UFOs, spiritism, reincarnation, possession, etc. As scientific knowledge expands, satisfactory answers may be found to some of the questions posed by these phenomena. Naturalia and naphology are intimately related. The first is the subject matter of the second.

See: Naphology.

NATURE. Man usually thinks of nature as the whole material world which surrounds him and in which he exists. He sees it as something intimately tied in with his existence, and not as something which is independent of him and his activities. In its broadest meaning, however, nature is synonymous with the Universe and all its varied phenomena. In another sense, nature is regarded as the totality of forces and laws at work throughout the Universe. Man can understand nature to the extent that he understands these laws.

Science has as its goal the study of nature. By discovering the laws of nature, science hopes to be able to control them and to use them for man's benefit.

The study of UFOs is especially interesting because UFOs appear to defy the laws of physics as presently known. Unraveling the UFO phenomenon would lead to tremendous technological advances, especially in the field of propulsion.

NAZCA. A dry, arid plain in the mountains of Peru. Etched into the soil of this plain are various geometric and animal figures. These are huge and, interestingly, visible only from the air. On the ground the lines look meaningless.

Some ufologists hold that these etchings must have been directed from the air. The theory has been advanced that the plain served as a landing field for ancient astronauts.

Critics dispute this. They speculate that the lines may be calendrical, astronomical, or astrological in nature. As to their manner of construction: In *Gods in Chariots and Other Fantasies,* Dr. Clifford Wilson points out that alongside some of the huge figures are small-scale models which were apparently used to proportionately construct the larger versions without the need for guidance from the air.

NEBECISM. A naphological theory which argues that there are other advanced beings in the Universe, that these beings landed on Earth in the remote past, and that during their stay on Earth they influenced the course of man's evolution. By its very nature, this hypothesis possesses many factual gaps because most of the facts which are necessary to substantiate it are simply not available. Instead, these gaps are filled in by probabilities and possibilities.

Nebecism is divided into two main schools, both of which are united in the basic belief that befapian astronauts influenced the cultural and biological evolution of man. Each nebecian school presents evidence to substantiate its claim.

The first school of nebecian thought advances the proposition that superior benevolent astronauts arrived on Earth at some point in the past. No definite time-period is proposed, but the most often cited time span for this landing ranges from 24,000 B.C. to 12,000 B.C.

According to this nebecian school, these befapian astronauts played a determining role in the evolution of life on Earth. Some supporters of this school argue that by genetic manipulation these astronauts may have given the social instinct to ants and certain other insects. More importantly, however, these befaps are said to have influenced human life and development. Some adherents of this school advance the idea that man as he exists today was shaped and molded by these astronauts. In his ignorance, primitive man mistook these befaps for gods. Religion is traced to this original misconception.

Adherents of this school are divided on the question of what the befaps did after influencing the evolutionary processes. One group believes that these beings, having performed their experiments, and thus having helped to spread intelligent life through the Universe, abandoned Earth and left life on Earth to its own resources.

The second school of nebecian thought also supports the proposition that benevolent astronaut-gods landed on Earth and influenced the evolution of life on this planet. Where this school of thought differs from the first is in the belief that these befaps did not completely abandon Earth, but that they still make periodic visits. This, they argue, may explain the UFO phenomenon. Because of their solicitous interest in Earth's development, these UFO beings are thus assumed to be benevolent.

It is on this last point that the two schools of nebecism coalesce. The underlying assumption is that these beings are advanced in all aspects of life: technological, cultural, moral, scientific, and biological. The philosophical basis for the common belief of both nebecian schools that the befaps are benevolent lies in the assumption that any beings who have conquered space and who are capable of interstellar travel cannot be evil or malevolent.

Believing that man has much to learn form these beings, nebecists hope that man may one day establish contact with them. They are accordingly strong supporters of the space program because they see its primary purpose as the search for intelligent life.

Those nebecists who believe that UFOs are piloted by benevolent beings advocate the cessation of all hostile acts against them. They argue that a serious attempt to establish communication with them should be tried instead. Those nebecists who doubt that UFOs are genuine spacecraft argue that man should expand the space program. Believing that befaps definitely exist somewhere in the Universe, they argue that serious attempts should be made to contact them by radio, laser, and if man's technology can advance rapidly enough for interstellar travel, by spacecraft.

On the other hand, opponents of nebecism argue that the fundamental aspect of nebecism is its loss of faith in man's ability to solve his own problems. Nebecists, they argue, seek solutions for human problems from intelligent beings who are supposed to exist somewhere in the Universe. They point out that nebecism is basically a defeatist position, and that the nebecists would willingly abandon human culture and submit mankind to whatever the befaps would deem proper for man. This, maintain the opponents of nebecism, is wrong and potentially dangerous. Whatever may be the origin of the human mind, whether created by God or by Nature, it separates man from animals. With his mind and intellectual faculties, man should attempt to solve his own problems. He has done so in the past, and he can do so presently and in the future. To do otherwise would be to betray man's nature.

Opponents of nebecism do not deny that there may be other intelligent beings in the Universe nor do they deny that these beings may be technologically superior to man. But they dispute the belief that these beings would necessarily have to be benevolent. They furthermore dislike the tendency of many nebecists, including ufologists, to regard these beings as saviors of mankind.

See: Aconin; Astronaut-God; Befap; Natural Quarantine; Philosophy; Seeding.

NEBECIST. Of or pertaining to nebecism. The term also designates an adherent of nebecism.

See: Nebecism.

NEGATIVE MASCON. An area beneath the lunar surface in which there is either a large cavity or matter much less dense than that found in the rest of the moon.

Nebecist Jean Sendy believes that in the past befapian astronauts landed on Earth and that they may have left a base on the moon. If they did leave such a base, Sendy holds, then it might possibly be located in this negative mascon area. According to Sendy, such a find would prove two things. First, it would prove that interstellar travel is possible. Second, it would bolster the theory that man's evolution was influenced by befaps. As a corollary, such a find would also prove that the ancient legends, myths, and stories describing the activities of gods on Earth were based on factual occurrences rather than on imagination.

A thorough exploration of the moon will provide a definitive answer to this possibility.

NICAP. Acronym for National Investigations Committee on Aerial Phenomena. NICAP is a private organization, founded in 1956, dedicated to investigating and determining the facts of the UFO phenomenon. It has branches in all fifty states and in over thirty foreign countries. It maintains a huge library of all reported UFO sightings and cooperates in all serious attempts to study the phenomenon. Its basic assumption is that UFOs are real and objective objects and not merely hallucinatory or illusory in nature. It is opposed to government censorship of the UFO material and has long advocated release of governmental records on UFOs. One of its major goals is to convince the government to undertake a serious and objective scientific study of UFOs. The Colorado University Project, the last major study of UFOs, was criticized by NICAP as being biased.

See: Colorado University Project.

NUCLEAR FISSION. The breakdown of the nucleus of an element with high atomic number into nuclei of lower atomic numbers. In the process there is a conversion into energy of part of the mass of the nucleus. In an atomic (or nuclear) power station, there is a controlled reaction so that the energy which is released is channeled into industrial use. In an atomic bomb the reaction is uncontrolled with the result that an explosion takes place, creating much devastation.

The biggest potential danger posed by nuclear fission is the deadly radiation which is released. Even nuclear power stations have a problem in disposing of deadly radioactive material. A major debate is in progress on whether the benefits provided by atomic energy outweigh the dangers. Opponents point out that alternate sources of safe energy, like solar energy, are available. The dangers notwithstanding, nuclear energy possesses great advantages. For example, controlled nuclear fission can provide the energy needed to power submarines and ships for months without the need for refueling. Perhaps one day it could even be used to power spaceships.

Radiation which indicates the presence of fission has also been detected in some UFOs. This has led ufologists to speculate that nuclear energy is somehow involved in the propulsive system of some, perhaps all, UFOs.

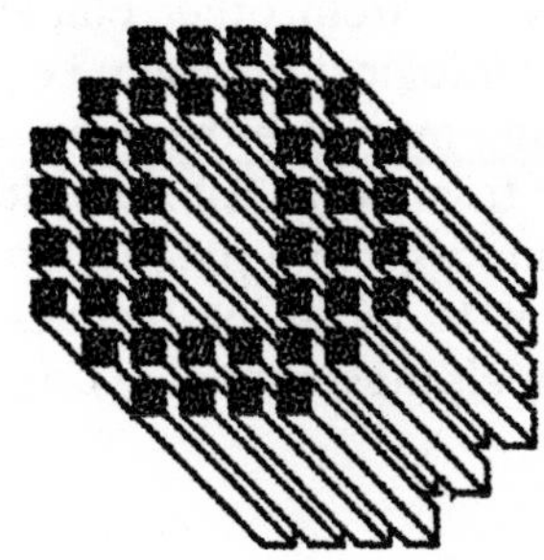

OBJECTIVE REALITY. The term refers to something which has real existence in the natural world. The existence of such a thing is independent of the mind which perceives it. The mind is the medium through which this thing or object is perceived, but the existence of this thing or object is not dependent upon the existence of a receptive mind.

This scientific and philosophical concept has relation to the UFO phenomenon because many critics doubt the reality of UFOs. They argue that UFOs have only a subjective reality, i.e., that they exist only in the mind of the person who claims to see them.

See: Subjective Reality.

OCCULT. Knowledge beyond the bounds of ordinary, empirical, scientific, and rationalistic knowledge. Specifically, occult involves the pseudosciences and the black arts or the black sciences, which claim knowledge of or the ability to communicate with and to use secret, mysterious nonmaterial agencies or beings to accomplish certain things. The occult presupposes the existence of powers and forces beyond the reception of man's senses. As such, it touches upon the concept of a supersensible world or supernatural reality and the concept of a parallel universe. It also involves the UFO problem, as dimensionalists argue that UFOs are creations of occult forces.

See: Dimensionalism; Naphology; Naturalia; Parallel Universe; Supersensible.

OINT. This term is short for "o(ther) int(elligence)." The term is used by Ivan T. Sanderson to refer to those beings who he believes exist alongside man but who are beyond the perception of man's senses. Sanderson believes in the reality of UFOs but doubts whether they are from other planets. He believes that some UFOs may be biological in origin, i.e., a type of life form. Other UFOs, he argues, may be either from an intelligent underwater civilization or from an invisible world existing within our space-time continuum or from a parallel universe. *OINTS* is the term he uses to refer to those intelligences which pilot these UFOs and which he feels most probably originate from the invisible world.

See: Invisible.

OPERATION LURE. In his UFO work *Aliens From Space,* Maj. Donald E. Keyhoe, USMC (Ret.) suggests a plan, Operation Lure, by which contact might be established between ufonauts and humans. The basic idea would be to construct a spacebase with various interesting and unusual structures. Hopefully, the ufonauts would be attracted to such a base and would land to examine it. Inside the base would be hidden cameras and recorders. These would permit a monitoring of the UFOs and any communication among its occupants by a control base some distance from the spacebase. Ideally, the UFOs would continue their landings at the spacebase and then direct contact would be attempted with them.

See: Ares.

OPTICAL ILLUSION. See: Illusion.

OPTIMAN. Voyages to other stars are a problem of both technology and biology. Stars are light-years away from Earth, the nearest being about four light-years away, and the most distant one being about 11 billion light-years away. Barring the existence of space gates, the more distant stars will never be reached by man. The near ones will probably be reached in due time. Even so, a human being would have a hard time enduring voyages lasting several years or tens of years. Among the various suggestions offered as to how to overcome this problem is one which suggests the creation of an optiman. Optiman is short for "opti(mum) man."

Unlike a bionic man, an optiman would not have any of his

vital organs replaced with artificial ones. An optiman would be a man in the full sense of the word. However, he would be a man whose physical, physiological, psychological, and mental characteristics, functions, and processes have been modified and speeded up in order to make him fit and capable of enduring the stress and tension of long, interstellar space voyages.

See: Bionic, Cyborg; Robot.

ORGEL, LESLIE. A world-renowned molecular biologist who together with Francis Crick jointly advanced the theory of the extraterrestrial seeding of life on Earth.

See: Crick; Seeding.

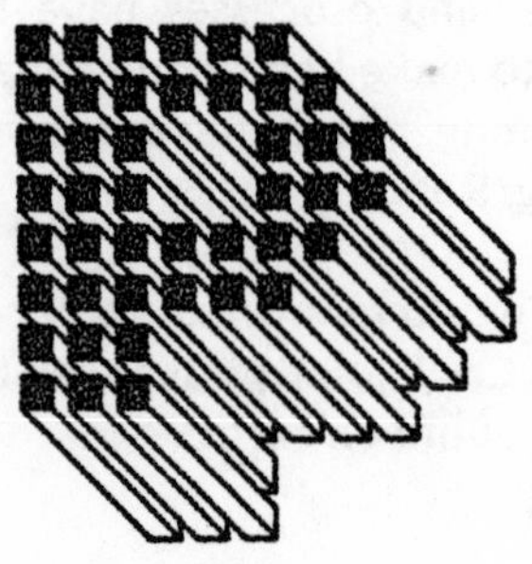

PALENQUE. The site in southern Mexico where in 1935 a stone relief was found on a tomb in the Temple of the Inscriptions. The relief on this tomb is said to represent a Mayan god. However, von Daniken states in chapter 9 of *Chariots of the Gods?* that a truly objective examination of this relief strongly suggests that it depicts an ancient space traveler sitting in what von Daniken maintains resembles a spaceship. He believes that this ancient depiction, said to date from about 692 A.D., illustrates a space traveler from another planet.

Many adherents of the extraterrestrial theory regard the Palenque relief as tangible proof that astronauts from another planetary system visited Earth in ancient times. Primitive man is said to have recorded their visit on this stone relief and on rock drawings.

However, Gordon Whittaker, in *Some Trust in Chariots,* edited by Barry Thiering and Edgar Castle, takes issue with this extraterrestrial interpretation of the Palenque stone relief. He points out that it cannot depict a space traveler and spaceship for several reasons. For one thing, that which von Daniken claims to be an antenna is in fact the individual's hair styled in the typical Mayan fashion. Secondly, despite von Daniken's claim, the figure is not shown wearing a tight-fitting jacket. In fact, his chest is bare and all he is wearing is a Mayan kilt. Whittaker also makes the interesting observation that the alleged space traveler is sticking his head out of the spaceship—a foolhardy and fatal thing to do on a space flight.

See: Daniken, Erich von.

PALMER, RAY. One of the pioneer ufologists and one of the most prominent during the 1940s and 1950s. From the early 1940s till 1948, Palmer was editor of *Amazing Stories* and was one of the first editors to show a genuine, active interest in the UFO phenomenon. In fact, years before Kenneth Arnold's sighting, Palmer was printing UFO-related material in the magazine. John A. Keel credits Palmer with keeping the UFO controversy alive during the 1950s when the topic was a subject of scorn and ridicule.

PARALLEL DIMENSION. See: Parallel Universe.

PARALLEL UNIVERSE. The concept that reality consists of a number of dimensions or space-time continuums. The dimensionalist branch of naphology believes that there exist one or more universes alongside ours. These parallel space-time continuums are said to occupy either the same space as our universe, but at a higher frequency or vibratory level than our universe, or a different curvature of space, thereby making it or them invisible to us. Dimensionalism further maintains that this parallel universe (or universes) is inhabited by intelligent beings, and that these beings can enter our space-time continuum and influence the course of events here.

See: Dimension; Dimensionalism.

PARALLEL WORLD. See: Parallel Universe.

PARAPSYCHIC. A term coined in 1969 by a scientist in the USSR as a collective term for the mass of invisible or intangible phenomena. Parapsychic phenomena should be distinguished from the parapsychological. The outward manifestations of the phenomena are quite similar in both cases, but the sources are believed by both scientists and naphologists to be different. The source of parapsychological phenomena which produce noises and images, such as telepathy, clairvoyance, psychokinetic energy, etc., is held to be in the mind. Under certain conditions as yet not adequately understood by science, the mind is capable of creating psychic phenomena or occurrences. These are all believed to be subject to physical laws

On the other hand, parapsychic phenomena, though similar in some respects to parapsychological phenomena, are believed to originate from nonmaterial beings or, if material, then from invisible ones. One group of scientists, scholars, and writers believes that there exists an invisible world around us and that this world is populated by beings. Though the exact mechanisms are not yet understood, these beings can and sometimes do create effects in our world. Some, if not all, poltergeists are believed to be of parapsychic origin.

The exact nature of this invisible world is not known, nor is it known whether there is more than one invisible world existing simultaneously at different frequencies or vibratory levels. There are also a number of other questions for which there are unfortunately no definite answers. For example: Is the concept of an invisible world the same as the idea of a parallel universe? How many different types of beings inhabit this world, assuming of course that there is only one such world? Can we enter into this world?

Most dimensionalists do not believe that these beings inhabit an invisible world which exists within our space-time continuum. They maintain that these beings originate from a parallel universe. Most dimensionalists also believe that there exist at least two groups of such invisible beings.

The adherents of this view also advance the opinion that these beings play pranks on men, create illusions, and mislead men by telling them lies and false predictions. Dimensionalists even hold these beings responsible for UFOs, which they create, it is said, in order to trick men into believing, for reasons known only to themselves, in the objective reality of UFOs. Adherents of this position do not deny the possibility that intelligent life may exist on other planets, but they do doubt whether genuine befapian astronauts have ever landed on Earth.

In short, these beings are generally regarded as evil, untrustworthy, mischievous, and harmful to man. Whatever their game is, it certainly is not motivated by altruism for mankind. Recognition of this fact raises a corresponding question. If these evil beings exist, what keeps them in check? The obvious conclusion is that other beings must keep these evil ones in check.

This is a very complex field and any examination of it engenders many questions, some of which have been dealt with here. Basically, the problem exists because there is a lack of sufficient knowledge and data. The facts are too few and the connections between them too uncertain. Of course, there also exists the possibility that there are no genuine parapsychic phenomena. With the advance of science perhaps it will be found that parapsychic phenomena are also subject to physical laws, though to ones about which man presently knows very little.

See: Dimensionalism; Parapsychology; UFO; UT.

PARAPSYCHOLOGY. A branch of psychology which studies such psychic pheonomena as clairvoyance, extrasensory perception, and telepathy. These mental or psychological functions have application to several disciplines, including religion, theology, psychology, and ufology. One school of scientists and scholars denies that parapsychological phenomena are truly supersensory mental functions. They believe that these phenomena are also subject to physical laws, but admit that at present man still does not adequately understand these laws.

Another school of parapsychology maintains that these parapsychological phenomena are supersensory and that they are functions of spiritual nonmaterial laws.

Many complicated scientific and metaphysical problems and questions arise with regard to the psychic phenomena studied by parapsychology. For example: Is there a spirit world? If so, how does it relate to the physical world? And, what is the relation between mind and brain?

Discussion of psychic phenomena also involves questions of determinism and free will. For example: If clairvoyance is true, does this mean that the world is deterministic? On the other hand, if the world is not deterministic, then how is clairvoyance possible? Can free will exist in a universe subject to physical laws? If it cannot, then what is the source of the universally held belief that man possesses free will? Are there some spiritual beings who know the future and who communicate it to certain persons? If so, how is this communication possible?

These are but some of the unanswered questions with regard to parapsychological phenomena. They are important because if the world is deterministic, then ultimately all human effort is futile and free will is a mere illusion. Unfortunately, however, no definitive answers can be given.

Nevertheless, men hold some sort of beliefs about these matters. Such philosophical beliefs about the nature of the world and the presence of good and evil, even if they are only partly true, fulfill an important function in helping man to live in and to understand the world.

Parapsychological phenomena are either directly or indirectly involved in many areas of human life and endeavor. They also touch upon the UFO phenomenon. Of special interest in this regard is telepathy. Contactees report that communication with ufonauts is often by telepathy. One question which then arises is that of how telepathy functions. According to ufological research findings, animals seem to be able to sense the presence of UFO beings or of approaching UFOs before most people can, though similar foresensing is also evident in some people. It is not known, however, how this ability functions.

In conclusion, we see that parapsychological phenomena pose many difficult and important questions to which there are presently no definite answers. Hopefully, future scientific research will remedy this situation.

See: Determinism; Extrasensory Perception; Free Will; Parapsychic; Technological Telepathy; Telepathy.

PARENT SHIP. *See:* Mother Ship.

PASCAGOULA. A small town in Mississippi. It was the site of the reported spectacular abduction of Charles Hickson and Calvin Parker by ufonauts in late 1973 and their subsequent examination aboard a UFO. Like the alleged Hill abduction, the Pascagoula incident continues to be a source of controversy.

See: Hill.

PHILOSOPHY. An organized system of knowledge and belief which seeks to explain the Universe, the natural forces operating within it, the purpose of existence, the right manner or organizing and living one's life, man's relation to the world, and man's relation to man.

Philosophy is essentially a world view shared in common by many people belonging to the same nation, culture or civilization. Being an important and indispensable component of man's life, it determines to a significant degree the manner in which man relates to and views the natural world. Philosophy also shapes and directs a person's and a society's political and economic organization, structure, and life.

Those people who have shared a philosophy which emphasizes self-reliance, knowledge, and the necessity to master nature, have made the most significant advances in the political, economic, and technical fields. The people in these societies invariably have more freedom and a higher standard of living than the people in societies which lack such adaptable philosophies.

Societies which have shared a philosophy which believes in evil or in powerful invisible deities, and which considers life on Earth as insignificant, tend to be stagnant in the technological, political, and economic fields. Barring the drastic changes which can be made possible only by the introduction of new ideas, such societies remain basically dead-end cultures. Its members lack self-reliance and even the desire to master nature because they either fear offending some deity or because they consider this life so insignificant that it is not worth the effort to improve it.

The advent of the space age has introduced a new element into philosophy. It poses the question of how man would or should react to the idea of the existence, probable or definite, of beings on other planets. At the same time, it also poses the question of whether there may be parallel univeres and whether these universes may also be inhabited. An even more fundamental problem with which philosophy must now deal is the question of how man will view and react to a possible visitation to Earth by beings from other planets. The experience thus far has not been very encouraging.

The world is beset with problems. Ironically, all these problems—overpopulation, war, pollution, depletion of natural resources—are manmade. Problems are inherent in development. It is not the existence of problems that destroys a society, but the manner in which men react to the problems. Throughout the ages, man has in the process of his development also created problems. Importantly, however, man also had faith in himself and in his ability to overcome his problems. This very faith in himself often showed him solutions which led to a better life. These solutions often caused residual problems. But these man again tackled confidently and resolutely.

In the mid-twentieth century, however, man began to lose faith in himself and, specifically, in his ability to solve problems. As a result, these problems have become more enormous and overbearing than they should be. Man's loss of confidence in himself had one other effect. He bagan to look for a savior, for someone to solve the many problems which became seemingly insurmountable. The advent of the space age opened up the possibility of saviors in the form of astronauts from other planets.

Though there are exceptions, there is nevertheless a fundamental consensus among ufologists that the ufonauts who are believed to be arriving on Earth are benevolent. Among ufologists there is the ubiquitous desire that these ufonauts may perhaps tell man how to find solutions to his problems. More fundamental than even this is the desire that such beings exist and that they will prove to be benevolent.

On the basis of fact, however, no justification exists for such a belief. If anything, the nature of ufonauts must be considered hostile or potentially hostile. At best, it must be considered neutral with respect to man. Though it is true that there have been no recorded large-scale hostile actions taken against man by ufonauts, this lack of hostility does not by itself prove their benevolence. They may merely be biding their time.

The *expectation* that ufonauts are benevolent and will solve the problems on Earth portends ill for mankind. If man has lost faith in himself, then he cannot continue to grow, develop, and learn by his mistakes.

Man's basic guiding philosophy of the world and of his nature is undergoing a change. It is unfortunate that in this time of doubt, internal crisis, and loss of faith in himself, man should be reaching toward the stars. In this condition man would not be able to relate to any alien beings as an equal. Yet, if there are ufonauts, then man must meet them and relate to them as an equal. Otherwise, mankind and human civilization are doomed.

In short, man's cosmic philosophy or his view of his place in the Universe should and must become more positive. Otherwise, man will miss out on the adventure and the possibilities of the space age. Man should venture forth into the Universe in a spirit of adventure and quest for knowledge, and not in the search for astronaut-saviors from other planets.

If in the process man should encounter aconins, such contact should not necessarily be avoided. But the contact must be between equals. Man must not have the inferior civilization. If he does, then man is doomed just as certainly as the primitive cultures here on Earth were doomed when they came into contact with superior civilizations. This is why man, as he is stepping forth into space, needs to rekindle the progressive philosophy which permitted him to enter the space age in the first place. He must adopt a positive world outlook.

See: Starism.

PHOBOS. See: Martian Moons.

PHYSICS. The branch of science which studies the natural laws and processes, and the states and properties of matter and energy. Its study does not, *however,* extend to biological processes or chemical changes. The unusual flight characteristics of UFOs would fall within the interest of physics.

PILLAR OF CLOUD AND FIRE. The term used in the Bible to denote the divine presence as the Israelites were guided out of Egypt by Moses and as they wandered through the desert. Exodus 13:21-22 states: "And the Lord went before them by day in a pillar of cloud . . . and by night in a pillar of fire."

Barry H. Downing in *The Bible and Flying Saucers* advances the theory that the pillar was actually a UFO with which Moses had the means to communicate. He also speculates that it may have been the pillar, i.e., a UFO, which caused the parting of the Red Sea, and notes the defensive measure taken by the pillar against the pursuing Egyptian army (see Exodus 14:24-25).

Such a hypothesis is of course related to the premise that the angels and gods of antiquity were actually ancient astronauts whom man in his relative ignorance mistook for supernatural beings.

See: Astral God; Nebecism.

PIRI REIS MAP. A map named after the Turkish Admiral Piri Reis (Reis means admiral) which is supposed to have been based on ancient maps and which purportedly depicts an accurate representation of the Americas and of Antarctica prior to the time when it was covered by ice.

Interestingly, the map has been used by persons in various fields of study to support their particular claims. Brad Steiger argues in *Atlantis Rising* that the Atlanteans, being remarkable sea-explorers, may have provided the original maps. Nebecist Erich von Daniken and ufologist Major Donald E. Keyhoe have seized upon the map as proof that astronauts from distant stars visited Earth during its remote past and that it was they who drew the original maps upon which the Piri Reis map is based.

However, the Piri Reis map has been severely criticized as an untenable proof in support of both the Atlantean theory and the extraterrestrial theory.

In *Crash Go the Chariots,* Prof. Clifford Wilson discusses the map at some length, as does also Prof. A.D. Crown in a chapter in *Some Trust in Chariots,* edited by Barry Thiering and Edgar Castle. According to these authors, there is nothing mysterious about the origins of the map. After analyzing the map, they also came to the conclusion that it was extremely crude and not at all as accurate as von Daniken and others would make it seem.

Admiral Piri himself stated that he had consulted twenty different earlier charts in the preparation of his own work. Furthermore, both authors point out that about a thousand miles of coastline are missing on South America's east side. Professor Crown also points out that, despite claims to the contrary, Antarctica is not even shown on the map.

The Piri Reis map continues to be relied upon by adherents of the extraterrestrial theory and continues to be repudiated by its critics. At issue here is the factual question of the map's origins. The Piri Reis map thus continues to be a source of controversy.

PLANETARY ECOSYNTHESIS. The artificial transformation of a planet's surface so as to render it capable of sustaining, first, basic life forms and, eventually, human life.

See: Terraformation.

PLANETARY SHIP. A type of spaceship which would operate solely in the interplanetary space within the solar system, traveling to the various planets, satellites, and asteroids in the solar system. Because they would always be near some planet or spacebase, planetary ships would not have to be self-sufficient. Interplanetary space would not hold as many hazards as would the dark, uncharted, and hostile regions of interstellar space. Planetary ships would be smaller in size and would not have to carry as many supplies and technological equipment as would starships. Since planetary ships would also be within visual sight of Earth, navigation would be simpler for them than for starships in interstellar space, and the possibility of being lost in space would be negligible.

Planetary ships are already within man's technological capability. He has both the technological knowledge and the sources of energy necessary to construct such spaceships. Indeed, the Apollo spacecrafts were crude prototypes of planetary ships, shuttling man from Earth to the moon. Still lacking, though, is the necessary desire and willpower to seriously explore and conquer the solar system.

Exploration of the solar system and the construction of planetary ships are two technological prerequisites of interstellar journeys and the construction of starships. That which man learns from his interplanetary travels will make it possible for him to create the first serious models of starships. This in turn would make serious discussions about interstellar journeys possible.

PLANETARY SYSTEM. A generic name referring to a particular star together with all the planets, moons, asteroids, etc., which revolve around it. Our planetary system is called the solar system. Solar refers to the sun, a specific name for our star. Other planetary systems might be called: taucetian system, after the star Tau Ceti; proximacentaurian, after the star Proxima Centauri; etc.

Scientists agree that other planetary systems probably do exist, especially around single stars similar to our sun, a Type G star. Scientists are almost positive that there exist one or more dark companions around Barnard's Star. Dark companion is the appellation given to a heavenly body which, though unseen, is believed to exist because of certain irregularities in the rotation of a star.

The examination of a star's rotation is one way to determine whether there are any dark companions, i.e., planets, which revolve around it. A second way to prove the existence of another planetary system would be to demonstrate the reality of UFOs. If UFOs exist, and if they are not from a parallel universe, then they must originate from another planetary system. Conversely, the discovery of a dark companion bolsters the argument in favor of the existence of UFOs. For where there are other planetary systems, there may also be intelligent beings who are capable of space travel.

The prospect that there are no other planetary systems in the Universe presents a frightening possibility. If our sun is the only star in the Universe with a planetary system, this would mean that man is all alone in the Universe—a chilling and depressing possibility, Also, if such should indeed be the case, the question of where UFOs *originate from* would still have to be answered. The only possible alternative then would be that they originate from a parallel space-time continuum.

The search for other planetary systems is one of the more earnest and primary pursuits of astronomers. Because planets are not sources of light, they are invisible to Earthbound man and will forever remain so. Astronomers must therefore rely on other methods of detection, methods less certain and reliable than that of optical observation. The presence of an irregular "wobble" in a star's rotation is one proof of the existence of one or more planets; the presence and reality of UFOs is another strong proof.

See: Barnard's Star; Dark Companion.

PLANETOID. A minor or small planet. The term is also frequently used as a synonym for asteroid.

See: Asteroid.

PLASMA: A stream of ionized particles. According to one scientific theory, some UFOs may be atmospheric plasma. If confirmed, this theory could very well explain some UFOs. However, the UFO phenomenon is too varied and complex to be explained by only the plasma theory. The plasma theory could not, for example, explain sightings of UAOs.

See: UAO.

PLASMA CLOUD. A cloud of plasma.

See: Plasma.

PLEIADES. In chapter 6 of *Chariots of the Gods?,* Erich von Daniken states that the pre-Inca peoples of South America possessed religious legends relating the story of how gods came to Earth from the constellation Pleiades. To von Daniken, these legends indicate that these people knew that the stars were inhabited.

If befaps did in fact land on Earth in ancient times, one of the pertinent questions involves their place of origin. If these pre-Inca legends are indeed correct, then the Pleiades may in fact be the home of these ancient astronauts. However, von Daniken's conclusions are disputed by scholars.

POLAR DESERT. See: Antarctica.

POSTHYPNOTIC SUGGESTION. A suggestion or command given to a person under hypnosis. The suggestion or command may be that the person should perform some act at a future time or that he forget some past experience. This has relation to ufology because ufologists claim that at times contactees are given a posthypnotic suggestion to forget the experience.

See: Hypnosis.

PRECESSION OF THE EQUINOXES. The term used to designate the difference between the sidereal year (365 days, 6 hours, 9 minutes, 9.6 seconds) and the appearance of the sun at the horizon (and at the vernal point). The sun appears annually at the vernal point 20 minutes and 20 seconds before the sidereal year has ended. The zodiac is based on this phenomenon of nature, and the zodiac is of course one of the prime tools of astrology.

The zodiac divides the heavens into twelve signs. The signs of the zodiac turn in a clockwise direction. As the difference in time is accumulated, the zodiac turns to a different symbol, which means in effect that the sun rises in a different vernal point.

Construction of the zodiac requires prior knowledge of the precession of the equinoxes. Knowledge of the latter requires a great length of time plus an accurate calendar. Nebecists argue that ancient man did not possess this knowledge but yet he somehow knew of the precession of the equinoxes. The existence in prehistoric times of this knowledge of the precession of the equinoxes means, hold the nebecists, that some other source established it. In the nebecian philosophy as propounded by Jean Sendy, knowledge of this phenomenon constitutes one of the proofs that Earth was visited in ancient times by befapian astronauts. It was they who discovered this phenomenon of nature, and it was from them that man acquired the knowledge of it. However, not fully understanding it, man nearly lost that knowledge in historic times. According to nebecists, it was not until about 200 years before the birth of Christ that learned men were able by their own means to determine the phenomenon of the precession of the equinoxes.

See: Zodiac.

PROJECT BLUE BOOK. One of the official Air Force investigations into the UFO phenomenon. It came into existence in 1952. Critics argue that its main function was not to investigate the UFO phenomenon but to debunk UFO sightings and to ridicule witnesses. It is also maintained that Project Blue Book was merely a cover operation and the mouthpiece for the Air Technical Intelligence Center, which conducted the real investigation into the UFO phenomenon. Because of the existence of Project Blue Book, the ATIC was spared the necessity to make any public comments on UFOs. Critics note that both Project Blue Book and the Air Technical Intelligence Center were located at Wright- Patterson Air Force Base in Dayton, Ohio. Project Blue Book was officially terminated in December 1969, after the appearance of the Condon Report. Critics, however, maintain that the Air Force is still continuing to investigate the UFO phenomenon.

See: Colorado University Project; Ruppelt, Edward J.

PROJECT GRUDGE. The code name of the Air Force's investigative probe into the UFO phenomenon which succeeded Project Sign. This took place on February 11, 1949. With the change in name came also a change in personnel and attitude toward the UFO phenomenon. The basic premise of Project Grudge was that UFOs did not exist, and facts and explanations offered the public were tailored around this premise.

Many of the Project Sign personnel who refused to participate in this cover-up and official debunking policy were "purged."

See: Estimate of the Situation; Grudge Report; Project Blue Book; Project Sign.

PROJECT OZMA. The possibility that intelligent life may exist on other planets has fascinated man for a number of centuries. One of the ways of detecting or establishing contact with befaps would be via radio. In 1960, Dr. Otto Struve stated that he believed there were a million planets in the galaxy capable of sustaining life. He also announced the start of a program called Project Ozma which would attempt to establish contact with these befapian civilizations.

The director of Project Ozma was Dr. Frank Drake, who was quite enthusiastic about the project. In 1961, Project Ozma focused in on two stars, Tau Ceti and Epsilon Eridani. These two stars were chosen because of their similarity to the sun. It was believed that a star similar to the sun stood the best probable chance of sustaining intelligent life and that it was therefore the best place to search for it.

The radio telescopes were turned on Tau Ceti and within two minutes strong signals were being picked up. According to ufologists, there is no doubt that the scientists had tuned in on a civilization on a planet of Tau Ceti. The scientists were stunned, and the story of the discovery was officially suppressed. Nevertheless, news of the discovery managed to leak out. The Pentagon quickly denied the report, however, explaining that Project Ozma had merely picked up signals from a secret military station. But if this were merely the case, then the program should have been continued after adjustments had been made to avoid intercepting further secret military messages.

What threw suspicion on the Pentagon explanation was the abrupt announcement by Dr. Struve that Project Ozma was being terminated. Even though he had originally been enthusiastic about the program, he now stated that it was a waste of time to search for intelligent messages from other planets. Suspicion that Project Ozma had tuned in on a befapian civilization was strengthened when shortly after the cancellation of the project, the same scientists came forth with the Green Bank Formula.

An interesting point made by Maj. Donald E. Keyhoe, USMC (Ret.) is that Project Ozma was not actually terminated but merely shifted to a station in Arecibo, Puerto Rico, where it continues to listen for radio signals. The project is now under Air Force control and any significant findings are being kept secret.

See: Green Bank Formula.

PROJECT SIGN. The code name of the first Air Force investigative probe into the UFO phenomenon. It was set up in September 1947 upon the recommendation of the chief of the Air Technical Intelligence Center (ATIC). A letter to the Commanding General of the Army Air Forces stated that, after a preliminary study, it was concluded that the UFO phenomenon was real.

Originally, most members of Project Sign were open-minded to the possibility that UFOs could be interplanetary craft. In February 1949 Project Sign was changed to Project Grudge.

See: Estimate of the Situation; Grudge Report; Project Grudge.

PROJECT TWINKLE. The name of a project established in the late summer of 1949 by the Air Force's Cambridge Research Laboratory to photograph the UFOs known at the time as "green fireballs." The project was to employ three special cameras, cinetheodolites, stationed at different points near White Sands, New Mexico. Cinetheodolites are basically 35mm movie cameras which also record three dials which show the time the picture was taken, the azimuth angle and the angle of the camera. Should two or more of these cameras photograph the same object, it would be possible to determine quite accurately the object's altitude, speed and size.

The project turned out to be a dismal failure. Only one camera was made available, and nothing was ever photographed. With the advent of the Korean War and the disappearance of the green fireballs, Project Twinkle was terminated.

See: Green Fireballs.

PROJECTION. One theory which seeks to explain UFOs argues that they are projections. Though this theory answers the question of what UFOs are, it raises other questions; namely, those of who is responsible for the projecting, what does the disc shape signify, and why is a disc-shaped object usually projected instead of a differently shaped object.

See: Hologram.

PROTOPLANET. Planets are believed to be fragments which are torn from the contracting mass of a new star's matter. The torn fragments are hurled into space away from the star but are still held within its gravitational field. Such a fragment is a protoplanet, i.e., a planet in its nascent stage.

PROTOTYPE. An original or model after which anything of the same type is formed. Technically, there can also be prototypes of planets, i.e., one planet can serve as a model for how other planets should look. Already, scientists are advancing the notion that Venus and Mars can be terraformed to create planets similar to Earth, thereby making them habitable for humans.

Technically, advanced biology would also be able to create certain life forms based on a prototype. Nebecists, in fact, advance such a position. According to them, befapian astronauts landed on Earth in ancient times, and during their stay influenced the course of evolution on Earth, perhaps changing the environment of the planet and certain life forms to conform to their preconceived image of the ideal forms.

PSYCHIC. Pertaining to mental or extrasensory mental functions or qualities.

See: Parapsychology.

PULSAR. A rapidly rotating neutron star. A neutron star forms when a star, several times the mass of the sun, suddenly implodes or collapses in on itself, forming an object so incredibly dense that its gravitational force crushes the very atoms of which the star's matter is composed. The density of a neutron star is said to be a million billion times the density of water.

The discovery of a pulsating neutron star, or pulsar, was first announced in 1968. Jokingly, it was named LGM, for "Little Green Men," because it was thought that the strong signals being received from it might be coming from an alien civilization.

The reason why pulsars radiate so much energy is presently still unknown, but it is believed to be due to their quick rotation. The relatively small size of neutron stars and their incredible density keeps centrifugal force from ripping pulsars apart.

To date, more than a hundred pulsars have been discovered. Their pulsating rhythm is fantastically precise, though ultrasensitive instruments have detected very slight decreases in speed, a result of the fact that they are using up their energy.

Pulsars are interesting because each one emits a different identifiable signal. It has been suggested by some ufologists and scientists that neutron stars can be used by man in the future, or that they may have been used or are presently being used by befaps, as celestial beacons or signposts, facilitating and enabling intergalactic navigation because they would provide identifiable points of reference.

PYRAMID. Gigantic monumental structures found in Mexico, Central America, and Egypt. They vary in size and shape. In Egypt the pyramid base is polygonal, usually square, with triangular sides, generally in one plane, sloping to an apex. However, there are also stepped pyramids with smaller layers structured upon larger layers.

Archaeologists and historians are positive that the pyramids were constructed by men through their own efforts, using the tools available at that time. Nebecists have suggested that either supertechnological knowledge was required to build pyramids, or that befapian astronauts had a direct hand in their construction. This, however, is a weak point in the nebecian theory.

The usual explanation is that the Egyptian pyramids were gigantic tombs. Other explanations advanced have been that the pyramids were astronomical observatories, standards of measurement, or repositories for storing treasures. Less mystery surrounds the pyramids in Central America and Mexico. These are known to have been used as observatories, temples, and as altars for human sacrifice.

Some nebecists, notably Erich von Daniken, have attached great significance to the pyramids. Many nebecists, however, do not rely on the pyramids as proof of their position. The nebecian position on the pyramids is criticized by Prof. Clifford Wilson in *Crash Go the Chariots,* and by a number of authors in *Some Trust in Chariots,* edited by Barry Thiering and Edgar Castle.

Pyramids constitute one of those classes of ancient monuments which have also attracted the attention of others besides nebecists, archaeologists, and historians.

One group of scholars championing the theory of a lost civilization on Earth, notably that of Mu and of Atlantis, claim a common origin for the pyramids of both Central America and of Egypt. They argue that there was contact between the Americas and the Mediterranean world in ancient times. The contact was either direct or, more likely, via a now lost people who served as an intermediary. Though some evidence exists in support of the contact theory, the evidence is not so overwhelming as to constitute conclusive proof for most scholars.

Occultists are also fascinated by the pyramids and by pyramid shapes in general. They argue that pyramids possess special cosmic powers; specifically, the cosmic powers are channelled through the pyramids, which serve as conduits.

There is also the curious relation of the Egyptian pyramids to UFOs. Some UFOs are described as triangular in shape. This leads to the interesting question of whether the pyramid shape has any hidden significance or relation to UFOs.

Scientists and scholars presently have reasonable explanations for many questions relating to the pyramids. The advise us to rely on theories which explain pyramids as the products of human endeavor and not as the works of nonhuman agencies. Admittedly, some questions still exist, and as long as there are gaps in our knowledge, various explanations for these mysteries will be proposed. Hopefully, though, an advance in scholarship and better scientific techniques will one day help provide definitive answers to some of the questions, such as, for example, whether there exists a relationship between the pyramids of the New World and those of the Old World.

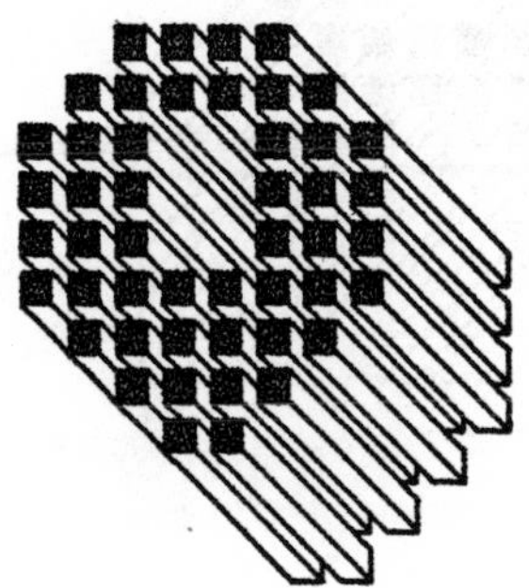

QUASAR. The name applied to the immense, extremely luminous conglomeration of stars found at the edge of the Universe, 11 billion light-years away. Quasars were only recently discovered. Their genesis and function is still unknown. Some theories exist about quasars but they are purely speculative.

In 1967, two USSR scientists, Prof. Iosif Shklovsky and Dr. Nikolai Kardashov, developed a hypothesis concerning the Universe, after studying the quasars. They concluded that the Universe is almost 70 billion years old and that it has a radius of about 15 billion light-years.

The most distant quasar marks the limits of the Universe.

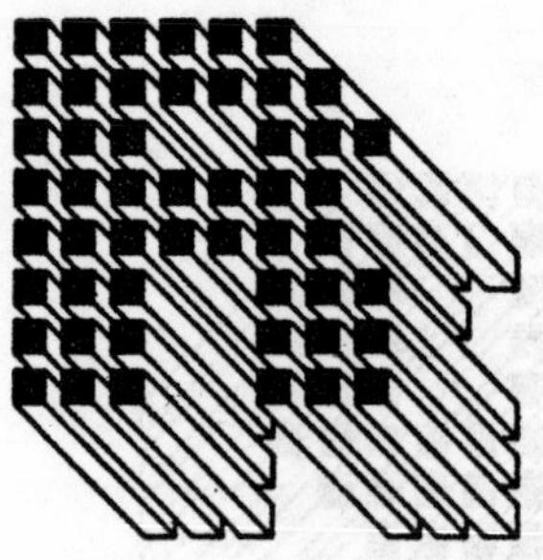

RADAR. An electronic device, first invented during World War II by the British, which determines the presence and location of an object by measuring the time that it takes the echo from a radio wave to return from the object to the source, and by determining the direction from which the echo returns. The word radar is an acronym derived from "ra(dio) d(etecting) a(nd) r(anging)."

According to ufologists, radar sightings of UFOs constitute an important and objective proof of their existence. Critics, however, point out that radar is not infallible. Adverse weather conditions can play tricks on radar, as can also air inversions which may be picked up and misidentified as UFOs. They also point out that under adverse weather conditions, radar can pick up objects (cars, trucks, etc.) beyond its normal range, and that these objects can be misidentified as UFOs.

The speed of an object spotted on radar is determined by the distance that the object moves on the radar screen per each revolution of the scanner beam. By this method, UFOs have been clocked at incredible speeds of up to 18,000 mph. Critics point out, however, that there is no way to be certain whether an object sighted at two different, widely-spaced points on the radar screen during separate revolutions is in fact the same object.

Therefore, the reliability of radar in substantiating the existence of UFOs is debatable. Ufologists tend to put greater emphasis on its credibility than do the skeptics. At best, radar remains a supplementary proof. The best indisputable proof of the existence of UFOs would still be either a mass sighting at close range or clear photographs.

RADIOACTIVE. See: Radioactivity.

RADIOACTIVITY. The product of the natural breakup of nuclei which results in nuclear changes and in spontaneous emissions by atoms of primary particles. Elements such as thorium, polonium, radium, and uranium are naturally radioacitve. Radioactive elements emit three types of rays: alpha, beta, and gamma.

Radioactivity, which can be fatal to man and other life forms, has been associated with UFOs, some of which have exhibited high radioactivity. In 1953 a UFO over Ontario disintegrated in a shower of brilliant particles. Afterwards, a blue rain fell, samples of which proved to be highly radioactive. Various examinations of ground areas where UFOs are said to have landed showed the areas to be radioactive. In *Aliens from Space,* Donald E. Keyhoe states that in 1956 UFOs ventured into an Air Force test area, location undisclosed, and that Air Force instruments showed the UFOs to be abnormally radioactive.

The abnormally high level of radioactivity associated with UFOs may indicate that they are natural phenomena, for the radioactivity, which would be dangerous to man, should also be dangerous to any beings inside. On the other hand, it is possible that UFOs are real spacecraft. The beings inside may be insulated against radioactivity.

The emission of radioactivity by UFOs implies that some sort of nuclear material is used in their propulsion systems, which may emit the radioactivity simply as waste material.

The radioactivity of UFOs presents a potential danger. Therefore, persons sighting UFOs should take precautionary measures to avoid possible radioactive contamination and damage to their vital organs. A Geiger counter would be the best way to test for the presence and level of radioactivity. It is not known whether the beings who pilot the UFOs are also radioactive. It seems highly unlikely that they would be. However, if the UFO beings are paraphysical in nature, as the dimensionalists claim, then the possibility that they could be readioactive should be taken into account before any attempt is made to establish contact with them.

See: Energy; Transmogrification.

RADIATION. The emission and diffusion of rays of heat, light, electricity, and sound, or the emission of rays by a radioactive substance. Some forms of radiation are harmful, others are not.

Certain forms of radiation, such as light, are necessary for the maintenance of life, but too great an intensity of light can also be harmful.

Stars and certain elements, such as uranium, radium, etc., naturally emit radiation. Radiation is also associated with UFOs, and some persons who have come into too close contact with them have developed radiation sickness.

See: Radioactivity.

RADIOASTRONOMY. A special branch of astronomy which studies celestial bodies through the energy received from them on radio frequencies. Radioastronomy supplements optical astronomy. One of its main goals is to search for intelligent signals from space.

See: Astronomy; Project Ozma.

RADIOCARBON. A radioactive isotope of carbon with an atomic weight of 14 and a half-life of about 5,760 years. It is used in the dating of organic material.

See: Radiocarbon dating.

RADIOCARBON DATING. The process used in establishing the age of dead organic material by determining the amount of carbon-14 that is still present in the remains. Radiocarbon dating is an important tool of paleontology and archaeology used to date bones and artifacts made of organic material. The process provides a good estimate of when an object was made. Concurrently, it establishes an approximate date for the culture which fashioned the artifact. It also helps to determine whether certain cultures were contemporary and in which time period each culture existed. This permits a determination of whether one culture appeared prior to another or after it. By providing a timetable, radiocarbon dating helps to show how cultures evolved, vanished, or influenced the development of one another. The method is not absolutely reliable, however, and is always used in conjunction with other scientific methods of establishing approximate age.

RED SPOT. See: Great Red Spot.

ROBOT. A mechanical "being" which would exhibit many of the attributes of his creator. A robot would have a memory bank, be capable of locomotion and possibly of speech. In function and purpose a robot would be an extension of a man's hands and mind. As a manmade machine, its primary and ideal function would be to perform tasks which would be too monotonous or too hazardous for man. Robots might be used to explore ocean bottoms or to land on other planets. Simple types of robot-machines have already been created and are being used for limited purposes. However, a sophisticated robot capable of complex functions is still beyond man's technological capability to construct.

Robots have been the subject of many science fiction stories and films. Some have depicted robots as helpful to man, others have stressed the dangers, both potential and real. With a memory bank and a capability to receive, analyze, and store data, a robot might in time also develop a mind with the faculty of intelligent thought. Such a possibility raises the complex scientific and philosophical concept of the mind, its origins, structure, and ability.

Should a sophisticated robot acquire the instinct for self-preservation and also the ability to reproduce itself by manufacturing more robots, the possibility would be very strong that such a robot might eventually revolt against its creators, i.e., against man. Such a possibility has been the subject of a number of science fiction movies and presently exists only in the realm of science fiction. However, if in the future sophisticated robots should be created, such a possibility could then be a very real danger.

Robots may also have an important connection with UFOs. A number of persons who have sighted UFO beings have reported that the beings exhibited deliberate physical movements. These descriptions would indicate that the UFO occupants might be mechanical in nature. For example, on May 24, 1962, Argentine government officials reported that reputable witnesses had seen a disc-shaped UFO land near a house. Two figures, described as robotlike, were seen to emerge from the vehicle. When they saw that they were being observed, these figures reentered the UFO and sped away.

There have also been sightings of UFO beings whose appearance was humanlike but whose movements were deliberate and mechanical. This raises the further frightening prospect of androids, robots which externally would resemble human beings.

See: Android; Cyborg.

ROCKETSHIP. A vehicle capable of traveling in space. Such a vehicle might also be used for travel on Earth.

Rockets have been known to man for centuries. From this it was only a small step for imaginative minds to conceive of a special compartment which when attached to a rocket would make it possible for men to travel in them. It was not long before science fiction writers had men traveling on rocket ships to the moon and other planets.

Rocketship was the original name for a vehicle capable of undertaking space journeys. It remained popular till the late 1950s. When the first official government-sponsored attempts at space travel took place around that time, the term "rocket ship" gave way to a new term to describe a vehicle capable of space travel—spaceship.

Nonetheless, the term "rocketship" still possesses a charm of its own and remains as a romantic reminder of man's flights of fancy when he first reached out for the stars. The rocketship of science fiction became the father of the spaceship of reality.

RUPPELT, EDWARD J. From early 1951 until September 1953 he was head of Project Blue Book, the official U.S. Air Force investigation into the UFO phenomenon. Ruppelt coined the now widely used term "UFO" (Unidentified Flying Object) to replace the popular though misleading designation "flying saucer." Ruppelt's book *The Report on Unidentified Flying Objects* appeared in 1956. The book is one of the best of its kind, and remains a standard reference in the field till this day.

See: Project Blue Book; UFO.

RYLE, SIR MARTIN. A prominent British astronomer and a Nobel laureate in physics. In 1976 he proposed a global ban on communication attempts by radio astronomers to broadcast to other stars the fact that life exists on Earth. He argued that extraterrestrials, if they exist, might prove to be hostile, and as a security precaution, mankind should not broadcast its existence to other intelligent beings in space.

See: CETI; SETI.

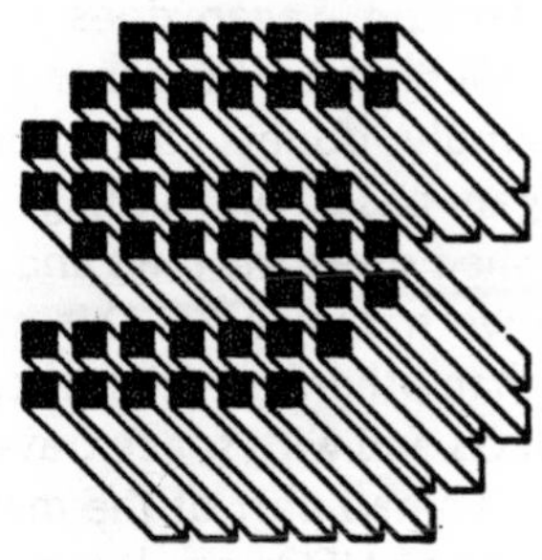

SAGAN, CARL. Renowned astrophysicist at Cornell University. He is articulate, intelligent and well learned in his field. He has published books, appeared on talk shows and news interviews, discussing various topics relating to space. His books are enjoyable, well written and readable, and provide much interesting scientific information on various topics: the exploration of the moon; Venus and Mars; the birth, evolution and death of stars; the existence of prebiological molecules in space; etc. The books present a panoramic view of space, its interaction with life on Earth, and man's expanding view of the cosmos. Sagan feels that the space adventure is revolutionizing man's view of himself and of his world. In his discussion of space he also treats the UFO problem.

Ufologists often cite Sagan in support of UFOs. Sagan, however, doubts the existence of UFOs. His rejection of UFOs is based on several grounds. One is mathematical probability: the Universe is simply too vast. An intelligent civilization seeking to explore other parts of the Universe would simply find the costs staggering and, considering that there are billions of stars and probably planets, could not possibly visit most of them.

The second argument against UFOs hinges on the technological level. UFOs, whatever they are, utilize a technology that is, if not fully understandable by humans, at least within the general level of present cultural and technological possibilities. A true alien (befapian) culture, on the other hand, would possess vehicles beyond our comprehension.

Sagan presents his facts in an objective, scientific manner, demanding rigorous proof and reaching cautious conclusions where proof is lacking. Sagan does not, however, dismiss the possibility that there may be other intelligent beings in the Universe. He simply doubts that contact has as yet been established. Sagan bases his findings and conclusions about space on established scientific laws and draws possibilities based within these known frameworks. This makes him more cautious in certain areas than other less scientifically oriented writers who also deal with UFOs and with space travel.

UFOs are only a small part of the material covered by Sagan. In fact, discussions of UFOs are largely incidental to his works, appearing more as something that must be mentioned because of public interest. But he does supply invaluable scientific information in an easily understandable fashion which provides background information for dealing with the UFO phenomenon.

SAGITTARIUS. Some ufologists believe that if ancient befapian astronauts did in fact land on Earth in ancient times, they most likely would have originated from one of the planetary systems in the constellation Sagittarius. This constellation contains a high concentration of stars similar to, but older than, our sun. Therefore, nebecists argue, life could have developed on such a planetary system millions of years before it developed on Earth. Consequently, by the process of evolution, intelligent life may also have arisen on such planets millions of years before intelligent life arose on Earth. Such intelligent beings may then have begun the conquest of space, and in their explorations may have discovered Earth, where intelligent life was only beginning to arise.

SANDERSON, IVAN T. A biologist by training, he brought his scientific background into the examination of UFOs. His scientific training and skills are clearly evident in his works, which are well researched, well written and thoroughly documented, and his discussions are presented in a professional manner. When evidence is insufficient, he discusses the various possible explanations. Some of his statements and conclusions reflect scientific caution, and in other instances he reaches reasonable conclusions based on available data.

On one point, however, he is certain. He believes in the existence of aconins, whom he calls *"oints"* (other intelligences). On the question of aconins in general and UFOs in particular he is a dimensionalist. He firmly believes that there is an invisible world around us populated by intelligent beings who can enter our visible world and influence events. However, he is vague about whether this invisible world is located within our space-time continuum (but is invisible to us), or whether it is located in a parallel space-time continuum. He believes there may be space-time holes through which these beings enter our visible world and through which objects such as UFOs can enter into our world from another world.

UFOs are, he feels, constructions or creations of these beings. They are real, but their reality (physical essence) is of a temporary nature. Simultaneously, he also suggests another possible explanation for UFOs. His biological background and meticulous scientific examination of UFOs led him to the tentative conclusion that some UFOs may actually be living creatures, i.e., forms of life.

Mr. Sanderson's works on the existence of aconins in general, including the UFO phenomenon, are invaluable for another reason. His works are some of the most scientifically oriented in the field of naphology. His scientific background and vast knowledge enabled him to relate findings from other scientific fields into helping understand some of the reported mysterious phenomena. As a result he presents an in-depth examination of the subject matter. He presents a convincing case that there are nonhuman intelligent beings who are involved in the manipulaton of human affairs. And he poses one frightening possibility; that is, that these beings are not rational. They may be so advanced, so overcivilized that they have gone mad and get their thrills from playing tricks and pranks on humans. Like other dimensionalists, he is not certain if there are several kinds of beings or merely one kind which is able to assume various forms. However, along with other dimensionalists, he sees these beings, manadims, as potentially dangerous to humans.

See: Dimensionalism; Manadim; Oints; Zeroid.

SARGASSO SEA. A calm area in the North Atlantic, northeast of the West Indies. There is an abundance of free-floating algae there. The seaweed is from the genus *Sargassum,* hence the name Sargasso Sea.

At one time, mariners feared this stretch of the ocean because of the belief that the seaweed could trap a ship. It was believed that if a ship became entangled, it would never escape, and the crew would eventually die of hunger. There is no basis to this superstition. Except for very small boats, no other type of vessel would be endangered in this area.

In more recent times, some writers have attempted to link the seaweed of the Sargasso Sea with the numerous mysterious disappearances of aircraft and ships in the North Atlantic. Some of these disappearances are indeed veritable mysteries, but there is no scientific basis to link them with the seaweed.

SASQUATCH. The name applied by the Indians of British Columbia more than a century ago to the creature popularly known in the U.S. as Bigfoot.

See: Bigfoot.

SATAN. In the Jewish and Christian religions, Satan is the chief evil spirit. He is synonymous with Lucifer. Religion maintains that Satan is a real being and not just a personification of evil. In the religious view, Satan is man's greatest adversary. Religion hints at the fact that at one time Satan and his demons lived on and ruled Earth, but were later expelled for violating God's commandments, and man was then bequeathed possession of Earth. Ever since that time, Satan has attempted to recover Earth and has despised man for being the present master over it.

The evil spirits or demons over whom Satan rules bear many similarities to the invisible beings from the other space-time continuums whose existence is maintained by the dimensionalist theory. Demons and the other dimensional beings are similar in that both are said to be evil, and capable and desirous of hurting and of deceiving man.

See: Demon; Devil; Dimensionalism; Elemental; Lucifer; Manadim; UFO; UT.

SAUCER CULT. Critics and debunkers of the UFO phenomenon have pointed out that some believers in UFOs have started a saucer cult. There is no evidence at present, however, that a large, organized saucer cult does indeed exist. Rather it is an amorphous and loosely organized group composed of people who share certain beliefs about UFOs.

Such beliefs have arisen because UFO beings are alleged to have presented to human contactees much arcane knowledge about themselves, warnings about the future, and warnings that man must change his ways. A few persons have even claimed that they received special powers from these UFO beings. There have also been several reported cases of persons who, when a UFO passed by, recovered speedily from injuries from which they were suffering. One elderly man claimed that a new set of teeth began to grow after he was caught in the glow of a passing UFO.

This brilliant glow which is emitted by UFOs figures prominently in many contact cases. A number of persons have claimed sudden illumination or understanding after being exposed to a UFO's light. Illumination is, of course, a subjective claim. It leaves open the question of the quality of knowledge or perception which a person claims to have acquired.

It is also claimed by most contactees that the UFO beings communicated with them via telepathy. If true, this suggests that these beings are mentally more advanced than humans. There are also reports that UFOs interfere with electromagnetism. This interference has been held partly responsible for power failures, poor radio transmission, and stalled cars when UFOs were in the vicinity. More important, however, is their reported ability to interfere with the human mind, which functions in part on electrical energy. Many scientists believe that ESP functions according to some sort of electromagnetic or psychoelectric basis. UFOs would therefore be able to interfere with the functioning of the brain, and via their ability to manipulate electromagnetism, would be able to induce hallucinations in people.

All these phenomena suggest the awesome power of the UFOs. But they also raise one question. With all this power why have the UFOs not conquered Earth? No answer is readily apparent.

This seeming lack of hostility on the part of the UFO beings, together with the awesome powers which they possess, has impressed some UFO buffs to the point where they worship the UFO beings as saviors of mankind. The UFO buffs who fall into this category constitute only a small group. Furthermore, they are not even serious students of ufology. They are more like those primitive men who worshipped the sun and the moon instead of studying them. Naphologists, on the other hand, seek to study the phenomenon, and by studying it to understand it. They are not awed by the UFOs nor do they worship them.

SAUCERIAN. A general term referring to those intelligent beings who pilot the UFOs. Compared to the number of reported UFO sightings, the number of actual sightings of UFO beings is rare, while actual contact with such beings is extremely rare. These saucerians or UFO beings have been variously described as being either humanoid or mechanical or hideous. The various differences in description may be due to the fact that more than one group of aconins pilot the UFOs, which themselves may originate from different places. On the other hand, it is also possible that saucerians may bring mascots or pets along with them or that they may send out robots from the UFOs. These pets and robots may then be mistaken for the actual beings.

At the same time, it must be admitted that some of the reported descriptions and sightings of UFO beings may be hoaxes, illusions or hallucinations.

A third explanation is also possible. Perhaps the saucerians want to keep their real identity a secret, and therefore assume various disguises in order to confuse man.

No definitive answer to the problems posed by the various descriptions can be given until either direct contact is finally established on an official basis or until one of these beings is captured. It is interesting to point out in this regard that there have been several reports claiming that UFO beings have actually been captured. No official confirmation, however, exists of these reports.

One thing is clear, though. Whoever these saucerians are, they are at the present time desirous of avoiding prolonged and official contact with humans. Various reasons have been suggested for this avoidance. One theory maintains that man is too low on the evolutionary scale to warrant any serious consideration or treatment by the advanced saucerians. Another theory proposes a more sinister possibility. It advances the idea that the saucerians wish to keep their identity a secret because their real motives are hostile, i.e., they are presently engaged in an extensive surveillance of the planet, possibly in preparation for some sort of concerted action in the future.

Hopefully, as ufology accumulates more data and develops better research methods, more definitive answers will be found to these vexing questions.

See: Aconin; Befap; Manadim; UFO.

SCIENCE. A systematic method of discovering and acquiring knowledge. Its most distinctive feature is the experimental method, the use of which has permitted the discovery of the laws of nature. The result has been an extraordinary cumulative gain in practical knowledge. The key element in science is the experimental method. By trail and error, by duplicating phenomena under controlled conditions, knowledge has been and is being acquired. Science has not yet directly tackled the UFO phenomenon. In addition to the current anti-UFO bias of many scientists who dismiss UFOs as insignificant, a major problem in studying UFOs is that science cannot recreate them in the laboratory, nor can it anticipate when and where UFOs will next appear.

However, because UFOs represent an unexplained challenge, new methods and concepts will probably have to be created in order to deal with them. Ultimately, in order to understand UFOs, science will have to take extensive tests and measurements.

Some UFOs may be mere light manifestations. Because these light manifestations violate all known laws of physics, much useful knowledge about the laws of physics could be gained by studying and understanding such phenomena. On the other hand, some UFOs may indeed be spacecraft from other planetary systems. Much valuable scientific knowledge could be gained by capturing and examining a UFO. Even if one cannot be captured, valuable scientific knowledge could still be gained by conducting an extensive and serious study of the UFO flight characteristics.

By refusing to seriously study the UFO phenomenon, science is only delaying the discovery of the final solution to this mystery. The UFOs are very real phenomena; simply denying that they exist or dismissing their existence as insignificant will not make them disappear.

Presently, ufologists, among whom there are many scientists, are engaged in a serious study of the UFO phenomenon. Naphology is an organized systematic study of unexplained natural phenomena, but unlike science, it lacks the experimental method. Basically, naphology is concerned with the accumulation of data and with the formulation of theories on the basis of that data. One day, it will hopefully have enough data and will be able to resolve the UFO mystery. If not, perhaps it will at least have enough convincing data to seriously interest the scientific community as a whole into studying UFOs.

See: Naphology; [illegible].

SCIENTIFIC IMMORTALITY. See: Technological Immortality.

SCIENTIST. A person committed to acquiring knowledge through science.

SEEDING. The concept of seeding is a major element of the nebecian philosophy. Nebecism holds that life on Earth either originated somewhere else in the Universe or that, if it did arise naturally on Earth through evolution, its development was influenced by outside forces.

There are several variations of this theory. One group of nebecists believes that life first originated in some other part of the Universe. A planetary system in the center of Sagittarius is often advanced as a likely place. The center of Sagittarius is believed to contain stars similar to the sun, though older and thus more suitable and likely places for the origin of life. Responding to the cosmic moral imperative to spread intelligent life, the intelligent beings on this alien planet then began to spread life throughout the Universe. This was done in one of two ways.

The first method would involve astronauts from this befapian civilization who personally visited other planets and introduced life there. If necessary, these befaps would even terraform a planet in order to make it suitable for supporting life. Once life was introduced, evolution would take over. More complex life forms would then arise.

The second way that these beings could have introduced life into other parts of the Universe was by indirect seeding, i.e., by merely shooting either simple forms of living organisms or prebiological molecules into space, there to be carried by stellar wind, gravitation and other cosmic forces throughout the Universe. Eventually, some of these life or prelife forms found their way to suitable planets. Once introduced to the planet, evolution then took over and more complex life forms began to arise. By this method, the befapian beings would not have been directly involved in introducing life to other planets.

Another group of nebecists adheres to the position, also advanced by some biologists, that life arises at a suitable stage when certain conditions are met. Accordingly, they believe that life evolved naturally on Earth. However, they maintain that the evolution of life was influenced and affected by befaps. There are several branches of this particular theory.

One branch believes that the technologically advanced befaps were able to detect the presence of life forms on Earth. They subsequently influenced the evolutionary course of these basic life forms by bombarding them with cosmic rays or other types of radiation. Some nebecists believe, for example, that dinosaurs died out on Earth because of cosmic explosions, either natural or artificial, which occurred somewhere in the Universe and which sent deadly cosmic rays to Earth.

Another branch of this theory believes that befaps arrived on Earth after detecting life forms here, and then influenced the evolutionary development of these life forms by genetic manipulation and by the extirpation of some species.

The third nebecian theory on seeding combines features of both the first and second theories. It maintains that life is a natural phenomenon, originating naturally in those parts of the Universe where conditions are right. But the origin of intelligent, sapient life is a rare phenomenon, requiring many billions of years and a series of favorable events. Therefore, this theory holds that intelligent life must have arisen in some planetary system similar to our solar system, but in a much older one. In response to the cosmic moral imperative, the intelligent beings which arose there then began to seed the Universe with intelligent life.

There were two methods of accomplishing this. The first one involved astronomy which located favorable planets. Radiation was then beamed upon these planets. The radiation would hopefully stimulate the development of life. Once life was started, evolution would then take over. The rise of intelligent beings would then become possible.

The second method called for those befaps to personally wander through the Universe in search of suitable planets upon which life had already arisen and had evolved into complex forms. Upon arriving on such a planet, these befaps would by genetic manipulation on a suitable higher form of life—an ape, for example—give rise to intelligent, sapient beings. It was not necessary to fully develop the intelligence, but merely to provide the spark for it. Since intelligence was biologically superior to other biological endowments, the intelligent beings would, by the process of natural selection, overcome their adversaries in the animal world. They would multiply and become the dominant and the creative life form on the planet. Eventually, they would also become technologically advanced and would enter into the exploration of space. Responding to the cosmic moral imperative, these beings would then also help spread intelligent life to other parts of the Universe.

There is a slight variation to this theory. Nebecists who ascribe to this theory disagree on the length of time that the befaps were supposed to have stayed on Earth, and on the degree of biological interference which they carried out in influencing the evolution of suitable life forms on Earth.

See: Evolution; Life; Nebecism.

SELF-AWARENESS. See: Consciousness.

SELF-CONSCIOUSNESS. See: Consciousness.

SENDY, JEAN. A firm adherent of nebecism, he places great emphasis on the Bible, especially on the Book of Genesis, as an accurate historical record of the activities of superadvanced befaps on Earth. On the interpretation and understanding of the Bible he is a cabalist, a believer that the Bible contains a hidden esoteric meaning. The Bible, he believes, is the best available record of past befapian presence on Earth. He parts company with other nebecists in advocating that befapian interference in human affairs ended with the Flood. Their experiment a failure, the befaps, known as Elohim, decided to destroy life on Earth and depart. But Noah intervened and asked for one more chance. They reluctantly agreed. The goal of man has been to regain the lost golden age when befaps ruled Earth and there was peace and tranquility. He believes that the befaps, before departing, left some tangible evidence of their presence on a nearby celestial body, most likely on the moon.

Sendy does not deal with the subsequent chapters of the Bible, except in the general sense that it is the story of man's attempt to regain and understand the lost knowledge. Someday, when man has advanced to the point where through technology he can duplicate the feats of the Bible, man will then, believes Sendy, realize the true meaning of the Bible. Already, man is reaching out for the stars and is developeing a new philosophy of life, viewing himself as master of natural laws rather than their victim.

On the UFO question, Sendy is ambiguous. He acknowledges their existence, but believes that they are some sort of cryptic messages which people have not yet deciphered. Sendy postulates that when the befaps left Earth several million years ago, they may have established a machine somewhere which would be triggered when mankind advanced to a certain technological level. The result would be that UFOs, which may perhaps only be images, would be sent or broadcast into Earth's atmosphere. The technological breakthrough which Sendy feels triggered the UFOs was the detonation of the nuclear bombs. It was only after the advent of the nuclear age, Sendy points out, that the UFOs began arriving in vast numbers.

See: Bible; Cabala; Elohim; Nebecism.

SENSE. A special bodily faculty by which man and other animals perceive external objects. Biologists list five senses: sight, hearing, smell, taste, and touch. Zoologists and psychologists believe that some species of animals possess a sixth sense which warns them of approaching danger. Humans are also believed to possess a latent sixth sense. This sixth sense, or ESP as it is called in humans, is believed to work by electromagnetism. Since senses are intimately involved in the UFO phenomenon, the quality and nature of the senses are especially relevant in the attempt to unravel at least part of the UFO mystery.

See: ESP; Sight; Telepathy.

SENSE WORLD. That part of reality which is perceivable via the five senses. Sense-data are received from the external world by the senses and are transmitted to the brain. There they are analyzed and stored. On the basis of this sense-data, intelligent beings are then able to form ideas about the sense world and to respond according to this perception.

Theologians, and some naphologists and philosophers, contend that there is a world or reality beyond the realm of the senses. The problem becomes more complex when the possibility is taken into consideration that this realm beyond the senses may be inhabited by intelligent beings who may be able to influence events in our world.

See: Dimensionalism; Invisible; Objective Reality; Supersensible.

SETI. Acronym for Search for Extraterrestrial Intelligence, the current name of the U.S. program to locate extraterrestrial messages via radio astronomy.

See: CETI; Ryle.

SHOOTING STAR. A synoym for meteor.
See: Meteor.

SIGHT. The process by which sense-data are received by a person via the medium of the eyes and then registered and identified by the mind. The retina's sensitivity to vibrations of radiant (light) energy is the basic process by which this works. Differences of intensity and of wavelength are picked up by the retina. The sense-data are then transmitted to the brain, which then determines the color, position, and other characteristics of the object. The end result of this process, i.e., the actual identification and contact established with the external object, is called sight.

Any impairment of the eyes naturally affects sight. Misidentification then becomes possible. Color blindness, myopia, hyperopia, and astigmatism are just some of the eye diseases which affect sight. There can also be a related mental inability to properly register, identify and distinguish among the sense-data. At times, this may result in illusions, mirages, hallucinations, and other failures of the mind to properly process sense-data.

Sight is also the single most important element in UFO sightings. At the same time, it also remains the most vulnerable proof. The credibility of witnesses is usually attacked by stating that they misidentified what they saw. In discrediting witnesses, the Air Force frequently claims that they were victims of illusions or hallucinations. On the other hand, a photograph of the object which is seen is a more reliable form of evidence. A photograph provides a permanent, objective record of an event. It is more reliable because it is not subject to a person's subjective analysis of sense-data.
See: Hallucination; Illusion.

SKYQUAKE. Among the unexplained mysterious phenomena are the explosions or quakes heard emanating from the upper atmosphere. These skyquakes, also known as airquakes, received widespread publicity in early December 1977 when on several different occasions, residents along the east coast of the United States reported loud aerial explosions.

Sonic booms from passing jet planes and nuclear explosions were ruled out as possible causes by scientists. Three other possibilities remained. One was that the military was testing some sort of secret weapon. The second was that skyquakes were a natural phenomenon as yet unidentified. The third was that

UFOs were responsible. Despite attempts to pinpoint the source of the skyquakes, neither the government nor the scientists were able to identify them.

As a matter of fact, these skyquakes are not recent phenomena, but have been reported for a long time. Charles Fort makes mention of skyquakes from the nineteenth century. As there were neither jet planes nor nuclear bombs in those days, it is obvious that skyquakes are not caused by human action. By the process of elimination, skyquakes must either be a natural phenomenon as yet unidentified or may be caused by other intelligent beings.

The mystery of the skyquakes persists. No definitive answer is possible at this time. However, one ufological theory suggests a possible explanation. If a UFO or some other object from another dimension were suddenly to appear or to materialize in our atmosphere, it would cause a displacement of air with a resultant noise or quake.

Skyquakes which can be recorded are tangible proof that something mysterious is happening in Earth's upper atmosphere. Skyquakes may be component parts of the proof that UFOs are real.

SMELL. The sense of smell has been involved in UFO sightings. Some persons who claimed to have encountered UFO beings, described an obnoxious sulfurous odor that emanated from these beings. It would seem that this odor is emitted either to repel humans or when the creature or being is excited or frightened. If the accounts are true, it is possible that these odor-emitting creatures are mascots or pets of the UFO beings rather than the UFO beings themselves.

Another possible explanation is that these mephitic creatures belong to an unidentified species of anthropoid apes inhabiting North America. The northwestern states of America and the western provinces of Canada are held to be the home of Bigfoot or Sasquatch. A strong case has been presented for the existence of this animal. Many persons who have encountered Bigfoot have described a rancid sulfurous odor that seems to emanate from the beasts. Momo, the Missouri version of Bigfoot, has also been known to release a sulfurous odor when humans have approached too close. These creatures may be animals indigenous to Earth that have been mistaken for UFO beings.

A third possiblity also exists. Dimensionalists point out that various apparitions have often been accompanied by a sulfurous odor. It seems that this type of odor is intimately associated with evil manifestations.

In any event, more study is needed in the entire field in order to unravel these interlocking problems and mysteries.

SOLAR SAILING. Sunlight radiation and the protons and electrons in the solar wind could provide a novel means of traveling within the solar system. A spaceship could be constructed to which tens of miles of golden gossamer-thin sails are attached. These sails would catch the solar wind and thus propel the spaceship. The fascinating feature of this means of propulsion is that it resurrects the exciting era of the sailing vessels on Earth. With the invention of the engine, it was believed that sailing vessels were a thing of the past. It was hardly imagined that the existence of solar wind would make the sail a feasible form of propulsion once again. A sail-spaceship would, of course, be cumbersome to construct and would be slow in speed. But it would be a reliable craft, propelled by natural means, thereby saving on fuel costs, and would be best suitable for freighting minerals from one celestial body to another.

SOLAR SYSTEM. The particular name given to our planetary system. Each planetary system is named after its parent star. The name of our star is the sun. Solar is the adjectival form of the sun and refers to the sun. The solar system is composed of our sun and of all the heavenly bodies that revolve around it; namely, the nine planets, the planets' moons and the asteroids.

SONIC GUN. *See:* Sound.

SONS OF GOD. Genesis 6:2 makes mention of "the sons of God." Erich von Daniken and other nebecists have focused on this line as one of the proofs that Earth was visited in ancient times by befaps. Primitive man, according to these nebecists, mistook befaps for gods and angels. Basically similar to man in their biological and physical nature, these gods and angels, some nebecists maintain, had sexual relations with humans. The offspring of this union were hybrid beings who were mentally and physically superior to the offspring of the purely human stock. Verse 4 of chapter 6 of the Book of Genesis is said to record the existence of these hybrid children.

This nebecian interpretation has been subjected to severe scholarly criticism by adherents of the theological school. Their fundamental argument is that there is no need to look to nebecian explanations when confronted with Biblical stories and accounts. In chapter 6 of *Crash Go the Chariots,* Prof. Clifford Wilson argues that chapter 6 of The Book of Genesis was trying to stress the fact that two lines of man had developed in human history. The first was the godly line of Seth, and the second was the ungodly line of Cain, who killed his brother Abel. Many Biblical scholars accept the interpretation that "the sons of God" referred to men and women from the line of Seth, who intermarried with "the daughters of men"—the ungodly line of Cain.

SOUL. In religion, soul refers to that essential indestructible part of man which survives death and which will be rewarded in an eternal existence by either happiness in heaven or misery in hell, depending on the kind of life the person lived on Earth. Scientists are divided as to the existence of the soul.

One school of scientists denies the reality of the soul, arguing that there is no proof for it. They claim that man misidentifies the vital life force as a soul. They claim that the term "soul" is applied to what is only the sum total of the animate activities of a living organism. In their view, the soul has no separate existence apart from these animate activities. When the body dies, the soul also dies.

Another school of scientists believes in the existence of the soul, but identifies it with consciousness. They also suggest that this consciousness acquires a separate identity, and that it retains this identity even after physical death.

The debate over the existence of the soul also involves naphology. Throughout man's history, various beings are reported to have appeared to man. Some of these beings have informed man that there is no immortal life. Other beings have reassured man that there is indeed a life after death.

Naphologists must therefore inquire not only about the reality of these beings, but also about their place of origin and their motivation for informing man of the things they reveal to him. The naphologist also needs to inquire about the motivation of these beings in bringing up the subject of the soul, and about the reason why conflicting statements concerning the soul's nature and existence were told.

Ultimately, man is left with only his intellect to decide on the merits of each claim. No statement or belief should be accepted without first being subjected to critical review. Otherwise, any belief, whether it relates to the soul or to other matters, would be of equal validity.

See: Consciousness; Naphology; Technological Immortality.

SOUND. Vibrational energy. Sound has both frequency and amplitude. It has various sources and has different effects on the type of person or animal hearing it. Musical sounds are the simplest sounds and the most pleasant to the hearing organ.

Prolonged exposure to sound causes both physiological and psychological changes. Over a long period of time and at sustained high decibels, sound can, for example, bring on heart attacks. Loud and unusual noises affect a person's psychological balance and can drive him to commit rash acts. Beginning in the early 1970s the harmful effects of sound were recognized, and laws were proposed and passed attempting to regulate sound pollution.

Sound also has a connection with UFOs, but until science began to study the effects of sound, this relationship had not been recognized. UFO witnesses often reported dizziness, nausea, headaches, exhaustion, and, in some instances, memory blackouts. Ufologists and psychologists originally assumed these effects were caused by the fear and excitement brought about by witnessing the mysterious UFO crafts.

However, when scientists began a serious study of sound in the late 1960s, they discovered that, like audible sound, infrasonic and ultrasonic sounds were also able to cause disturbing and dangerous effects. These included fatigue, nausea, headaches, loss of consciousness, and loss of equilibrium. The relation to the UFOs became immediately evident, as a result of which the reports of the UFO witnesses were reexamined. Though it is not known for certain if UFOs can create inaudible sound waves, the evidence does seem to indicate that they could.

One curious feature of UFOs has been that, in nearly all cases, their movements were described as soundless. In some cases whistling noises were reported. It is possible that during their soundless movements the UFOs emitted either or both infrasonic and ultrasonic sound waves. The emission of such sound could explain the symptoms reported by persons who saw UFOs at a close distance.

If UFOs are able to emit inaudible sound waves,this presents another potentially dangerous possiblity. Concentrated inaudible sound waves could be used as weapons of war. Such weapons would cause only minimal damage to material things, but would be able to destroy living creatures, including man.

The question of whether or not UFOs emit inaudible sound waves can be answered very easily. All that is necessary is to have the right equipment at the right place at the right time. This again calls attention to the need for a serious sustained scientific study of UFOs. Every additional bit of information which can be acquired about UFOs will bring man one step closer to identifying and explaining the phenomenon.

SOUND-SPEED. This refers to a unit of velocity (a measurement of velocity) utilizing the velocity of sound as the standard. At sea level, the velocity of sound in the air is 730 miles per hour.

See: Mach.

SOUTH POLE. See: Antarctica.

SPACE. A fundamental scientific and philosophical concept. Though science deals with space, ironically, no satisfactory definition of space exists. Space is generally regarded as the unlimited receptacle in which all material objects are located. This does not, however, explain whether space has a limit and, if it does, then what lies beyond it. Another baffling problem is whether space is independent of the material objects located in it. Is space a separate material entity which is capable of containing other material entities or does space have reality only if there are material objects located within it?

Space is a fundamental concept of nature and a better understanding of it would lead to a better understanding of one of nature's fundamental laws. This may then lead to technological inventions of which man presently has no inkling. By mastering the laws of space and time, it may perhaps be possible to find short-cuts through space to various distant parts of the Universe. Some ufologists have speculated that UFOs may have conquered the laws of space and time, and that they may originate from distant parts of the Universe.

Though man's present knowledge of space is inadequate, man continues to deal with it and continues in his attempt to unlock its secrets. Hopefully, in the future his efforts will be rewarded.

SPACECRAFT. A general term referring to any vehicle which is capable of traveling in space.

SPACESHIP. A vehicle which is capable of traveling in space. There are two basic types of spaceships: starships and planetary ships.

See: Planetary ship; Starship.

SPACE-TIME CONTINUUM. A widely-used synonym for dimension. It is a more formal and technical phrase which refers to a particular dimension or level of existence. A basic premise of dimensionalism is that there is more than one space-time continuum.

SPACE ANIMAL. See: Zeroid.

SPACE APERTURE. See: Space Gate.

SPACE GATE. A hypothetical hole in the fabric of the space-time continuum which would be a short-cut through space and time. A spaceship entering such a gate would emerge in another distant part of the Universe, perhaps also at a future point in time. If space gates do indeed exist, they may make it possible to conquer space and to travel to distant parts of the Universe.

Some scientists and writers have suggested the possibility that black holes may be such space gates. On the basis of current scientific knowledge, however, the existence of space gates cannot be proven. At present, these short-cuts through space and time exist only in the realm of science fiction and in theoretical scientific speculation. The existence of space gates can be ascertained in one of two ways. The first way would be to actually find a space gate. The second way would be by making official contact with UFO beings who, being in possession of superior scientific knowledge, could provide a definitive answer as to how they were able to travel from their home planet to our planetary system, i.e., whether by using a space gate or via blisk-speeds.

See: Black Hole; Superspace.

SPACE STATION. Space travel would necessitate the establishment of strategically located bases for refueling and repairing spaceships, and also as places of rest and recreation for weary space crews. Such bases could be established on planets, on asteroids, and on manmade orbiting stations around planets. It is even possible to conceive of buoy-type space stations located between stars and/or galaxies. Any space-age civilization which has embarked on the exploration and conquest of space would have to establish such bases. This is also the crux of the nebecian theory about UFOs.

Some nebecists have advanced the theory that Earth may be a space station for voyagers from other planetary systems. Such may indeed be the case. American astronauts described Earth as an oasis in the sky. Earth is incredibly beautiful when viewed from outer space, while other planets in the solar system are plain and desolate. Earth's abundance of water makes it literally the waterhole of the solar system.

Water played a crucial role in the formation of life on Earth. If the laws of biology are as universal as the laws of physics, then water must also have played an equally important role in the formation and sustenance of life on other planetary systems. It may be the presence of water and of food supplies which attracts befaps to Earth. This presence of food and water may also explain why Earth has been saved from invasion by befaps, assuming that the ufologists are correct in their belief that befaps do indeed exist.

Earth is the only hospitable planet in the solar system. Ufologists point out that evidence points to the fact that UFOs exist, that they have been visiting Earth for centuries, perhaps even for millenniums, and that there may be more than one group of UFOs which visits Earth. Taking all these facts into consideration, it is possible that Earth has been spared an invasion because there exists some sort of galactic treaty which has declared Earth to be a neutral zone, one which is off limits to conquest and colonization. Such a galactic accord may also explain why, despite the numerous sightings of UFOs, no large-scale hostile actions have been initiated by the UFOs. However, isolated cases of aggression have occurred. These hostile actions are dismissed by most ufologists as either accidental or as retaliations for hostile acts against UFOs.

The use of Earth as a galactic space station may also explain the reason for the different reports on the physical appearance of the befaps. A number of befapian civilizations may have agreed that Earth is to be used solely as a space station. Any attempt by one civilization to conquer Earth would be met by resistance from the other befapian civilizations. Now that man has developed nuclear bombs and has in his possession the fruits of advanced technology which has given him guided missiles and lasers, man would also resist any befapian attempt to conquer Earth. The resultant nuclear holocaust would destroy Earth, rendering this invaluable piece of galactic property useless for future habitation.

SPEECH. The faculty or power of speaking or of carrying on communication by oral means. Speech is also involved in the UFO phenomenon. Contactees are divided into two groups, depending on the manner in which they communicated with the UFO beings. In some cases, the UFO beings are reported to have verbally communicated with the human contactees, while in other cases, communication was allegedly carried out by telepathy. A baffling problem is posed for ufologists by this difference in communication. One possible explanation may be that there is more than one type of UFO beings who have established contact with humans. One group of saucerians may communicate verbally, while another group may use telepathy. It is also possible that the saucerians may be able to communicate both by verbal and by telepathic means. The method of communication utilized may depend upon the particular circumstances of the contact.

SPENCER, JOHN WALLACE. Renowned and recognized expert on the area known as the Bermuda or Devil's Triangle. He has done extensive in-depth research on the various disappearances of airplanes, ships, and people in this mysterious stretch of water. In his work *Limb of the Lost,* he believes that UFOs may be involved in these disappearances.

SPRINGHEEL JACK. The name applied in ufological lore to a strange figure who appeared in Middlesex, England, in mid-November 1837. He earned the nickname because of his uncanny ability to leap to great heights from a standing jump. He was also known as Springheeled Jack.

Springheel Jack was described as tall and thin, though exuding a sense of agility and strength. He had a prominent nose, long, claw-like fingers, and pointed ears. Beneath a long, flowing cape he wore something that appeared to be metal mesh, and strapped to his chest was an unidentifiable lamplike device. His strange attire was topped off by a tall, metallic hat or helmet.

Though the police tried to capture Springheel Jack, it proved an impossible task. He was easily able to avoid capture by his ability to jump over high obstacles.

For three months Springheel Jack terrorized the inhabitants of the town, stalking them at night and knocking on doors, also at night. No one, as far as is known, was ever physically injured by Springheel Jack. But twice he is said to have spurted strange balls of blue fire into the faces of his victims, both women. This rendered them unconscious.

The last recorded sighting of Springheel Jack was on February 27, 1838. However, an individual similar to Springheel Jack was sighted again in England in 1877.

Some authors have suggested that Springheel Jack was an aconin trying to establish contact with humans. Others have suggested that Springheel Jack was a manadim playing another seemingly pointless game on humans.

See: Manadim.

SPUTNIK. The first artificial satellite, launched by the Soviet Union on October 4, 1957. The 184-pound sphere orbited Earth about every ninety minutes in an elliptical orbit ranging from 140 miles to 560 miles. Sputnik marked man's entry into space. It would rapidly be followed by other spectacular space achievements.

See: Starism.

STAR. A self-luminous celestial body, as distinguished from planets, comets, and meteors. There are different types of stars. They are classified in a decreasing order according to their temperatures. The clue to a star's temperature is found in its color. The hottest stars are the blue stars, the surface temperature of which is estimated to be about 30,000 degrees centigrade. At the bottom of the scale are the red stars. Their surface temperature is estimated to be about 3,000 degrees centigrade.

The different classes of stars are designated by letters arranged in the following order: O,B,A,F,G,K,M (O stands for the hot blue stars, M represents the red stars). Stars are further subdivided numerically, i.e., K0 (K-zero) to K9, G0 (G-zero) to G9, etc. The sun is a class G star whose surface temperature is about 6,000 degrees centigrade.

Of major concern to astronomy is the question of whether stars have planetary systems. Many astronomers and astrophysicists believe that they must. In 1963, Professor Lloyd Motz of Columbia University stated that planetary systems must appear and develop around stars of a given type. Walter Sullivan also believes that any star the size of our sun could also have planets, one of which would then be about 92 million miles from it. Under such conditions life would probably also arise.

This conclusion is reached on the basis of the Assumption of Mediocrity. Its basic premise is the universality of the laws of nature. Since the laws of physics and chemistry, for example, have been found to be universal, the fact that the sun has a planetary system strongly indicates that other stars of the same class as the sun must also have planetary systems. This same assumption leads to the conclusion that some of the planets within these planetary systems would have life. If there are intelligent beings on these planets, it would also follow that they would have to be similar to man in many physical and mental aspects. It should be emphasized that these conclusions are tentative and are based on deductions from an assumption whose basic premise concerning the universality of natural laws has yet to be proven.

See: Assumption of Mediocrity; Barnard's Star; Dark Companion.

STAR OF BETHLEHEM. At the time of the birth of Jesus Christ, a bright luminous object appeared in the sky, and led the wise men to Bethlehem, the village where Jesus was born. The origin and nature of the Star of Bethlehem has been a long-standing subject of discourse and wonder. Some ufologists claim that it was a UFO. In their view, Jesus Christ was not God, but a befap whose celestial place of origin is unknown. Adherents of the Christian theological school argue that the Star of Bethlehem was put up in the heavens by a miracle of God to herald the birth of Christ. In Christian theology, Jesus Christ is the Son of God and is of divine origin and nature. Other explanations have ventured that the Star of Bethlehem might have been a comet or a rare kind of celestial phenomenon. The subject is delicate and complicated, and touches on several scholarly disciplines.

STARISM. The advent of the space age has created a new direction, a new goal for imaginative individuals. This goal is to reach the stars and spread human civilization there. Starism refers to and identifies that system of thought and belief which holds that mankind should enter upon the exploration and conquest of space, because only through this exploration and conquest does mankind have a future.

Starism is not at present an organized movement. It is only in its nascent stage and may remain so for some time. The desire to reach the stars is present, but it is incapable of being fulfilled without the necessary technology. And such technology is presently beyond man's ability to develop.

But the undercurrent of starism runs deep through both the scientific and ufological endeavors. Whereas scientists hope to acquire the necessary knowledge through laborious, piecemeal experiments, ufologists hope that by establishing contact with UFOs, the knowledge of how to achieve interstellar travel can be given directly to humans.

Though proceeding along different routes, both scientists and ufologists are working towards the same goal, or at least are helping to nurture the desire for the same goal. Humans have already been in space and have walked on the surface of another celestial body (the moon), and space probes have been sent to other celestial bodies. The value of the space program is no longer being seriously questioned. Satellites, for example, have provided worldwide communications. The pace of the space program may vary, but mankind is now irrevocably committed to it.

The scientists at NASA who are responsible for the successful and spectacular space achievements; the ufologists who raise questions about the origin and purpose of UFOs; and the science fiction writers who create fictitious adventures in space, all help to create and to generate a positive attitude towards space. All are helping to lay the foundations of a starist philosophy.

It is possible that in the distant future, when imaginative minds, spurred by science fiction stories and the UFO mysteries, develop the technology for interstellar space travel, starism will become the dominant philosophy of mankind. After limiting his interest to Earth, man may decide that the only viable solution is to reach the stars. The present generation will not live to see interstellar space travel. Nevertheless, we are living in a grand time. It is the present generation which is laying the foundation for starism; and for this, generations yet unborn will owe us a debt of gratitude.

STARMAN. A generic designation of an interstellar astronaut. It is used by some nebecist writers to refer to astronauts from other planets who reportedly came in the past or who still may be coming to visit Earth. However, the designation is not strictly limited only to befaps. If humans could travel to other stars, the designation "starman" could readily also apply to them.

See: Astronaut; Befap; Celestial.

STARSHIP. A special type of spaceship which would be able to undertake voyages to other stars. Such spaceships would have to be huge, would require a high level of sophisticated technology, and would have to be capable of blisk-speeds. They would have to be completely self-sufficient for long periods of time. Because there would be no nearby space bases, starships would have to carry all necessary supplies and equipment. Their primary area of operation would be the dark, desolate regions of interstellar space. Of course, such sophisticated spaceships would also be able to operate in interplanetary space. Presently, the construction of starships is beyond man's technological abilities. Assuming that man continues in his efforts to explore space, there is no doubt that with the advance of technology starships will be constructed.

STEADY STATE THEORY. A cosmological theory which maintains that our Universe or space-time continuum is, as a whole, eternal. That is, while stars and galaxies do eventually die, there have been and always will be other stars and galaxies to take their places. In this view, originally proposed by Hermann Bondi and Thomas Gold, the Universe is in a state of continuous creation and this process of birth, evolution and death of stars will continue for eternity.

See: Big Bang Theory; Superspace.

SUBJECTIVE REALITY. Something which lacks objective existence but exists only in the mind of the person. Sense-experience forms the basis of all ideas, concrete, imaginative and fantastic. The mind possesses categories like space and time, by which it analyzes and stores sense-data. It is then able to combine this data to create new ideas. Such ideas may have no corresponding reality in the natural world. For example, the mind may perceive from the sense world a pink rose and a black mountain. Imagination may then combine these two sense experiences and create th idea of a pink mountain. Such a pink mountain would have no objective reality; it would exist only in the mind of the person thinking of such a mountain, i.e., it would have subjective reality.

Imagination is a faculty common to all intelligent people, though it is more pronounced in some people than in others. The personal experiences and mental processess which cause one person to be more imaginative, to fantasize more, and to daydream more than another person are complex and involve many factors.

Some critics and debunkers of the UFO phenomenon argue that UFOs have only subjective reality. The memory of each person stores a variety of experiences, ideas, fears and desires. Something in the sense-world or perhaps a person's mood at a given moment may trigger these memory-data to combine in such a way as to create a UFO. No doubt, some reports of UFOs may have only subjective reality. However, as ufologists emphasize, the UFO phenomenon has been too pervasive and too complex to be explained away as simply a construction of the mind.

See: Hallucination; Illusion; Objective Reality.

SUN. The name of the star around which Earth revolves. Its attractive gravitational power keeps Earth and the other eight planets orbiting around it. Life on Earth is dependent on the sun's light and heat. The sun is about 93,000,000 miles from Earth. Compared to other stars, the sun is average in mass, volume, composition, and temperature. It is a Class G star with a surface temperature of about 5,700 degrees centigrade and with a diameter of 865,000 miles. On the basis of the amount of matter which the sun is calculated to possess, scientists estimate that it still has a life of 6–10 billion years.

SUPERNATURAL. Something which lies beyond or which originates from beyond the natural sense-world. In its most general meaning, supernatural refers to anything beyond the sense-world. The term is often used by religion to refer to the fact that God and other spiritual beings are supernatural in character or that they exist in a supernatural world. The term is also used in the disquieting sense that whatever lies beyond the natural world lies beyond man's knowledge and thus beyond his ability to understand or to control, and therefore it should be feared or deferred to if ever one encounters it.

Occultists and initiates of various secret societies claim the ability to communicate with the supernatural world and to achieve cosmic consciousness, i.e., mental excursions into the supernatural world. As a result, they claim powers and knowledge beyond that available to ordinary men. However, scientists and scholars remain dubious about many of their claims. Science can neither prove nor disprove the existence of a supernatural world. One possible explanation of how cosmic consciousness works is that it is an illusion. An illusion of being in another plane of existence may possibly be created when people who claim to experience it shut off the sense-world via drugs or volition and thus reflect on their own minds.

Scientists are quick to point out that the rise of science has increased man's knowledge of the Universe, and that because of this increase in knowledge the area of the supernatural is shrinking in size. Science has found and proven that the Universe is governed by laws which can be discovered and utilized by man. In such an orderly rational Universe there is no need for the supernatural.

SUPERSENSIBLE. Referring to or belonging to that part of reality which lies beyond the senses. In naphology, the concept of supersensible is synonymous with the religious concept of the supernatural or with the occultist concept of cosmic consciousness. The whole question dealing with the existence of and the attributes of the supersensible world is a very complex issue. There are a number of unanswered questions about the supersensible world. Does there really exist such a world and, if so, how large in scope is it? If such a world does exist, is it inhabited by intelligent beings? If it does exist, does it exist within our Universe or space-time continuum, but in such a manner that it is undetectable by either the senses or sensitive instruments? Or, does it exist as a parallel universe, the inhabitants of which are aware of and can enter into our space-time continuum, though man cannot enter into their dimension or even prove its existence?

This question of a supersensible world has a peripheral relation to many disciplines and areas of interest, including: spiritualism, ufology, cosmic consciousness, and dimensionalism. In theory and in practical usage, supersensible and supernatural are synonymous. However, the terms possess different connotative meanings.

Supersensible implies that even though something is beyond the senses, it is still within man's ability to know by the use of sophisticated instruments. Supernatural, on the other hand, implies the idea of something above and beyond nature, and thus totally alien to our space-time continuum. It also carries with it the implication of something frightening, something which can overwhelm man, but of which man can never really have a grasp unless it, the supernatural, desires to reveal things about itself. Supernatural also carries with it a religious connotation. God, the angels, and the demons are spoken of as supernatural beings. The term supersensible lacks this intimate religious connotation.

The supernatural carries with it the connotation of something both invisible and infinite. The supersensible is also invisible, but it is thought of as being merely above the sense-world and not completely out of its reach. Each term creates a different effect. However, these differences in connotation are not that important in naphology. The term "supernatural" is almost never encountered in naphological writings, whereas the term "supersensible" is used by a few authors, as, for example, Trevor Ravenscroft in *The Spear of Destiny*. Most naphologists prefer to use more neutral and scientific terms, such as: space-time continuum, dimension, and parallel universe.

See: Dimensionalism; Parallel Universe.

SUPERSPACE. A parallel universe which is believed to encompass our space-time continuum (or universe). The existence of superspace has not yet been conclusively established, but that it may indeed exist is a strong possibility based on known scientific principles. Its existence is suggested by the general theory of relativity. Furthermore, though scientists are cosmologically divided between the Big Bang theory and the Steady State Theory to explain the Universe, the existence of superspace is indispensable to both theories. Thirdly, the discovery of "black holes" has also bolstered the argument in favor of the existence of superspace.

On the basis of known scientific laws and principles, scientists who believe in the existence of superspace have deduced several of its characteristics. If it exists, it is believed to contain at least ten times more mass than the visible universe (our space-time continuum). Secondly, time would not exist in superspace. Thirdly, it is believed that there are "holes" in the structure of our space-time continuum through which matter or an object can enter into or exit from superspace. Adrian Berry in his superlative popular scientific work *The Next Ten Thousand Years* devotes a whole chapter to the discussion of superspace and how it affects interstellar space travel.

A practical application of superspace would be the conquest of space. Humans would be able to travel instantaneously to distant stars via superspace. If the existence of superspace could be proven conclusively it would be a tremendous advance in science and in man's understanding of nature.

The concept of superspace has direct application to naphology in general and to ufology in particular. Ufology is divided into two main theories, dimensionalism and nebecism. And the concept of superspace raises questions relating to both theories.

If superspace did not exist, then dimensionalism would definitely have the stronger case. Even at a speed near that of light and with a long life span, travel to distant stars would be complicated; the possibility that befaps could visit Earth would likewise be remote. Dimensionalism, which believes in the existence of a parallel space-time continuum or world which is populated by intelligent beings, would then emerge as the only viable alternative to explain the UFO phenomenon.

Superspace, however, would make interstellar travel feasible and probable. This in turn makes nebecism a viable ufological theory. UFOs could be coming to Earth from a distant star via superspace. However, the existence of superspace, if it indeed exists and if travel is indeed possible through it, does not as such substantiate nebecism. It merely makes it a viable explanation.

The existence of superspace also helps to bolster and possibly to substantiate in a positive manner the dimensionalist theory of a parallel universe or world. For there exists the frightening possibility that superspace, if it exists, is populated by intelligent beings who are able to enter our space-time continuum and influence human events.

Superspace can therefore be used as an argument in support of both ufological theories. Unless and until more scientific facts about superspace become available, any and all ufological ramifications of superspace must remain tentative.

See: Black Hole; Dimensionalism; Gravity II; Nebecism; Space Gate.

SUPERSTITION. Basically, a superstition is a blindly accepted belief or notion about the natural world without any rational basis to justify it. Specifically, it is a belief that a particular thing, circumstance, or event has an ominous significance. Conversely, it is also the belief that the performance of certain rituals will have a significant effect in controlling future events. In essence, superstition results from a lack of knowledge and from a failure to apply reason. With the rise of science, superstition begins to vanish.

Superstitions have only an indirect relation to the UFO phenomenon. In particular, they are connected peripherally to the dimensionalist explanations of UFOs. This theory argues that in man's past beings from another dimension may have entered our space-time continuum. These beings or manadims, as they are called, influenced the course of events and affected human ritualistic behavior. Primitive man feared these beings and desired to placate them. In the process, this contact with manadims gave rise to certain superstitions, as, for example, the belief that by wearing amulets evil could be warded off.

As man's knowledge increased, the methods employed by these beings, whose purpose has always been to deceive man, also became more sophisticated. In the dimensionalist theory, the idea that UFOs are spaceships from other planets is an example of a modern, highly sophisticated superstition which possesses the basic accouterments of scientific respectability. Dimensionalists like John A. Keel and Clifford Wilson, for example, believe that beings from another dimension may in fact be responsible for creating many of the UFOs.

The widespread appearance of UFOs has given rise to many unsubstantiated beliefs about them. Among them are the beliefs that: a) UFOs are from hell, b) UFOs are from God, and c) UFOs are spaceships from advanced planets whose mission, if only man would give them a chance, is to teach man many beneficial things. Prior to the discovery by Pioneer 10 that the Giant Red Spot on Jupiter was an 18,000-mile vortex, some UFO buffs maintained that it was actually a giant spaceship waiting to evacuate surviving humans if a disaster struck Earth. Some persons who have come into contact with UFOs have claimed sudden illumination or sudden recovery from injuries and infirmities. Claims such as these have led to the belief that UFOs are benevolent and solicitous about man's welfare.

Dimensionalists maintain that these are all examples of modern sophisticated superstitions, i.e., beliefs without any solid scientific basis in fact. They do not know for certain what UFOs are. But they are convinced that UFOs are not spaceships from other planetary systems and that they do not have man's welfare in mind. Nebecists, on the other hand, possess a more positive attitude about UFOs. They share a common belief that UFOs are from another planetary system. Most nebecists discount the more extravagant claims about UFOs, as the belief that the saucerians are maintaining a UFO fleet somewhere in space to evacuate Earth if a catastrophe struck. However, nebecists do share the common underlying belief that UFOs are nonhostile, and are potentially friendly and benevolent.

See: Saucer Cult.

SUSPENDED ANIMATION. A state of existence similar to hibernation, but medically induced. In such a state, all vital bodily processes would be kept to an absolute minimum functional level. By prolonging life in this manner, suspended animation would overcome the biological problem which would be encountered when undertaking long interstellar voyages, ones that would last for several or more light years.

The possibility of using suspended animation was in vogue during the early days of the space age when man first became interested in the conquest of space, but had not yet actually embarked on a manned exploration of space. It is no longer considered a viable solution and has vanished from the list of options open to scientists whose task it is to formulate plans for space missions.

But even if suspended animation were medically possible, it is highly doubtful whether scientists would prefer it as the answer to long space voyages. If UFOs are actually spaceships from other planetary systems, it is also highly unlikely that the saucerians undertook the journey to Earth in a state of suspended animation.

Suspended animation has two major drawbacks. Firstly, it would be an extremely costly operation. Secondly, too many things might go wrong. The spaceships would have to rely on automatic controls to get to the desired destination. Automatic controls, however, are liable to error without periodic checks by intelligent beings. Without these checks and corrections, the spaceship might go off course or its hull might be pierced by meteoroids. The list of possible things that could go wrong is almost endless. Therefore, the safety factor alone would require that one or preferably two astronauts remain awake. The problem with this is that these astronauts would age normally, while the one in suspended animation would age at a much slower rate. It is possible to have two crews, one to be placed in suspended animation and the other to monitor the flight. After a specified period of time, the crews would reverse roles. But even here the potential problems and drawbacks are enormous. If something should go wrong, for example, there might not be enough time to awaken the crew members who were put in suspended animation.

Scientists are, therefore, considering other possibilities as being more practical. Interstellar space travel is a problem of both biology and technology. The technological aspect is easier to solve; yet the solution of this aspect may also provide the answer to the biological problem. If the spaceship can attain a great enough speed, then less time would be required to make the journey. This would mean that even within man's present life span he would be able to undertake long space voyages. Scientists are presently working on the speed aspect. Other viable biological alternatives to suspended animation which have been suggested are the use of bionic humans and optimans. The use of robots has also been suggested. Initial exploration of distant planets within our solar system or initial journeys to distant stars could be undertaken by robots. However, the real goal is for man to undertake the journeys. Man has only recently entered the space age. One day, however, he will undertake a voyage to another star. How he will resolve the biological problem posed by such a journey will be definitively answered at that time.

See: Bionic; Optiman; Robot.

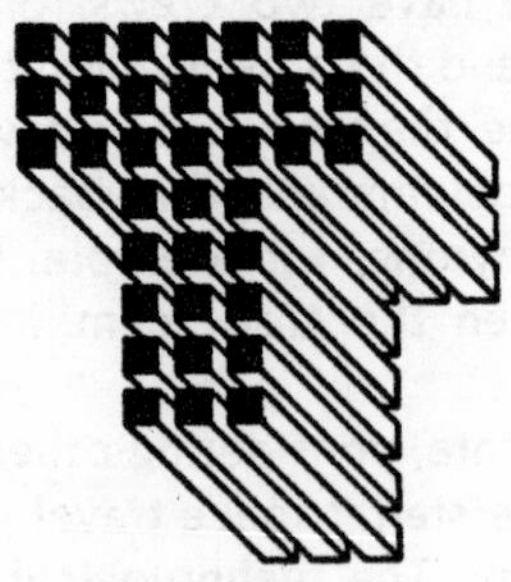

TACHYON. A particle which travels faster than the speed of light. Tachyons, whose existence is believed proven by some scientists and disputed by others, do not contradict the laws of physics. The laws of physics, specifically the theory of relativity which was formulated by Einstein, state that an object cannot accelerate to the speed of light. However, an object or particle which from its first moment travels at a speed greater than that of light does not violate the theory of relativity. The problem in studying such particles and in conclusively proving their existence lies in the fact that their tremendous speed makes them difficult to detect.

If tachyons can indeed travel faster than light, then it may also be theoretically possible for a spaceship to travel at the speed of light or at a speed greater than that of light. The alleged existence of these particles gives a big boost to the argument that sometime in the future it may be possible for man to undertake interstellar journeys. It also gives a boost to the nebecian theory which maintains that in the distant past technologically advanced beings from other planetary systems visited Earth.

A spaceship traveling at Blisk 2 or Blisk 3 or Blisk 4 could cut down tremendously on the time needed to travel to other stellar systems. Unfortunately, at the present time such speeds remain only in the realm of the hypothetically possible. But tachyons do suggest that such speeds are possible.

See: Momentum.

TAU CETI. One of the two stars which Project Ozma, organized to search for intelligent life, examined by radio astronomy in 1961 for intelligent radio signals.

See: Project Ozma.

TECHNOLOGICAL IMMORTALITY. A fundamental belief of religion is the concept of immortality or an afterlife for those persons who are good and fulfill their religious obligations while living in this world. In many cases, the origin of the concept of immortality can be traced back to a divine revelation from a supernatural god or to a direct message from the god worshipped by that particular religion. The exact nature of immortality, and the quality and condition of the afterlife vary from religion to religion. For example, one religion may believe that the individual soul, which is held to be the indestructible essence of man, will live in the afterlife. Another religion may believe in the resurrection of the physical body of the deceased person in an afterlife.

Many nebecists deny the idea of a supernatural or spiritual afterlife for man. They do not deny that in ancient times men were promised immortality by the gods. But to a nebecist these ancient gods were befapian astronauts and the immortality they promised was technological and not spiritual. Furthermore, such immortality was to be achieved by man himself and not by or through the intervention of a spiritual or a supernatural being or beings. Technological immortality would not eliminate deaths entirely. Accidental deaths would still occur. However, life could be prolonged indefinitely by either stopping the aging process or by replacing the vital biological organs (the heart, the lungs, the liver, etc.) with artificial ones, and by finding medicines to combat infectious diseases. Artificial organs and medicines to cure all diseases are already potentially within the reach of man's scientific knowledge. It is just a matter of time now before they are perfected.

The possibility of achieving technological immortality raises fundamental philosophical, ontological and metaphysical questions. For example: Who were the gods, or who was the God, who millenniums ago promised immortality to man? Does man have a soul? Is there a plane of existence above the sense-world? If there is, then what is the relation between the sense-world and this spiritual world? Is it perhaps an error to separate the sense-world from the spiritual world? Could it be that there is only one Reality, embracing all different aspects or levels of existence?

The possibility of achieving technological immortality also involves the question of what will be the future of the Universe. Most scientists are currently leaning towards the view that the Universe is not infinite. The Big Bang theory states that at one time all matter in the Universe was compacted into one giant mass. An explosion caused this matter to be hurled out into space, thus forming the Universe, which is still expanding. However, because the matter will not be able to attain escape velocity, the Universe will one day begin to fall back on itself. If the Big Bang theory is true, then the question is raised of how technological immortality can be possible in a finite Universe. In other words, true immortality cannot be possible in a Universe which is not itself everlasting.

Has man been deceived? Or are the nebecists wrong in maintaining that only technological immortality was promised to man? The answer is obvious. If, millenniums ago, man was indeed earnestly and truthfully promised immortality, it must follow that such immortality would require the existence of an eternal or infinite Universe. This, of course, presupposes the existence of a supernatural world, one whose existence is not dependent on the natural laws which govern our universe. However, the existence of such a world or different space-time continuum is disputed, and it is precisely the question of the existence of such a world which forms the crux of the problem under discussion.

See: Space-Time Continuum; Supernatural; Supersensible.

TECHNOLOGICAL TELEPATHY. Telepathy or mental communication would theoretically be possible to accomplish by the use of sophisticated machines. A machine could pick up thoughts, i.e., the psychoelectrical brain waves which carry them, reprocess them and then either translate them into another language or else beam them, i.e., the psychoelectric brain waves, directly to another mind.

On a very primitive level such a machine already exists in the encephalogram. However, man is nowhere near constructing a true telepathic machine. If it were possible to construct a telepathic machine, then it would also be theoretically possible to create an image-telepathic machine, i.e., a machine that would project mental images onto a screen. Such a machine would probably be able to pick up only conscious brain waves. The unconscious waves would undoubtedly remain hidden, and other means, such as drugs or hypnosis, would be required to reveal them.

The successful operation of a telepathic machine between humans and aconins would presuppose a universality of psychoelectric brain waves. Though there is no evidence that the psychoelectric brain waves of aconins are similar to those of man, theoretically, assuming that biological laws are universal, they should be.

Because the laws of physics and of chemistry have been found to be universal, i.e., the same throughout the Universe, the laws of biology, because they depend on physical and chemical processes, should also be universal. Furthermore, since psychological processes arise from biological functions, they should also be similar. Images, thoughts, concepts, feelings, etc., should be basically similar in all intelligent beings no matter where they may live in the Universe. If such similarity of mental processes is indeed the case, then the construction of a machine capable of performing telepathic functions between humans and aconins should theoretically be possible.

Some ufologists believe that this is in fact the way in which the saucerians communicate with selected humans. Contactees have reported that communication was conducted via both verbal and telepathic means, though the latter method has been the more frequently reported. If these contactee stories about telepathic communication are correct, these experiences would indicate that technological telepathy may indeed have been involved.

See: Telepathy.

TEKTITE. The generic name of a geological formation of several kinds of small glassy objects. They are found in various forms and are found from Australia to Southeast Asis, but are most prevalent in Australia. Their exact origin is unknown, though some experts believe that they were hurled to Earth from the moon when the crater Tycho was formed by a meteorite impact which, it is believed, occurred about 700,000 years ago. Potassium-argon and fission-track dating indicate that these tektites melted at approximately the same time.

Another possible explanation offered is that tektites are of celestial origin and that they crashed to Earth millenniums ago. This possibility is not seriously considered for one main reason. Firstly, if they are of celestial origin, then similar objects should have been detected in the solar system. But such objects are not known to exist anywhere else. Furthermore, it would have to be explained why and how so many of these objects could have fallen to Earth when the probability is that they would have fallen on some other planet or that planet's moons, or that they would have been captured by the sun's gravitational field.

Whatever their origin, one thing is clear. Extreme heat was required to produce them. Those scientists who believe that tektites originated from the moon argue that they melted and hardened while passing through Earth's atmosphere. As further proof of their lunar origin, scientists point out that some of the tektites are ball-shaped, a condition which could have occurred only if the original material had melted in a vacuum such as on the moon.

Some nebecists offer another possible explanation. They point out that detonation of nuclear bombs in the atmosphere turns sand into glassy material at ground zero. On this basis, they cautiously suggest that Earth at one time may have been the scene of a series of nuclear detonations, of either natural or artificial origin. The obvious implication of this nebecian theory is that intelligent beings were involved. Various theories have also been offered as to the identity of these beings, their place of origin, their purpose on Earth, and the reason for the detonation of nuclear bombs. In short, according to the nebecian theory, tektites are one of the main proofs of the arrival to Earth of intelligent beings in the remote past.

TELEPATHY. The mental communicatory process involving direct contact with other minds. Not only is the existence of telepathy accepted, but scientists even have a general theory of how it works. In order to understand this theory, a few observations must first be made. The brain is a complex transmitting and receiving unit which by complex chemical and electrical impulses sends and receives messages to and from the body. Though chemical and electrical impulses may also be involved in the thought process, scientists are leaning more and more towards the possibility that there may be another form of energy, psychokinetic energy. But it is possible that psychokinetic energy has no separate identity. It could merely be a function of chemical and electrical energy.

Whatever the exact nature of psychokinetic energy, psychologists have discovered that the mind is capable of producing this type of energy, which can then cause external effects. For example, psychokinetic energy can cause noises and even project three-dimensional objects.

Telepathy must obviously then involve the ability of one mind to pick up electrical or psychoelectrical impulses, the carriers of thoughts and emotions, from another mind. It is known that telepathy can and does occasionally function. Though some individuals possess greater telepathic abilities than others, no person seems to be able to possess or to exhibit this ability at all times. It is not yet known what sort of stimuli are required to trigger the sensitivity of one mind to the thought waves of another.

In a moral sense, the prospects of telepathy are frightening. Perhaps man will one day achieve it. Still unknown, however, is whether telepathy would be able to pick up only conscious thoughts or whether it would be a total mind probe, capable of picking up even unconscious thoughts and of probing the mind's memory banks.

Interestingly, UFO contactees have often reported that conversations with saucerians were carried on telepathically. In fact, some saucerians were described as lacking mouths. If true, this feature alone would indicate that these beings do not have the physical means to carry on verbal communication.

There exists an alternative to the theory that telepathy will develop through evolution. The development of a genuinely permanent telepathic ability may be a stage too complex to achieve through evolution or through genetic or mental manipulation. If such is the case, telepathy may still be possible by technological means.

See: Technological Telepathy.

TELEPORTATION. The ability of instantaneous movement of a body from one place to another, irrespective of distance. The question of whether teleportation, or Instant Transference (ITF), as it is also called, is actually possible is purely speculative at present. Teleportation is a popular concept in science fiction, but it is not so far-fetched as it might seem at first glance. It is grounded on two scientific theories, and some scientists also give it serious consideration.

The first of these theories is the time-dilation principle inherent in Einstein's theory of relativity. This states that, inter alia, as an object approaches the speed of light, its mass increases and time begins to slow. At the speed of light, time would stop. Thus an object moving at the speed of light would arrive at its destination instantaneously, for time would have stopped for that object.

The second theory is the postulated existence of superspace, a concept derived in part from Einstein's theory of relativity. Superspace, essentially a different dimension which encloses and envelops our space or universe, is postulated to contain much more matter than our space-time continuum. However, because time supposedly does not exist in superspace, a journey through superspace would be instantaneous. That is, a journey between two points in our space-time continuum (universe) via superspace would be instantaneous.

However, neither the existence of superspace nor the time-dilation principle has been conclusively verified through experimentation. Consequently, teleportation has neither been proven nor disproven. Nevertheless, were it possible, it would most probably utilize superspace or the time-dilation principle.

The concept of teleportation figures prominently in ufology. It is a concept which gives credence to the nebecian theory of UFOs. If teleportation is possible, the theory that beings (befaps) from distant stars could be visiting Earth is scientifically plausible, assuming of course that such beings actually exist.

The concept of teleportation also has application to man's space exploration. For teleportation, if it is indeed possible, would mean that some time in the future humans could travel to distant stars.

See: Nebecism; Starism; Superspace.

TERRAFORMATION. The word literally means "the formation of a terrain." It refers to the ability to change the environment of a planet so as to make it suitable for the needs and purposes of the civilization which effects such change. As a particular application of astroengineering, terraformation is no longer in the realm of science fiction. Man already possesses the know-how to be able to terraform Venus and Mars. In fact in 1961, Carl Sagan, astrophysicist at Cornell University, even outlined a plan to change the deadly environment on Venus. The plan involved releasing millions of algae plants in the Venusian atmosphere. Through photosynthesis the algae would transform the carbon dioxide atmosphere of Venus into one containing life-sustaining oxygen.

One of the tenets of nebecism is that Earth in its remote past was also unsuitable for the maintenance of life. Astronauts from other planets arrived and terraformed Earth. However, nebecists disagree on the time of the arrival of these befaps and on the degree of influence that they exerted in forming the physical environment and affecting the biological development of living organisms, including man.

See: Astroengineering; Nebecism.

THEOLOGY. The branch of science, philosophy or knowledge which has as its subject the study of God, His attributes, and His relation to the Universe. In a broader sense, theology studies and seeks to discover religious truths and the means to better express this religious truth. On a practical level, the findings of theology, i.e., the particular type of theology or religious philosophy that a people possesses, would have application to and would affect many areas of the political and social system. It would determine the basic standards, goals and values of society. One of the main topics of conversation among ufologists over the years has been the question of whether saucerians also have a religious philosophy of God.

THEOSITE. In the nebecian philosophy, theosite is one of the infrequently used generic names which refers to the befaps who allegedly arrived on Earth in its remote past, and whose stay on Earth has been recorded in myths, legends and stories. "Theo" is a word element meaning "pertaining to the gods" or "divine." The primary reason that the nebecists use this appellation is to convey the implication that these befaps were mistaken by primitive or ancient men for gods or God.

TIME. Although man is able to measure time, he has not been able to define it or to adequately understand it. There has long existed a metaphysical and scientific debate over the nature of time. Specifically, the debate has centered on whether time has objective or subjective reality. Immanuel Kant proposed that time is one of the categories of the mind, i.e., the mind is so structured that it perceives time. In other words, the mind perceives reality in sequence where one event follows another. Events occur in time. Perception of time is the perception of the sequence of events.

Another major breakthrough in the perception of time occurred when Einstein, in the special theory of relativity, proposed the dilation of time. According to this theory, if an object, including a person, were to travel at or near the speed of light, time would slow down for that object.

Whatever the real nature of time, one fact seems clear. Time is progressive, i.e., it seems to be a law of nature that man can travel only forward in time. Time travel into the past would be impossible and contradictory to the laws of nature. For example, a man traveling into the past would meet himself when he was younger, an obvious impossibility. But time travel into the future is not only possible but very real. In actuality, each person is always traveling into the future from one moment to the next. Though man may be able to slow down or speed up this process, he cannot stop it altogether or reverse it. When scientists speak of traveling into the future, they are speaking of speeding up or slowing down the progress of time.

Time is definitely one of the most important elements involved in space travel. Because the distances to the stars are so great, interstellar space travel requires that man must first better understand and manipulate time. Also in this regard, what is true for man is equally true for other intelligent civilizations which may exist somewhere in the Universe. Any civilization capable of interstellar travel—and this includes UFOs, if they do indeed originate from other planets—must of necessity have conquered or at least partially mastered the secrets of time.

TRANSMOGRIFICATION. It is an established scientific fact that energy and matter are interchangeable. Dimensionalists apply this fact to explain numerous strange phenomena. The concept of transmogrification, or energy manipulation, is central to the dimensionalist theory. Some dimensionalists suggest that there exist superior, nonhuman intelligent entities who, being forms of conscious and intelligent energy, are able to control and manipulate energy in such a way as to create temporary physical (material) forms. The resultant ephemeral forms thus created can include fairies, UFOs, monsters, Bigfoot, etc. This manipulation and control of energy by these beings is designed to deceive and confuse people about the true nature of reality and, possibly, of God.

See: Dimensionalism; Keel, John; UFOs.

TRIDENT. An ancient symbol of unknown origin. A ubiquitous symbol, it has appeared in many cultures and in many epochs. It has probably been most intimately associated as a maritime symbol. In their most basic forms, anchors are trident-shaped.

The three-pronged trident was an accouterment of the Greek sea-god Poseidon and of his Roman version, Neptune. Because of this association with Poseidon, the trident, in Greek mythology, was the symbol of might and of power over the seas. It is still a mystery, however, as to why the Greeks chose a trident and not some other device for Poseidon's symbol.

Tridents have also been associated with other meanings. In Germany, the trident was symbolic of a dove descending from heaven; that is, of the Holy Spirit. French researchers propose that the trident was a symbol of freedom. In the provinces of Transcarpathia and Hutzulia, the trident was regarded as a symbol of protection from evil. These are but some of the meanings attached to it.

Britannia, the female representation of Britain, is always depicted holding a trident. Presently, the island-state of Barbados utilizes the trident as its symbol and has reproduced it on its coins.

Occultists maintain that the trident was the symbol of Atlantis, and whenever they depict or represent any aspect of Atlantis, they invariably include a trident.

The advent of the UFO era has added a new theory regarding the trident's significance. One person who sighted a UFO reported seeing a trident symbol on it. Specifically, he saw a half-circle with a line through it.

By far, the most mysterious use of the trident symbol occurs in Peru. Carved on the side of a mountain in the Bay of Pisco is a huge 820-foot trident. It points to the Plain of Nazca. Nebecist Erich von Daniken associates it with extraterrestrial significance and suggests that it could have been an aerial marker formed by ancient befapian astronauts.

It is impossible to say with any degree of certitude what the true and original meaning of the trident was. What is certain, however, is the fact that it was associated with something grand and powerful, something so magnificent and out of the ordinary that it caught the attention of early man. It was a widely used but mysterious symbol, and perhaps it holds a clue to some secret message. It is also possible that all the diverse meanings may have a common origin.

Speculations and theories abound as to the origin and significance of the trident. Perhaps a definitive answer will be found someday. For the present all that can be said about it with any degree of certitude is that it is a mysterious though quite common symbol.

TROJAN ORBIT. See: Lagrange orbit.

TYPE I CIVILIZATION. A system of categorizing intelligent civilizations on the basis of their control of energy sources. It is based on the necessary relationships between technological sophistication and the consumption of energy. Such energy is the total amount which is ideally available for communication purposes, specifically for communication with other civilizations. A Type I civilization would be able to harness and control an amount of energy equal to the total energy sources of its planet.

By definition, Earth is not yet a Type I civilization. Carl Sagan, astrophysicist at Cornell University, estimates Earth to be a Type 0.7 civilization. The question of whether there exists a Type I civilization in the Universe is a fascinating one, though relatively simple to answer. If UFOs are indeed from other planetary systems, then they must, at the very least, be from a Type I civilization.

See: Civilization.

TYPE II CIVILIZATION. A system of categorizing intelligent civilizations on the basis of their control of energy sources. See definition of Type I civilization. A Type II civilization would he able to harness and control energy equal to the total energy output of its home star. The existence of a Type II civilization is possible, but such a civilization would be incredibly advanced in technology. It would be capable of such complex tasks as astroengineering. If such civilizations exist, they are undoubtedly few in number and would most definitely be able to undertake interstellar voyages. The existence of such a civilization might be detectable by optical telescopes, assuming that the civilization undertakes those types of astroengineering projects that could be recognizable at a distance of many light-years. To date, however, no such civilization has been detected by astronomers. Some ufologists, though, believe that the government has proof of the existence of befapian civilizations and that it has intercepted radio signals from such civilizations. They accuse the government of keeping these findings secret so as not to alarm the people.

See: Civilization; Dyson Sphere; Green Bank Formula; Project Ozma.

TYPE III CIVILIZATION. A system of categorizing intelligent civilizations on the basis of their control of energy sources. See definitions of Type I civilization and Type II civilization. A Type III civilization would be able to harness and control an amount of energy equal to the energy output of the entire galaxy.

In order for such a civilization to develop, a long period of peace, a high level of prosperity, a stable government, and a high level of technology would be required. Therefore, it is doubtful if such a civilization could arise. If such a civilization does indeed exist somewhere in the Universe, it would most assuredly be capable of interstellar travel and most probably also of intergalactic travel. If such a civilization exists, its presence should be detectable by telescopes. No such civilization, however, has been detected by astronomers. It is possible that earthbound instruments are not sensitive enough and may not be able to detect such a civilization. But one thing is certain. If such a civilization exists, it must be in a distant galaxy. A Type III civilization cannot possibly exist in the Milky Way galaxy because if such a civilization did exist, Earth would be part of it.

TYPE IV CIVILIZATION. A system of categorizing intelligent civilizations on the basis of their control of energy sources. See definitions of Type I civilization, Type II civilization, and Type III civilization. A Type IV civilization would be able to harness and control an amount of energy equal to the energy output of the entire Universe. It would have conquered the entire Universe and thus would only be able to communicate with itself. A Type IV civilization is merely what is possible in theory of classification. The enormous distances involved, the large number of stars which constitute the Universe, and the time required to explore and to bring the Universe into a unified system make the attainment of such a civilization an impossible task. By definition, a Type IV civilization would have nothing further to do. It would have learned everything there is to know and would have conquered both space and time. A civilization with no other goals to attain, a civilization in which there was no possibility of further progress or advancement, could only stagnate and eventually begin to decay.

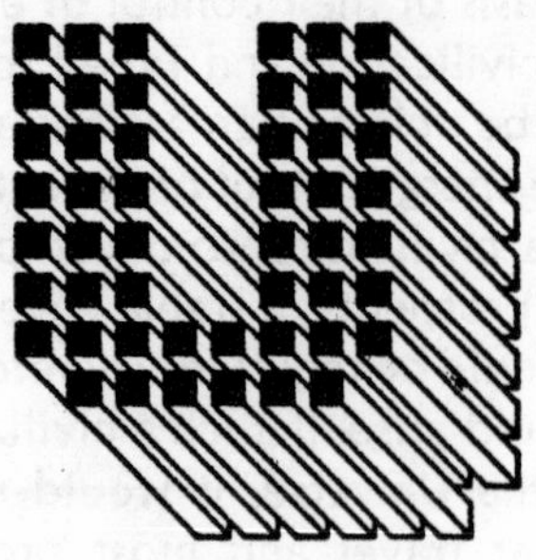

UAO. Acronym for Unidentified Aerial Object. This constitutes the most interesting type of UFO. In this case, witnesses report sighting the actual craft. Unlike the UAPs, which may be of natural origin, UAOs presuppose the existence of other intelligent beings who could construct and pilot these crafts.

See: UFO.

UAP. Acronym for either Unidentified Aerial Phenomena or Unexplained Aerial Phenomena. This official Air Force designation refers exclusively to that particular class of UFO sightings in which only light manifestations or phenomena were visible. A UAP may be a natural phenomenon and thus may eventually be explainable without reliance on the extraterrestrial origin theory. Indeed, some progress has been made in this direction. During an experiment conducted at the Melpar division of E-Systems, Inc., in Falls Church, Virginia, scientists ignited ammonia vapor with a high-voltage spark. The glowing gas quickly assumed the characteristic disc-shaped form of a UFO. Conclusive experiments have not yet been carried out, but it is possible that certain types of atmospheric gases may also be ignited by natural means and then assume a shape and behavior pattern similar to that reported for UFOs. However, even if conclusive tests were to prove this to be true, this theory would not explain all UAP sightings, but it would probably explain many, if not most, of them.

UFO. Acronym for Unidentified Flying Object. It is an official Air Force designation for a class of aerial phenomena. Though the original term "flying saucer" is still in use, it was superseded by the designation "UFO" when the Air Force began to investigate the phenomenon after Kenneth Arnold's sighting.

It is not known positively when UFOs first appeared. There are some ancient and medieval records which indicate that UFOs may have been present even during these times. The first definite recorded sightings of UFOs occurred during World War II. These UFOs were dubbed "foo fighters" by the Allied pilots. The official starting date for the UFO phenomenon in America is given as June 24, 1947. It was on that date that Kenneth Arnold, flying in his private airplane, saw a formation of UFOs over Mt. Rainier.

If UFOs are indeed space vehicles and not some sort of natural aerial phenomena, then their place of origin is unknown. There are three major theories as to their place of origin. The first states that UFOs originate from another planetary system. The second states that UFOs originate from a parallel universe. The third states that UFOs are indigenous to Earth and are in reality vehicles from an advanced subterranean civilization.

The place of origin of UFOs could be more accurately determined if their nature were better understood. The Air Force has divided the UFO phenomenon into two distinct groups, the UAPs and the UAOs.

The UAP (or Unexplained Aerial Phenomenon) class of UFOs is believed to be caused by natural, though not yet fully understood, forces. UAP sightings are of light phenomena only. These light phenomena exhibit movements, such as sharp turns at high speeds, which defy known laws of physics. There have also been cases in which UAPs have broken up into several smaller units which then duplicated the movement characteristics of the original UAP. Scientists theorize that UAPs may be formed from ionized gases, plasma, unusual forms of energy, or perhaps from other natural phenomena which man has not yet identified. On the other hand, it is also possible that some UAPs are indeed solid objects which are merely camouflaged by the light manifestations.

UAPs present a fascinating area of study, but it is the UAOs or Unidentified Aerial Objects which present the real challenge. In the UAO phenomenon there is an actual sighting of an object which exhibits several distinctive characteristics and which is unlike any type of craft known to man. Such objects could either be remote controlled or else personally guided by intelligent beings. UAOs have actually been seen to land on Earth and have been observed in the atmosphere, in space, and underwater (known as USOs). All this raises the very disturbing questions of who controls them and what is their purpose.

It is possible that UAPs and UAOs are related. The one feature common to both is the light phenomenon. Both types of sightings exhibit unusual light patterns. UAPs are often reported as being able to change shape and color. Such changes in shape are usually related to changes in color. UAOs exhibit a definite shape, but are at times described as being surrounded by or as emitting light. The exact nexus, if any, between UAPs and UAOs is unknown, as is also the nexus between the light phenomenon and the UAOs. It is believed by most ufologists that there is a nexus between color changes exhibited by UFOs and their changes in velocity.

Another strange feature of UFOs is their speed and maneuverability. They have been clocked at incredible velocities, the fastest being 18,000 mph, and are able to make sharp turns at great speeds. Though UFOs have never been clocked at blisk speeds, ufologists maintain that UFOs are capable of attaining them. There has been some speculation that through the light phenomenon UFOs become in effect light and thus can travel at blisk speeds. Another possibility offered is that UFOs operate on some form of antigravitational device.

Much more study needs to be done on the UFO phenomenon. One reason why scientists cannot understand it is because they attempt to study it with scientific tools created for other types of phenomena. Because UFOs do not fit into any known category, new tools and new theories must be devised in order to explain them and to study them.

There are a number of common UFO factors or patterns which could form the structural basis of research into the phenomenon. UFOs are intimately associated with a light phenomenon; they are usually seen flying in formation; they have unusual maneuverability; their shape is either disclike, cylindrical, triangular, or spherical (delta-winged UFOs have also been observed); they are able to materialize and dematerialize; they are able to change shape; animals, and sometimes humans, are sensitive to approaching UFOs, probably because of electromagnetic effects on the brain; fragments, ashes, and refuse, such as angels' hair, occasionally fall from them.

UFOs undoubtedly represent one of the greatest mysteries of modern times. It is, of course, possible that all UFOs do not represent the same type of phenomenon. Man may be classifying a number of different phenomena under the category of UFOs. Slowly, however, man's scientific knowledge is increasing; some questions about UFOs have already been answered, as, for example, the connection between color changes and velocity, and the fact that UFOs somehow utilize electromagnetism.

Ufologists believe that the government possesses much information on UFOs that it does not want to release. The ufologists argue that if UFOs were merely a form of aerial phenomenon, there would be no need for the government to hide its findings. But because the government does withhold information, ufologists believe that it has positive proof that at least some UFOs are types of spacecraft.

Everything else aside, one fact about UFOs remains clear. They are a real phenomenon and will not disappear simply because some men do not want to accept their reality. Man must deal with them, and it is inevitable that someday the truth will become known.

See: Dimensionalism; Nebecism; UAO; UAP; Ufology.

UFO. A bimonthly UFO magazine devoted to the examination of all aspects of the UFO phenomena. Its coverage includes both the current UFO cases and the possibility of UFO manifestations in past history.

UFO CULT. See: Saucer Cult.

UFO REPORT. A UFO magazine published ten times a year. The magazine, available by subscription and also sold at newsstands, provides coverage of all aspects of the UFO phenomena as well as related psychic and parapsychic phenomena.

UFOLOGIST. A person who studies and is versed in ufology.

UFOLOGY. The branch of naphology which studies the UFO phenomenon. Ufology believes in the objective reality of UFOs and seeks to determine their origin and purpose for coming to Earth. Through various organizations, ufologists are also engaged in an educational program to make the public aware of the reality of UFOs and to combat attempts by the government to keep findings about UFOs secret.

UFOMANIAC. A disparaging term occasionally applied by UFO

skeptics and debunkers to persons reporting UFO sightings and to those who follow the UFO phenomenon. This designation arises because of the propensity of some UFO buffs to rashly apply the UFO label to any reported aerial phenomenon without first checking and verifying the facts. Ufology has also had its image tarnished by contactees who claim to have engaged in telepathic or verbal conversations with UFO beings. Descriptions of such beings have varied greatly. While some are reported to be humanoid, others are reported to be robotlike or grotesque. Contactees often claim that these UFO beings provide them with information and warnings about the future. Consequently, a hard-core group of individuals has blended UFOs with the occult. Such beliefs have led to further charges of ufomania by critics and skeptics.

It is primarily because of these seemingly wild contact reports, and the resultant occult aspects, that many persons who would otherwise believe in the UFO phenomenon or who would at least be willing to admit the possibility of their existence, shy away from the problem.

Ufologists who ascribe to the nebecian theory have been hard pressed to explain these latter reports of contacts with UFO beings. However, ufologists who ascribe to the dimensionalist theory see no fundamental conflict. They believe that UFOs are an occult phenomenon created by beings from a parallel world or from a supersensible world.

The circumstances of the reported contacts are invariably unusual and present many questions. Various theories have been proposed, but presently no generally accepted one exists. Ufologists are themselves critical of sensational UFO contact reports. Nevertheless, they are quick to point out that ufology as a whole should not be branded as nonsensical simply because of the irrational activities of some. They emphasize that they are engaged in a serious study of the phenomenon and argue that, in order to be understood, UFOs should be approached in a serious and scientific way. The UFO phenomenon, they point out, is very real and will not go away simply because it may be branded as the result of a mania.

Ufologists feel that the disparaging appellation of "ufomania" has been applied too readily and too frequently by skeptics who do not take the time to examine the relevant facts and data on the subject.

See: Contactee; Saucer Cult.

UFONAUT. A general term referring to and identifying any and all intelligent beings who pilot UFOs. Literally, the word means "one who travels in a UFO."

See: Befap; Saucerian.

ULTRACOM. One of the most puzzling aspects of the UFO phenomenon has been the failure to positively record or monitor—or at least the lack of verification that this was done—any communication between UFOs. This lack of verified communications is one of the main arguments against the theory that UFOs are piloted by befaps. It suggests that UFOs are nothing more than such unexplained or unidentified natural aerial phenomena as fireballs, bolides, etc.

Ufologists offer several explanations for this lack of communications. Firstly, some UFOs are admittedly drones, thus no verbal communications would be possible or necessary.

Secondly, if UFOs can travel at the speed of light, no communications would be necessary. Since they would be able to travel as quickly as radio waves, UFOs would not need radios to communicate. They could travel personally to deliver a message. Though this.argument may be applicable to some cases, it cannot possibly apply to all. UFOs would still need radios in the event of an emergency. And, though UFOs have occasionally been seen to experience difficulties, no verified communications to other UFOs were ever monitored.

Thirdly, it is possible that UFOs use a system of communication which cannot be intercepted. Credence is given to this theory because of the fact that the U.S. has already developed a similar system, an ultracom. Ultracom uses an ultraviolet beam to send messages. Its short wavelength is absorbed by the atmosphere and thus is almost impossible to intercept. For this reason, an ultracom system could not be used for communication purposes between Earth and a spaceship. On the other hand, spaceships in orbit around Earth could use an ultracom system without being heard on Earth. Such a system would explain why no messages can be monitored from orbiting UFOs which can be picked up on radar.

In Earth's atmosphere, however, an ultracom could still be monitored by sensitive instruments. In view of this, it has been suggested that the ultracom be used to contact UFOs when they are in our atmosphere. It is not known whether such contact has already been attempted. Officially, the government would never admit to such an attempt. The official position of the Air Force is to deny the objective existence of UFOs. And, if UFOs do not exist, then obviously the Air Force would not attempt to establish contact.

Still unanswered, however, is the puzzling question of why no communications between UFOs have been monitored. Though an ultracog system used by UFOs would be extremely difficult to monitor, it would not be impossible to do so. It is clear that some UFOs are either piloted by or controlled by intelligent beings. UFOs have been able to monitor communications between airplanes and air bases, for they have been able to alter their flight patterns after an intercept order had been given to pursuing jets.

One possible answer to the lack of monitored communications is the possibility that UFOs may utilize a system of communication even more advanced than the ultracom. Though only speculation, it has been suggested that such a system might employ brain waves. It is definitely known that electrical energy is involved in the functioning of the brain. However, scientists feel that there is yet another, presently unidentified, energy source which is responsible for, or which arises from, conscious thought. One theory maintains that brain waves are even quicker than light.

It may be possible to construct a machine which would be able to pick up and send out thought waves. Though such a method of communication is presently beyond man's technological ability, it is theoretically possible and may have been developed by the saucerians. Such a system, if indeed used by the UFOs, would explain why no communications have been monitored.

See: Technological Telepathy.

ULTRASONIC SOUND WAVES. See: Sound

ULTRATERRESTRIAL. See: UT.

UNEXPLAINED AERIAL PHENOMENA. See: UAP.

UNIDENTIFIED AERIAL OBJECT. See: UAO.

UNIDENTIFIED AERIAL PHENOMENA. See: UAP.

UNIDENTIFIED FLYING OBJECT. See: UFO.

UNIDENTIFIED SUBMARINE OBJECT. See: USO.

UNIVERSE. The totality of all existing or created things, including all energy and all matter located in space. The farthest known object is a quasar located some 11 billion light-years away. This signifies that the Universe is at least 11 billion years old, for it has taken that long for the light to reach us. The question of what lies beyond the farthest quasar is presently unanswerable.

Radio telescopes have enabled man to see the farthest limits of the Universe. But the Universe is too vast and complex for man to comprehend its nature. A series of unresolved and perhaps unresolvable questions arise. Did the Universe have a beginning or is it eternal? If it had a beginning, then who created it and why? On the other hand, if it was not created, then how did it start? Is there only one universe or are there a number of parallel universes? Will the Universe continue to expand into space? And if so, what is this space into which the Universe expands? Is this space infinite or is it finite?

Though rational thinking men do not have the answers to such questions, they must nevertheless ask them and seek the answers to them, knowing fully well that the answers they arrive at may be only partially true. Reflection on the Universe shows the limits of man's knowledge and intellectual ability. Yet, by pondering such questions, man remains true to his essence. The very act of thinking about such questions indicates that man is still curious and viable, and that he has not lost interest in his natural world. Thus man still has a future as a biological species. If man ever loses his curiosity, he will begin to decline and will eventually revert to his primitive ways.

The rise of science was made possible by the very act of systematically thinking about the natural world and then experimenting with nature. The knowledge gained made it possible for man to begin to master his environment. Though man will perhaps never learn the whole truth about the Universe, he can nevertheless learn some of its secrets.

Next to God, the Universe in its totality remains the ultimate mystery and challenge to man. He cannot hide from it nor can he ignore it, for he is part of it. Though the Universe is larger and more complex than he, man can nevertheless understand with his mind some of the laws which govern it. He can then use these laws for his own advantage.

See: Big Bang Theory; Nature; Parallel Universe; Space-Time Continuum; Steady State Theory.

UNKNOWN. A synonym used at times by military personnel, NASA officials, scientists, and astronauts to designate a UFO.
See: UFO.

USO. Acronym for Unidentified Submarine Object. This infrequently encountered term refers to that class of UFOs which have been detected under the waters of our planet. A USO does not seem to be fundamentally different from a UFO. USOs have been described as long cylindrical objects which vaguely resemble submarines, though unlike any type known to man. This description is very similar to the cigar-shaped aerial UFOs. UFOs have been reported to enter into and to emerge from water. This has led one group of ufologists to postulate that UFOs may have a base under the waters of our planet. If deep enough, such a base would be secure from interference by humans. Another group of ufologists has suggested that perhaps there exists an underwater civilization composed of beings who may be indigenous to our planet. Perhaps at one point in man's evolution, one part of the human family branched off and returned to the sea. Or perhaps they originated from another planet and at some time in the remote past arrived on Earth and established themselves here.

UT. Acronym for Ultraterrestrial. The designation is used by John A. Keel, who adheres to the dimensionalist theory to explain UFOs and other related parapsychic and parapsychological phenomena. This theory holds that there are two or more parallel universes and that these universes are inhabited by beings who can enter into our dimension where they are able to affect and influence man's actions.

In his book *Our Haunted Planet* John A. Keel calls these beings by several names, the most frequent of which are "UT" and "elemental." Keel does not, however, enter into great detail as to how many different kinds of beings there may be. Nor does he adequately describe the difference, if any, between a UT and an elemental. He frequently uses the terms interchangeably.

According to Keel and other dimensionalists, these beings are able to assume many forms and to deceive and play pranks on man. He describes them as evil beings who act contrary to man's interests. He also holds them responsible for creating UFOs in order to deceive man and to give him the false hope that salvation from the problems of mankind may lie in the hands of beings from outer space.

One interesting feature of his work is the similarity which emerges between his description of the UTs and elementals, and the Jewish and Christian concept of demons.

Keel presents a powerful case for the existence of a parallel universe and for the reality of UTs. He refers to these beings as ultraterrestrials, signifying that they inhabit a plane of existence higher in frequency than man's plane of existence. He often postulates that they must descend the frequency scale in order to appear to man. According to him, electromagnetic energy and volition seem to be the two factors associated with their appearance into the sense-world which man inhabits.

See: Aconin; Demon; Dimensionalism; Manadim; MIB.

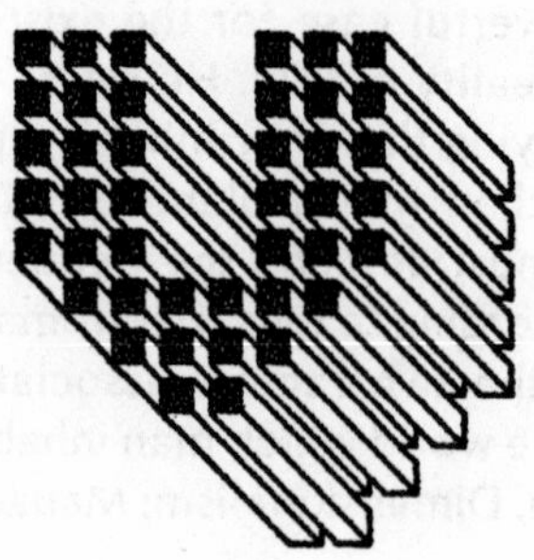

VELOCITY. The distance travelled by a body per unit of time.
See: Momentum.

VENUS. The second planet from the sun. In ufological lore, Venus has long figured prominently as one of the possible points or origin for UFOs. Some ufonauts told the contactees, as for example George Adamski, that they came from Venus. Some contactees even claimed that they were taken by the UFO on a trip to Venus.

U.S. and USSR space probes to Venus have not detected any visible signs of intelligent life. However, the spaceprobes have only conducted a perfunctory and general investigation of Venus. More thorough investigations and explorations of Venus are necessary before the question of whether Venus has or had any sort of life can be conclusively answered.

Nevertheless, on the basis of the information obtained by the *space probes,* it is clear that there are no gigantic cities or lavish civilizations on Venus, at least on the surface. The belief that Venus is inhabited by beautiful, sexy, blonde females has also been laid to rest.

The preliminary scientific explorations and investigations of Venus have, however, suggested a much more exciting prospect. It might be possible to terraform Venus so as to make it inhabitable.
See: Adamski; Terraformation.

VERY LOW FREQUENCY. See: VLF.

VILE VORTEX. See: Vortex.

VILLAS-BOAS, ANTONIO. One of the classic UFO sex-kidnapping contactee cases involves the seduction of Antonio Villas-Boas in Brazil. Villas-Boas was allegedly seized by little humanoid ufonauts and brought aboard an UFO. He was undressed and locked in a room. Waiting for him there was a beautiful, naked, humanoid female, about four feet tall, with white skin and slanted eyes. She began making sexual advances to which Villas-Boas succumbed, and they had sexual intercourse twice. Afterwards she patted her abdomen and pointed towards the stars, suggesting that the child would be born on another planet.

See: Abductee; Contactee; Hallucination.

VISION. The power or sense of sight. It also refers to the power of perceiving something which is not actually present in the external world. Such a perception may arise as a result of ESP. Drugs and physical deprivation may also give rise to these non-physical perceptions, but such mental perceptions would be purely hallucinatory. It is also possible that mental perceptions, i.e., mental visions, may be induced by external sources.

It is this latter possibility that involves naphology. Specifically, three questions arise with regard to the possibility of external inducement of hallucinations: How can such visions be induced? By whom are such visions induced? Why are such visions induced?

The problem of external influence on hallucinations also involves the dimensionalist view, which maintains that beings from a parallel universe can enter into our space-time continuum and affect events there. These beings are also said to be able to possess or to take control of man under certain circumstances by somehow entering into his being and taking over his mind and willpower. At times, these beings can also give man hallucinatory visions. A curious aspect of the UFO phenomenon is the claim by some contactees that they experienced visions.

The nebecian explanation for the origin of UFOs also concerns itself with visions. One group of nebecists argues that UFO beings are able through their superior technology to induce visions in selected humans. For example, R.L. Dione argues that Ezekiel's vision (Ezekiel 1:4–28) of a flying object was induced by a UFO.

The problem of induced visions by UFO beings is exceedingly complex. There is presently a lack of sufficient facts concerning the origins of UFOs to justify the conclusion that they may cause visions. At best, the possibility should remain open that beings with a superior technology might be able to induce visions in order to influence human behavior.

See: Determinism; Dimensionalism; Ezekiel; Hallucination; Nebecism; UFO.

VLF. Acronym for Very Low Frequency. This designation refers to very low radio waves. They have a highly specialized use. Their ability to penetrate water makes VLF waves ideal for communicating with submarines. The CIA also uses VLF for sending messages to its agents. In fact, the frequency is used by intelligence agencies around the world for secret communications. However, because direct voice transmission is very difficult on VLF, messages are usually sent in code.

The CIA, which is directly involved in the UFO problem, has instructed its agents to report any VLF anomalies and aerial phenomena. VLF anomalies may be caused by natural sources, or by attempts made by foreign governments to intercept secret American messages or to send their own coded messages on the American frequencies. However, as John A. Keel hints, VLF may also be used by other intelligences.

Persons owning VLF receivers have occasionally been able to pick up strange and unexplainable radio waves. Consequently, ufologists have become interested in VLF. Though VLF may have some relation to the UFO problem, more data is necessary in order to establish a solid connection. The relation of VLF to the unexplained phenomena on Earth is discussed at length by John A. Keel in chapter 14 of *Our Haunted Planet.*

VORTEX. Naphologist Ivan T. Sanderson maintains that Earth possesses ten vortices, or vile vortices, as they are called. Of these ten, the so-called Devil's Triangle is the best known and most infamous. There are said to be five such vortices in the northern hemisphere and a corresponding five in the southern hemisphere. Contrary to popular belief, these areas are shaped not like a triangle but like a lozenge.

At certain times of the year and under certain conditions, something goes "abnormal" in these areas, with the result that material objects disappear in them. Some of the disappearances may be due to natural occurrences, but others, according to naphologists, may be engineered by intelligent beings.

What triggers the disappearances, how and why they occur, and where do the objects disappear into, are questions for which there are presently no definitive answers. Naphologists have offered some theories, but there are too few facts with which to approach the problem. The subject of vile vortices is discussed at some length by Ivan T. Sanderson in chapters 10 and 11 of *Invisible Residents.*

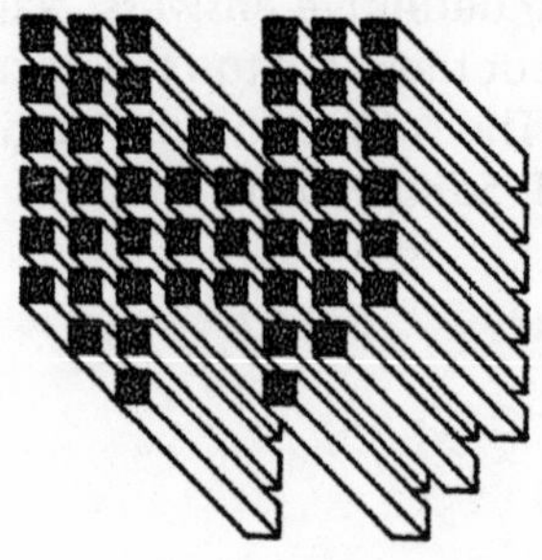

WALESVILLE. The site of an allegedly UFO-related disaster. On July 1, 1954, an F-94 Starfire was scrambled and sent to investigate an unknown flying object which had been tracked over New York State by radar from Griffins AFB. Spotting a gleaming disc-shaped object the pilot began to close in. Suddenly and unexpectedly, a tremendous blast of heat, presumably originating from the UFO, filled the cockpit. Both the pilot and the radar operator bailed out, but the jet went screaming down to earth, crashing into a home in Walesville, N.Y., and bursting into flames. Four people died and five were injured in the disaster. The dazed pilot, after parachuting down at the edge of town, informed a reporter of the strange heat. The Air Force later denied the heat incident and blamed engine failure for the crash.

The use of heat in this case by the UFO seems to have been a defensive measure. However, seemingly offensive uses of heat have also been reported.

See: Fort Itaipu.

WEIGHT. The force which gravitation exerts upon a material body. Weight is not a constant factor but is subject to gravitational variation. On the moon, for example, a man would weigh about one-sixth of what he would weigh on Earth. Though weight is variable, mass is believed to be constant.

See: Mass.

WILSON, CLIFFORD. On the UFO phenomenon, he is a dimensionalist. However, he believes that the true significance of UFOs is found by examining them in the light of Biblical teachings. He believes that UFOs form part of the empirical verification of the teachings of the Jewish and Christian religions about God and about the existing conflict between the forces of good and evil. Dismissing the nebecian theory as without solid foundation, he links UFOs with the millenniums-old conflict between good and evil forces. Like other dimensionalists, he believes that superior nonhuman intelligences, bent upon malevolence towards man, have throughout the ages deceived gullible people. Essentially, he sees UFOs as products of these nonhuman intelligences, especially tailored to the present cultural-technological level of man. By believing that UFOs are from another planet, maintains Wilson, people ignore their real intentions and significance.

His works are well written and provide a wide panoramic view of naturalia, interrelating and integrating the various naturalic phenomena into a coherent system. He parts company with other dimensionalists by presenting a teleological explanation for UFOs. Integrating the Biblical prophecy of an Armageddon, the final great battle between good and evil, to the UFO phenomenon, he believes that these beings, or manadims, though prescient in certain events, do not know the time of the final great battle. Therefore, fearful of their doom, they always have to be ready and thus have been attempting to win over men through the centuries. For, maintains Wilson, these beings are trying to get human allies for that final battle.

See: Angels; Demons; Dimensionalism; Manadim.

WINDOW. Though UFOs are a worldwide phenomenon, UFO activity is greater in some areas than in others. This type of area is known as a window. Ufologists believe that there are specific windows on our planet through which UFOs enter and leave Earth or our space-time continuum. The North Pole, the South Pole, and the Devil's Triangle are the three major areas. Ufologists believe that UFOs prefer to enter our planet via the poles in order to avoid the deadly Van Allen radiation belt which encircles our planet. Many ufologists also believe that UFOs have a base both at the South Pole and in the Devil's Triangle.

See: Antarctica; Devil's Triangle.

WINDOW AREA. *See:* Window.

WOW. Acronym for Wings over the World. In his novel *Things to Come,* H. G. Wells decribes a world ravaged by war and ruled by warring warlords. A small group of scientists then bands together and dedicates itself to restoring civilization. They call their organization Wings over the World (WOW) because of the fact that they accomplish their task by flying over the planet.

This plot has certain parallels to the UFO phenomenon. Some ufologists believe that UFOs may be engaged in surveillance work and in influencing man. Dimensionalist John Keel suggests that there may be a real WOW which has always existed and which has influenced man's development from the time when he first arose. However, he does not specifically link this WOW to the UFOs. Though he believes in the reality of UFOs, Keel is a champion of the dimensionalist theory for explaining their origin.

See: Dimensionalism; UFO.

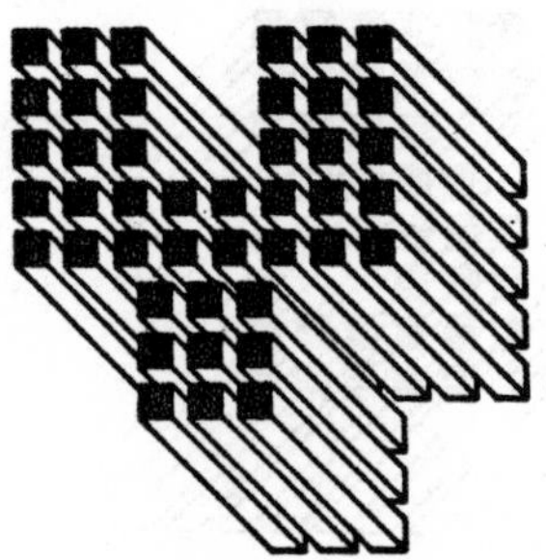

YAHWEH. In the Christian and Jewish religions, Yahweh is the name of God as it is written in the Hebrew text of the Old Testament. In the nebecian theory advanced by Jean Sendy, Yahweh is one of the Elohim, i.e., one of the befapian astronauts who arrived on Earth in ancient times. Sendy also suggests an alternate interpretation. Yahweh may refer not to a being, but to the unified fundamental principle of the Universe, i.e., to the Law. Belief in Yahweh, therefore, is merely belief in and adherence to those immutable laws which govern the Universe.

See: Elohim; Sendy.

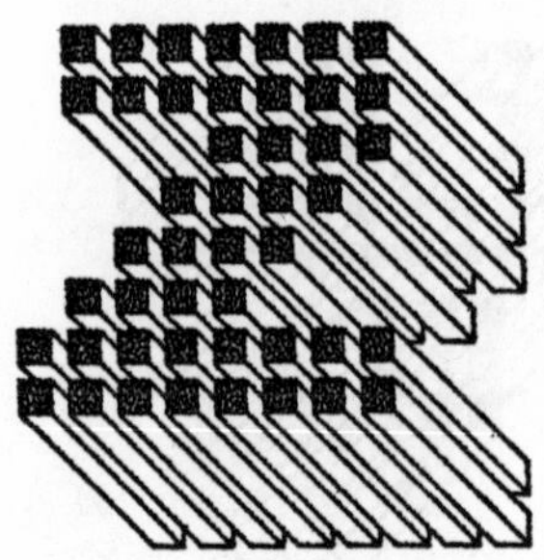

ZEROID. A generic term referring to and applying to the creatures or animals which some naphologists believe may exist and live in space. It has not been positively determined how many different kinds of these animals there may be or whether they even exist. But there is no scientific basis on which to preclude their existence. Life has adapted to and lives in many different types of environments. If zeroids do exist, they most probably feed on either direct light from the sun, much as plants do, or on the preorganic molecules which abound in space. It is also possible that they may have an energy (food) source presently unknown to man.

Some scientists and naphologists believe that many UFOs may in fact be zeroids (space animals). There have been several rare times when strange unidentified animals were found, usually on or near a beach. One such find occurred in Tasmania in July of 1960. Authorities never revealed any detailed information about this find. These animals may have been unknown marine animals or they may have been space animals. According to eyewitnesses, the curious feature about these animals was their very hard skin.

If zeroids do in fact exist, there should be nothing basically frightening or unusual about them. They would merely be another form of life, possibly even one which originated on Earth.

ZETA RETICULI. Based on the star map which Mrs. Hill believes she viewed aboard the UFO to which she and her husband were taken, Zeta Reticuli was the apparent point of origin of the ufonauts who carried out the abduction.

See: Hill.

ZODIAC. A chart of the heavens divided into twelve equal parts. Each section of the heaven is represented by an appropriate symbol, usually that of an animal. The zodiac is based on the natural phenomenon known as the precession of the equinoxes. The discovery of the precession of the equinoxes would have been a very slow and complex process. It would have required some advanced mathematical knowledge and a long period of time. Hipparchus in 128 B.C. is given the credit for discovering this phenomenon.

Nebecists, however, maintain that there is evidence that the use of the zodiac predated Hipparchus. But if man did not have the ability to discover the precession of the equinoxes before that time, then he must have acquired such knowledge from another source. For this other source, nebecists look to befapian astronauts. In their view, the existence of the zodiac based on the natural phenomenon of the precession of the equinoxes constitutes a strong argument in favor of the theory that befapian astronauts landed on Earth in prehistoric times.

The apparent use of zodiacal symbolism in ancient times does not prove that in prehistoric times the knowledge of the precession of the equinoxes was discovered by astronauts from another planet, and that this knowledge was subsequently handed down to man. It is also possible that scientists are mistaken and man had the ability to discover the precession of the equinoxes earlier than he has been credited, which would explain why the Egyptians seemed to follow zodiacal symbolism.

Nebecists rely on the zodiac as one of the proofs that befapian astronauts visited Earth. According to them, these astronauts during their stay on Earth charted the heavens, and while doing so discovered the precession of the equinoxes. They then drew up the zodiac. After these befaps left, the memory of their stay survived, along with some of the knowledge that they had discovered and had handed down to select Earthmen.

Their stay on Earth survived in the form of myths and legends. Because these befaps had come from the heavens and had departed into them, ancient man became interested in astronomy and began to scan the night skies. A priestly class arose both to study the heavens and to preserve the ancient knowledge. This interest led to the rise of astronomy, the first science, which was popular in Babylon and in Egypt. Astronomy, and astrology, which developed from it, owe their origins to these ancient pagan priests. The priests who cared for the knowledge left by the befapian astronauts did not fully understand it, but they preserved it as best as they were able. Among the knowledge preserved, maintain the nebecists, was the zodiac.

See: Nebecism; Precession of the Equinoxes.

ZOOLOGY. The branch of biology which studies animal life. As yet its study has been limited to animal life on Earth. Presently, there is no positive proof to justify the belief that animal life exists in other parts of the Universe. Should it be proven that such life does exist, it would be of immense interest to zoology. No doubt a specialized branch of zoology, exozoology, would then arise.

The discovery of animal life in other parts of the Universe would have immense biological significance. Comparative studies could then be made on anatomy, behavior, physiology, and on other features that such animal life may exhibit. With animals from more than one planet to study, zoologists might then be better able to understand or to discover the universal natural laws which govern animal life. This may lead to a better understanding of the general laws of evolution. A comparative study can show the influence that differences in planetary systems can have on the development of animal life. Simultaneously, it would also be possible to reach a better understanding of the complex interrelationship and influence of animal life on the natural environment of a planet.

Such comparative studies would also have great significance for a better understanding of animal life on our planet. The particular manifestations and attributes of animal life and behavior, as well as variations in animal behavior, could then be seen in better perspective.

Though no conclusive proof exists, it is possible that man has already seen some of these animals from other planets. Zeroids may be space animals. If UFOs are indeed spaceships from other planetary systems, and if they are indeed piloted by intelligent beings, then it's also possible that these beings bring pets, domesticated animals, or mascots, along with them. During UFO flaps it has been reported by some witnesses that they were attacked by strange-looking beasts. Such stories are rare and have been dismissed by the authorities and in the popular press as hoaxes and hallucinations. However, if the reports are true, these creatures would most probably be pets or mascots of the saucerians, as one would hardly expect the saucerians themselves to exhibit such wild behavior.

See: Biology; Exobiology; Zeroid.

BIBLIOGRAPHY

Berlitz, Charles. *Mysteries From Forgotten Worlds.* New York: Dell Publishing Co., Inc., 1973.

Berry, Adrian. *The Next Ten Thousand Years.* The New American Library, Inc., 1975.

Charroux, Robert, Translated by Lowell Bair. *Forgotten Worlds: Scientific Secrets of the Ancients and Their Warning For Our Time.* New York: Walker and Company, 1973.

Churchward, James. *The Lost Continent of Mu.* New York: Paperback Library, 1968.

Daniken, Erich Von. Translated by Michael Heron. *Chariots of the Gods?* New York: Bantam Books, Inc., 1971.

Daniken, Erich Von. Translated by Michael Heron. *Gods From Outer Space.* New York: Bantam Books, Inc., 1973.

Daniken, Erich Von. Translated by Michael Heron. *The Gold of the Gods.* New York: Bantam Books, Inc., 1974.

Dione, R.L. *God Drives a Flying Saucer.* New York: Bantam Books, Inc., 1973.

Dione, R.L. *Is God Supernatural?* New York: Bantam Books, Inc., 1976.

Downing, Barry H. *The Bible and Flying Saucers.* New York: Avon Books, 1970.

Edwards, Frank. *Flying Saucers—Here and Now!* New York: Bantam Books, Inc., 1968.

Edwards, Frank. *Strange World.* New York: Bantam Books, Inc., 1974.

Edwards, Frank. *Stranger Than Science.* New York: Bantam Books, Inc., 1973.

Edwards, Frank. *Strangest of All.* New York: The New American Library, Inc., 1974.

Goodavage, Joseph F. *The Comet Kohoutek.* New York: Pinnacle Books, Inc., 1973.

Hobana, Ion and Weverbergh, Julien. Translated by A.D. Hills. *UFOs From Behind the Iron Curtain.* New York: Bantam Books, Inc., 1974.

Hook, Sidney (ed.). *Determinism and Freedom.* New York: The Macmillan Company, 1961.

Jessup, M.K. *The Case for the UFO.* New York: Bantam Books, Inc., 1955.

Keel, John A. *Our Haunted Planet.* Greenwich: Fawcett Publications, Inc., 1971.

Keel, John A. *Why UFOs: Operation Trojan Horse.* New York: Manor Books, Inc., 1976.

Keel, John A. *The Mothman Prophecies.* New York: The New American Library, Inc., 1976.

Keyhoe, Major Donald E. (USMC Ret.). *Flying Saucers: Top Secret.* New York: G.P. Putnam's Sons, 1960.

Keyhoe, Major Donald E. (USMC Ret.). *Aliens From Space.* New York: The New American Library, Inc., 1974.

Kolosimo, Peter. Translated by A.D. Hills. *Not of This World.* Bantam Books, Inc., 1973.

Kolosimo, Peter. Translated by Paul Stevenson. *Timeless Earth.* New Hyde Park: University Books, Inc., 1973.

Lorenzen, Coral E. *Flying Saucers.* New York: The New American Library, Inc., 1966.

Norman, Eric. *Gods And Devils From Outer Space.* New York: Lancer Books, Inc., 1973.

Ravenscroft, Trevor. *The Spear of Destiny.* New York: Bantam Books, Inc., 1974.

Ruppelt, Edward J. *The Report on Unidentified Flying Objects.* New York: Ace Books, 1956.

Sagan, Carl. *Cosmic Connection.* New York: Dell Publishing Co., Inc., 1975.

Sanderson, Ivan T. *Invisible Residents.* New York: Avon Books, 1973.

Sendy, Jean. Translated by Lowell Bair. *Those Gods Who Made Heaven and Earth.* New York: Berkley Publishing Corporation, 1972.

Sendy, Jean. Translated by Lowell Bair. *The Coming of the Gods.* New York: Berkley Publishing Corporation, 1973.

Sendy, Jean. Translated by Lowell Bair. *The Moon: Outpost of the Gods.* New York: Berkley Publishing Corporation, 1975.

Spencer, John Wallace. *Limbo of the Lost.* New York: Bantam Books, Inc., 1973.

Steiger, Brad. *Atlantis Rising.* New York: Dell Publishing Co., Inc., 1973.

Stoneley, Jack with Lawton, A.T. *Is Anyone Out There?* New York: Warner Books, Inc., 1974.

Thiering, Barry and Castle, Edgar (ed.). *Some Trust in Chariots.* New York: Popular Library, 1972.

Tomas, Andrew. *We Are Not the First.* New York: G.P. Putnam's Sons, 1971.

Trench, Brinsley LePoer. *The Sky People.* New York: Universal-Award House, Inc., 1960.

Wilford, John Noble. *We Reach the Moon.* New York: Bantam Books, Inc., 1969.

Wilson, Clifford. *Crash Go the Chariots.* New York: Lancer Books, Inc., 1972.

Wilson, Clifford. *UFOs and Their Mission Impossible.* New York: The New American Library, Inc., 1974.

Wilson, Clifford. *Gods in Chariots and Other Fantasies.* San Diego: Creation-Life Publishers, 1975.

Zarkon. *The Zarkon Principle.* New York: The New American Library, Inc., 1976.